PIONEER
LEGACY

Skeena
River
Country ◆

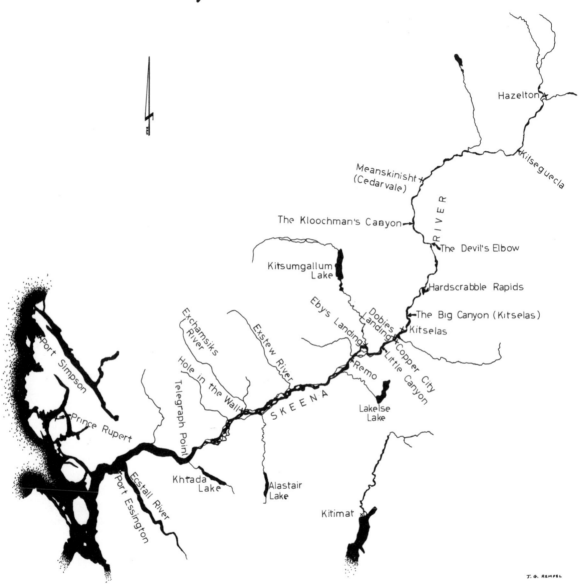

Hazelton

Kiseguecla

Meanskinisht
(Cedarvale)

RIVER

The Kloochman's Canyon

The Devil's Elbow

Kitsumgallum
Lake

Hardscrabble Rapids

Eby's Landing

Dobies Landing

The Big Canyon (Kitselas)

Kitselas

Copper City

Little Canyon

Exchamsiks River

Exstew River

Port Simpson

Hole in the Wall

Remo

Telegraph Point

SKEENA

Lakelse Lake

Prince Rupert

Khtada Lake

Alastair Lake

Ecstall River

Port Essington

Kitimat

J. G. REMPEL

•

PIONEER
LEGACY

Chronicles of the
Lower Skeena
Volume 1

Compiled by

Norma V. Bennett

"To everything there is a season,
and a time to every purpose under the heaven."
Ecclesiastes 3:1

Dr. R.E.M. Lee Hospital Foundation
c/o 4720 Haugland Avenue
Terrace, British Columbia V8G 2W7

Pioneer Legacy

Copyright ©1997 the Authors.

Published by The Dr. R.E.M. Lee Hospital Foundation, c/o 4720
Haugland Avenue, Terrace, BC V8G 2W7.

Cover of paperback edition: painting of *Mount Royal* by J.D. Kelly.
Cover of casebound edition: drawing of sternwheeler by C. Braam.
Page design and layout: David Lee Communications
Printed and bound in Canada

Canadian Cataloguing in Publication Data

Main entry under title:
Pioneer legacy

Includes bibliographical references and index.
ISBN 0-9683026-0-2

 1. Skeena River Region (B.C.)—Biography. 2. Skeena River Region
(B.C.)—History. 3. Frontier and pioneer life—British Columbia—Skeena River
Region. I. Bennett, Norma V., 1912– II. Dr. R.E.M. Lee Hospital Foundation.
FC3845.S59Z48 1997   971.1'8503'0922   C97-911003-3
F1089.S5P56 1997

Contents

This book is respectfully dedicated to the Pioneers, who, as they pass down the Corridors of Time, are ever distinguished, and distinguishable—a Breed apart.

IT IS MY SINCERE PLEASURE to convey congratulations to the Dr. R.E.M. Lee Hospital Foundation on another outstanding achievement.

In March, 1994 Norma Bennett offered her accumulation of research and stories of the Skeena River to the Foundation as a possible fundraiser. After many years of sorting, finding a publisher and all the other necessities to ready the book for publication, *Pioneer Legacy* has evolved. It is a quality product and will preserve for ever more an important part of our heritage.

The Dr. R.E.M. Lee Hospital Foundation was formed only a decade ago and in that short time a small band of volunteers has rallied the business community, service clubs, other organizations, employee groups and the community to open their hearts and their cheque books with a net result of almost $1,000,000 in capital donations made to date to Mills Memorial Hospital and Terraceview Lodge.

Proceeds from the sale of the book will also go toward much needed hospital equipment and the health care of Terrace and area.

I sincerely hope this project will be supported and that the readers will appreciate and learn from the many hours of research by Norma Bennett.

Norma Bennett has sufficient material for further volumes. I look forward to this first volume being a success so that readers can look forward to the stories of the building of the railroad and other pioneer stories in subsequent volumes.

In conclusion, thank you for your past support, congratulations on the publication of this volume and all the best in your efforts to bring future volumes into print.

Michael A. Leisinger
Chief Executive Officer
Terrace and Area Health Council

Foreword

◆ Norma V. Bennett

This is a history of the Skeena country, centering around what is now Terrace, up until 1920.

The purpose of the book is threefold:

(1) To provide a background of the history of our area and of the events that contributed towards its settlement.

(2) To examine the quality of pioneer life through the media of pictures, newspaper excerpts, and personal accounts.

(3) To assemble many of the scattered stories, articles, reports, etc. that have been written about this area and to make them available at a central location.

In some instances where a story has had its roots in our time frame, rather than cut it off at 1920, we have continued it to a more suitable termination date.

There are times when different versions of the same incident appear. In these cases all have been presented so the reader may better assess the situation from more than one viewpoint.

There are often different spellings of the same place name, particularly in those of Indian origin. We have retained whatever spelling was used at that time, and it is interesting to note how the more modern version has evolved.

We have retained the original wording of some of these pieces, but in doing so we ask that our readers excuse the use of expressions that are no longer tolerated.

◆

Early on, I was frequently asked such questions as: "How come you are so interested in pioneer life?" or "How come *you* are planning a history of pioneer Terrace?"

More than twenty years ago I was approached by the then-librarian of our public library with the request that I consider writing a pioneer history of Terrace.

Why me? I believe it was because of the success of an exhibit that Elsie Anderson and I had put on for a convention of the BC Chambers of Commerce and Alaskan Affiliates in 1962. I had gathered personal histories and photographs from many of the old-timers and we had set up a "log cabin" equipped with all the early furnishings that we could find by diligently combing the district. Dressed in period costume we greeted our guests at the old Civic Centre and the whole project was well received. It was entirely a community effort and the response was overwhelming.

Nadine Asante did the *History of Terrace* and I give her kudos for having done so. Here were people like Nadine and myself—virtual newcomers—showing an active interest in the beginnings of our community that pioneers or their families should have taken on.

Again I was urged to do something. I could work only within my own time frame but I decided to give it a try. It proved to be a very rewarding experience. Soon I knew the old-time population of the district far better than I knew my own contemporaries.

Twice a year I would go to Vancouver to stay for two or three weeks at the old Grosvenor Hotel near the public library, where I would spend my days and evenings doing research in their Northwest History Room. I was amazed at the vast quantity of material available. It seemed that anyone who had ever visited the Skeena River was so impressed one way or another that they had felt compelled to write about it.

I was also a frequent visitor to the provincial Public Archives in Victoria where the archivist at that time, Mr. Willard Ireland, became not only my adviser but a friend as well. With his whole-hearted co-operation and that of others who followed him, I was able to have the old photographs obtained from local residents copied for my use, with a second copy going to the archives to build up a library of Terrace pictures. The originals, of course, were returned to the donors.

The Northwest History Room yielded so much exciting and first-hand material that I felt only a compilation could do justice to my subject. Stories experienced by those who had actually been there would be so much more convincing than any second-hand attempts could ever be. I could add relevant accounts from the newspapers of the day and could, myself, write what I call "bridges" to connect the stories and thus allow the chronicle to develop in a more understandable way.

And so I did—still expecting the final product to be given to our local library.

Like Topsy, once it got going it seemed it "jes' growed." Before long I had over a thousand pages of material and some eight hundred fabulous pictures collected.

I was unable to work steadily on the project but that did not really concern me as I had no one to answer to but myself. At one phase of my life it was laid aside for more than six years. However, people kept asking about it and wanting to see it. Those who did, pressured me to have it published. I had planned to donate to the library the original that I had already typed and laminated but it was now evident that this was entirely impractical.

At last, in 1994, a small group of dedicated people got together to take the publication in hand and it seemed that there might be some hope of bringing this enterprise to a successful completion.

From its inception to its final disposition *Pioneer Legacy* has been a community undertaking. As its compiler I express my deepest gratitude for the assistance I have received in these important areas:

(1) MATERIAL: For permission granted by the owners of the various newspapers to use any stories, articles, reports etc. found relevant therein. I am especially indebted to the late Catherine M. Fraser of the Terrace *Omineca Herald* who made available to me the earliest files of the publication which she had so faithfully preserved.

My thanks also to the Terrace *Herald*, the BC Archives and Records Service (formerly the Provincial Archives of BC), the Vancouver *Province*, the Prince Rupert *Daily News*, The Victoria *Times-Colonist*, the Vancouver Public Library, The Hudson's Bay Company Archives, *BC Digest* (now *BC Outdoors*), *Paddlewheels on the Frontier* (Vol. I) and all others whose generosity and assistance I am happy to acknowledge.

A special salute to the pioneers of Terrace and area, those doughty originals who dreamed a dream of the future, the results of which others like myself have been able to enjoy. They have shared with me their trials, their hopes and their achievements and my association with them has enriched and inspired my life.

For additional information, confirmation and encouragement I am particularly indebted to the following:

Vina Eby, Floyd Frank, Ernest Hann, Claire Giggey, Jean Jefferis, Ted Johnston, Lloyd Johnstone, Edith Kawinsky, Ed Kenney, Ken Kerr, Onalee Kirkaldy, Emma Lindstrom, Gordon Little, Bill McRae, Edith Mitchell, Katie O'Neill, Adella Pohle, Hazel Schultzic, Mildred Skinner, Jack Sparkes, Gordon Sparkes and Elsie M. Whitlow.

(2) PICTURES: My thanks to all those who so graciously opened their albums and entrusted me with pictures that were priceless to them, to be copied and used as I saw fit.

To those who reproduced the pictures for me—Mr. Willard Ireland and later provincial archivists—Mr. J. Robert Davison and Ms. Share Mawson.

To Mr. Ken Fuergutz of our local Ken's Photo, who was ever generous with his time, his encouragement and his expertise.

(3) PUBLISHING: And now to the final area in which I have received immeasurable aid:

To the small committee who got things going and never gave up despite innumerable difficulties—Helene McRae, Yvonne Moen and Casey Braam, I owe this book's very survival.

Helene, with her eye firmly fixed on the goal of publication, was our liaison with the Dr. R.E.M. Lee Hospital Foundation, which, through her efforts, agreed to sponsor our project. Her knowledge of pioneer days (she is of the Durham–Adams lineage) has proved invaluable.

Yvonne, with her buoyant energy and tireless enthusiasm, has constantly spurred us on and has never allowed us to lag. Her ability to organize has been of the greatest assistance.

Casey, with his quiet common sense, his surprising background of pioneer knowledge, his perceptive eye and his fine artistic abilities has been an irreplaceable member of the group.

My committee joins with me in extending our sincere appreciation to Pat McGinlay who so generously offered to take on the onerous task of typing all this material onto the computer disks. It is an exacting and time-consuming operation and deserves our collective thanks.

(4) YOU, the PUBLIC: I shall thank in advance those of you who will purchase and, I hope, treasure these books. In this rapidly changing world our history is of supreme importance to all of us—not only those who can trace their roots back to the beginning, but those of us who arrived later to enjoy the benefits—without the hardships—of the beautiful area in which we live. It is a small price to pay to perpetuate knowledge and is a mark of respect to our founders.

Any monies received from the sale of this book will go to the Dr. R.E.M. Lee Hospital Foundation, in support of Mills Memorial Hospital and Terraceview Lodge, as I desire no compensation for myself. I have already been amply repaid by the associations I have made and the friendships I have enjoyed.

Norma V. Bennett

Skeena Country

◆ Norma V. Bennett

When God created Skeena country He did it with a prodigal hand. Range upon range of mountains march in seemingly endless parade, their snow-capped peaks glistening in the sunlight or rising semi-obscured through collars of chiffonous mist. Vast tracts of timber sweep along the mountain slopes and across the valley floors, their bases matted with an almost tropical verdure—fern and frond, brush and bramble, devil's club and ivy. The trees rise straight and tall, reaching upward and ever upward, the light sifting down through their branches in cool, emerald shafts to narrow cathedral aisles, deeply carpeted with spongy moss. Tones of green are everywhere, punctuated only by the seasons.

In the spring the tender jade of unfurling deciduous leaf contrasts sharply with the darker hues of evergreens and the sombre green-black shades of balsam. In autumn the countryside is ablaze with every conceivable vivid hue, brilliant and breathtaking in its flamboyant beauty—a panoramic explosion of colour. Then the leaves fall slowly, lingering with whispered reluctance until finally only the bare skeletons of trees are left to await the next miracle of spring. The evergreens stand sentinel over winter, dark, silent and brooding, occasionally herringboned with new-fallen snow.

It is a land of waters. There are lakes lying cradled like gleaming mirrors, embossed with cloud pictures and snow-topped mountain crests, giving back in faithful reproduction a perfect replica of all that is reflected therein, but never once revealing the secret mysteries of their own unsounded depths. There are rivers, swift and impetuous in their rush to the sea, sometimes cascading through rocky gorges, straining like mettlesome steeds against their confines; sometimes sliding smoothly but powerfully with whirlpools sucking in dangerous undertow, carrying trees or logs or any other obstruction that bars their progress as they swell their banks to overflowing and threaten to spill their waters far out over the valleys; sometimes merely trickling amongst the sandbars in low water, bearing little resemblance in this momentary insignificance to the relentless torrent of flood days. There are creeks, somersaulting in gay and reckless abandon, rushing in sparkling joyousness to their ultimate destiny—their complete loss of identity in the oblivion of greater waters.

Valleys, slung like giant hammocks, invite the herds to graze, the crops to flourish. It is as though this land, wooed by the warming winds, kissed by the ardent sun, charmed by the rune in the treetops at night, lay waiting. Waiting until the time when change, in the guise of white-skinned men, should, at first gradually, then with a tempo so quickened as to be almost fearsome, transform it to a state scarcely recognizable. The promise of the land is for the future—food in abundance, materials with which to build, work for man's practical needs and beauty for his spiritual yearnings. Perfect sites for towns and settlements, offering space and peace and plenty; a land of opportunity requiring men and women of strength, of vision and of faith. It is indeed a time for sowing.

The First People

There in the shadows of the mountains, close by the mighty waters, dwelt the First People. Theirs the lands, the forests and the streams, and all the bounty of nature contained therein—theirs from time immemorial "for the use of Man in the Garden of Earth." To adequately chronicle the life and customs of these people requires the most intensive research and the most skillful pen. It is a subject unto itself and quite outside the scope of this simple presentation.

May it suffice, therefore, to acknowledge their presence, their culture, and their rights.

One cannot be catapulted into any period of time with a view to appreciating it, without considering to some extent that which has gone before. History is a continuing process. The effects of the past are found in the present and this goes back, link by link, to the very beginning.

In the confusion and uncertainty of our beginning there is FOOD FOR THOUGHT.

In the Beginning

◆ B. A. McKelvie

When and by whom British Columbia was first inhabited is unknown. It is believed that there were successive races occupying the Pacific Slope in prehistoric days, but their identity and the order of their coming and going have not been determined. Evidences that have come to light in ancient burial mounds, in the speech of native tribes, in customs and ceremonies, and in occasional discoveries of primitive artifacts have led scientific investigators to agree that Mongolian influences have been a strong factor in populating the country west of the Rocky Mountains. Some research students advance arguments in an effort to establish that these Asiatic migrations included definite groups of Chinese, Japanese, Koreans and Northern Mongolians, while other anthropologists contend that traces of the impact of Polynesian culture may also be discerned.

Chinese
Japanese
Koreans
Northern Mongolians
Polynesians

There are some definite facts that give support to several of these contentions. In 1882, miners in Cassiar uncovered a number of Chinese bronze coins while running a tunnel into a hill. The coins were threaded on to an iron rod that disintegrated when exposed to the air. The money was brought to Victoria where it was identified as coinage of China such as was circulated about 2000 BC. Several years later, the Chinese interpreter of the Supreme Court at Victoria encountered Indians near Telegraph Creek who had in their possession several solid silver Buddhist ceremonial dishes. They asserted that they had found them beneath the roots of a large tree. The natives would not part with the vessels, but did give the interpreter one of several large brass disks—each some two and a half inches in diameter—that had been found in one of the dishes. The interpreter could not decipher the ideographic characters on the disk. Upon his return to Victoria he gave

1882: Cassiar discovery

Telegraph Creek discovery

Buddhist charm

Nanaimo—Japanese sword

Lytton stone figures

458 A. D.—Buddhist priests

Jews from China

Theory: A wind-drift to the Queen Charlotte Islands or the Nass River area.

Indian language suggests Hebraic influence.

it to His Honour Judge Eli Harrison, who submitted it to experts in New York, Philadelphia and Washington for study. They identified it as a Buddhist charm, of a type that had not been manufactured for more than 1500 years. This disk is in the possession of a collector in Oregon.

When the streets of Nanaimo were being laid out, the road foreman discovered, eleven feet underground, a Japanese sword. It was sheathed in a wooden scabbard that was protected by closely wound silvered copper wire. The handle was of sharkskin. The blade had not deteriorated by rusting. A Japanese archaeologist who inspected it declared the weapon to be of great antiquity. It is in the possession of the family of the road foreman. In different localities, and especially along the shore of the Gulf of Georgia and up the Fraser River as far as Lytton, quaintly carved stone figures have been found. They range from one of about two inches in height to a recent discovery fourteen inches high. They evidence the workmanship of a highly artistic and skilled people. The majority of these figurines depict a man holding a bowl. The features are well modelled and portray people of determined character, with prominent noses and protruding large round eyes, and with ears—and some noses—pierced for ornaments. Distinctive head-dresses are also featured. That these receptacles were for some special purpose may be inferred from the care and patience evident in their manufacture.

According to Li Yan Tcheou, a Chinese historian of the early seventh century, a band of Buddhist priests crossed the Pacific and followed the coast south from Alaska, finally settling in the Kingdom of Fusang (believed by some to have been Mexico). They left China in the year 458 A.D.—about the time that the Romans were leaving Great Britain—and in 499 A.D. the last of the priests, Hoei Shin by name, returned to China and his story was recorded. This written account would be roughly 1000 years before Columbus crossed the Atlantic Ocean.

None of the puzzles of the past is more interesting than the possibility that Jews from China were at one time located on the Coast, and remained there long enough to leave the imprint of their culture upon that of the tribes whom they encountered. It is an historical fact that Jews were once powerful in China. The theory has been advanced that when Kublai Khan made his ill-starred expedition against Japan—towards the end of the thirteenth century—his fleet was dispersed by a storm and was blown out into the Pacific Ocean, and junks bearing the Jewish contingent of his troops made the great drift and landed on the American coast—possibly in the vicinity of the Queen Charlotte Islands, or the Nass River.

The late Father Jean Marie Le Jeune, probably the greatest linguist who worked among the British Columbia Indians, recorded that he had found Hebraic words in every native language west of the Rockies.

Coast Indian customs that are suggestive of Hebraic ceremonies and usages include:

First fruit offerings: the ceremonials observed in taking the first salmon and oolichan (candlefish) of the season.

Purification rites: the fastings, social constraint, and frequent bathing of hunters and warriors preparatory to an expedition.

Wearing of the fringes: the ceremonial dress of the medicine man or chief of some Coast tribes is reminiscent of that of the Jewish priest, with a mitred head-dress, a blanket with its totemistic design giving the effect of a breast-plate, and with its fringes.

Fasting from sunset to sunset: this was meticulously followed by hunters and warriors in spiritual and physical preparation for their undertakings.

Measurement of time: the Indian system of division of seasons, months and days, was similar to those of the Jewish calendar.

Father Morice, the great historian of the Dene peoples, has noted in his examination of their habits that certain customs enforced upon female adolescents were similar to those of the Jews.

So it is, that numerous distinctive habits and ways of Coast Indians suggest that long ago, Jews from China—the most likely place—visited the North Pacific coast. There is no evidence for assuming that there is a biological relationship between the Jews and Indians—on the contrary, a race that had preserved its insularity in China during centuries when that nation was far advanced in learning and culture, would not be expected to intermarry with the untutored barbarians of the Coast; but any customs observed and the speech used by the strangers would be copied by the savages. Thus, it is possible that a lasting imprint of a stay amidst the tribes would be made. [1]

M ystery, conjecture and only partially substantiated claims continue to obscure the earliest history of the North Pacific coast of North America. Many questions, to this day, have yielded inconclusive information or remained unanswered.

Christopher Columbus made his historic voyage in 1492, after which Pope Alexander VI decreed that the New World be divided between Spain and Portugal.

In 1520 Cortez was in Mexico and the Spanish gradually began to advance northward from there along the Pacific seaboard.

The 17th century saw the Russians move eastward across Siberia. By 1697 they had reached Kamschatka. In 1728–29, Vitus Bering, a Dane in Russia's service, sailed to the Arctic through Bering Strait from the south, but because he did not see the American mainland due to bad weather, he did not realize the true import of what he had done. In 1741 he was on the southwest coast of Alaska, the Alaskan Peninsula and the Aleutian Islands. His party's explorations

Indian customs reflect Hebraic influence.

Jews from China

Unsolved Mysteries:
Did the Arab merchant, Sulaiman, actually sail on the Pacific Ocean in the 9th century? Did Marco Polo and his successors do likewise in the 13th and 14th centuries? Was Sir Francis Drake off Long Beach, Vancouver Island, in 1579? Did Juan de Fuca, in 1592, visit the straits that bear his name? Did he sail as far north as Vancouver Island? If he did—though many discredit his claim—he was two centuries ahead of Captain Cook . . .

gave Alaska to the Russians and introduced to her the sea otter. A brisk trade in furs ensued. In 1867 the United States purchased Alaska from Russia and has held it ever since.

With the Russians so active in the north, the Spanish roused themselves and in 1769 began northern expeditions. By 1776 they had reached San Francisco Bay.

By this time the search for the Northwest Passage was on. Attempts were being made from both sides of the continent. On the Pacific Coast another nation—the British—established a third area of influence between the Russians to the north and the Spanish to the South. They became the fathers of our own territory—what was one day to be known as British Columbia.

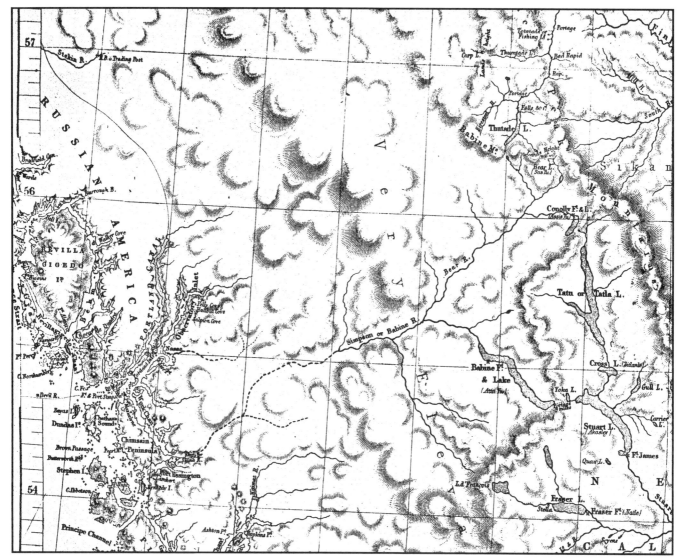

1862---British Columbia by MacDonald. In this detail, the mouth of the river is marked "Skina," the upper river "Simpson" or "Babine."

Stepping Stones in History

• **1774:**

Juan Perez, a Spaniard, sailed north from Mexico. His instructions were to claim for Spain all lands to which the Russians had already established their rights---approximately 60° N. Latitude. His trip was plagued by fog but land was sighted on July 17, 1774. The headland was named Cape Santa Margarita and was thought to be part of the mainland. Bad weather prevented Perez getting ashore to raise a marker. The ship was forced southward and although Vancouver Island was sighted, they could not land there either and so returned to Mexico.[2]

◆ 1775: Quadra

Juan Francisco de la Bodega y Quadra. Spanish. Sailed as far as Sitka.

◆ 1778: Captain James Cook.

Our first geographer. Established a general outline of the northwest coast of North America although he saw but little of what is now the coast of British Columbia.[3]

On the afternoon of April 26, 1778, after nearly a month spent at Nootka Sound and on the shores of British Columbia adjoining . . . ". . . he again put to sea. Captain Cook was therefore the first British subject to set foot on the shores of British Columbia." [4] He gave to the world a "complete idea of the configuration of the northern coastline of America with the exception that neither Vancouver Island nor the Queen Charlotte Islands were recognized as being separate from the main coastline." [5]

In his narrative, Cook mentioned the sea otter pelts obtained from the Indians at Nootka and how there was a ready market for them in China, at lucrative prices. This narrative, published after Cook's death (Cook was killed in the Sandwich Islands on his way back to England, following his third voyage), fired many traders with the lust for furs.

◆ Fur trading vessels:

A thriving fur trade developed along the Northwest Coast with English, Spanish and Russians taking prominent parts.

◆ 1785: James Hanna.

"The first expedition to the northwest coast after furs was conducted by one James Hanna." [12]

◆ 1787:

Captain Charles Duncan of the schooner *Princess Royal* mentions the (Skeena) river, referring to it as "Ayton's River."

◆ 1788: *North West America*.

A schooner of about 40 tons built by John Meares and his associates at Nootka Sound in 1788. The first vessel built on the west coast of Canada. Master—Robert Duffin. This vessel was on the coast again in 1789. [11]

◆ 1792–94: Captain George Vancouver.

Commissioned to map the northwest coast of North America. His surveys were the first detailed ones north of San Francisco.

◆ 1793: Whidbey.

Vancouver, himself, was not at the mouth of the Skeena River, but his first officer was. With a second boat Mr. Whidbey, Master of the *Discovery*, examined the estuary in July 1793. According to Walbran, he came "to the mistaken conclusion that the opening was of no importance." He refrained from examining farther than the Raspberry Islands, which were given that name by him, and on his return to the vessels then lying off Gil Island, reported to Vancouver that this river was a small stream and the inlet into which it entered not worth examination above the islands, being entirely filled from thence with sandbars and boulders. Thus the Skeena was overlooked in the same way as the Fraser, from ignorance as to what the entrance of a large river would be like when deploying into the sea.

"It seems strange that Vancouver, an officer of such an observing nature, should miss noting the three large rivers, Fraser, Skeena and Nass, yet such is the case." [6]

. . . so even the great err!

♦ **Compiler's Comment:**

To me the above seems even stranger when we consider that Vancouver was aware of Duncan's surveys, the latter's charts being on board the *Discovery* and mentioned by Vancouver in his diary. The men, no doubt, had met and discussed Duncan's trip before Vancouver left England in 1791. [6] Thus Vancouver should have known of and checked the existence of "Ayton's River."

♦ **1793: Port Essington.**

The Sound in the estuary of the Skeena was named Port Essington for one of Vancouver's officers.

♦ **1793: Nass River.**

"Survey work near the mouth of the Nass River was conducted by Mr. Johnson, on whose work Vancouver reported: 'In the morning of the 25th July, being assisted by a strong ebb tide, they quitted this small river, which, with the other in Port Essington observed in Mr. Whidbey's late excursion, are the only two streams that had yet been discovered to the north of the river Columbia. These are too insignificant to be dignified by the name of rivers, and in truth scarcely deserve the appellation of rivulets'." [7]

INDEED!

♦ **Tsimpsean traders:**

The Skeena River was a highway of trade for the Coast Indians, the Tsimpseans, who travelled by canoe to barter furs with the Interior Indians. Upon their return these were traded again to the vessels that plied the coastal waters for this purpose.

♦ **1793: Alexander Mackenzie.**

Mackenzie reached the Pacific overland at a point about 275 miles north of Vancouver (Bella Coola). This paved the way for the fur traders and trappers of the North West Company.

♦ **1805: Simon Fraser.**

Established Fort McLeod (Parsnip River).

♦ **1806: Simon Fraser.**

Fort St. James (Stuart Lake); Fort Fraser (Fraser Lake).

♦ **1807: Simon Fraser.**

Fort George (Junction of the Fraser and Nechako Rivers).

♦ **1811: D.W. Harmon; James McDougall.**

Harmon and McDougall were Hudson's Bay Company men in charge of

Fort St. James and Fort McLeod respectively. They were the *first* explorers of Skeena waters in the Babine country.

◆ 1821: Fur Companies amalgamated.

The North West Company and the Hudson's Bay Company united under the latter's name.

◆ 1822: More forts are built.

Fort Kilmaurs (Babine Lake) and Fort Connolly (Bear Lake)

These were built: (1) to compete with Tsimpsean trade to the west. (2) to provide fish for the Interior, from the Skeena.

◆ 1830: Fort Naas—Fort Simpson.

Fort Naas was established in 1830 by Captain A. Simpson of the Hudson's Bay Company. A few months later he died and the village was renamed Fort Simpson in his honour. Location proved unsatisfactory—moved to new site in 1834.

◆ 1832: Donald Manson.

"On October 19, 1832, Donald Manson embarked on the schooner, *Cadboro*, in accordance with instructions he had received from Peter Skene Ogden, for the purpose of examining the river. On his arrival at the entrance of the Skeena River, Manson decided to leave the *Cadboro* and continue his journey up the river in a canoe. Having ascended the river for about 50 miles, he decided to return and arrived back at Port Simpson in November." [8]

◆ 1834: (Fort) Port Simpson.

The new site was chosen about halfway between the Nass and the Skeena rivers. Later named Port Simpson, it immediately became the Canadian headquarters of the north coast fur trade.

◆ 1835: John Work.

Took charge of the Hudson's Bay post at Port Simpson.

◆ 1846: International boundary west of the Rockies established.

With settlers pouring into the Oregon country, a boundary became necessary. Foreseeing this, the Hudson's Bay Company moved its western headquarters from Vancouver, Washington to Victoria.

◆ 1849: Vancouver Island.

Vancouver Island was made a British Colony.

◆ 1858: Colony of British Columbia.

The mainland territory was proclaimed a Colony and was named British Columbia.

◆ 1858: Gold Rush.

Gold was discovered along the Fraser River and in the Cariboo.

◆ 1859: Major Downie.

At Port Simpson, Downie enlisted four other men (two natives) to make a trip up the Skeena River to the Forks. Travelling by canoe, this took them about two weeks.

◆ 1862: William Duncan.

Established Metlakatla.

◆ **1863: Charles Horetzsky.**

A Hudson's Bay Company man. Travelled on foot through the Yellowhead Pass, the Bulkley Valley and thence along the Skeena River to its mouth. Recommended this route as the site for a railway.

◆ **1864– 65:** *Union.*

This boat, captained by Tom Coffin, sailed up the Skeena 90 miles in 1865. Its attempt at navigating the river the year before was not successful. It took supplies up the Skeena for the Collins Overland Telegraph Company. When they could go no farther the journey was completed by canoe and goods stored in a cabin at the Forks.

◆ **1866:** *Mumford.*

Sailed with supplies for the Collins Overland Telegraph Company as far as the Kitsumkalum River, where they had to take to the canoes. She is said to have ascended the river 110 miles, which could even have been as far as Kitselas Canyon, but there appears to be some doubt that she actually got that far.

◆ **1866: Collins Overland Telegraph.**

Captain Butler and forty Collins men, who had come up on the *Mumford* as far as she could go, continued on to the Forks. They made contact with linemen advancing westward from the Fraser and work went on until news of the laying of the Atlantic cable spelled the end of the venture.

◆ **1866: Sir James Douglas.**

Colonies of British Columbia and Vancouver Island united, with James Douglas---a former Hudson's Bay Company factor---as Governor.

◆ **1866: William Manson & Thomas Hankin.**

Sent by the Hudson's Bay Company to explore the Upper Skeena.

◆ **1868: Robert Cunningham.**

In charge of the fort at Port Simpson.

◆ **1868: Hazelton.**

When the Overland Telegraph project was abandoned some of the men stayed on to winter at the Forks. The settlement grew and became known as Hazelton.

◆ **1870: Robert Cunningham & Thomas Hankin.**

In April, 1870, these men applied to Victoria for land at the mouth of the Skeena River.

◆ **1871: Skeenamouth, Skeena Bay or Woodcock's Landing.**

Woodcock had built an inn here. In 1871 twenty men spent the winter there.

◆ **1871: Gold Rush.**

Beginning of the gold rush up the Skeena. Cunningham and Hankin built a store on bank of river; Hankin was the first postmaster.

◆ **1871: Thomas Hankin.**

Hankin made a hurried trip to Hazelton via the Nass River and the old grease trail, to establish a store at that end to serve the influx of miners to the Omineca country.

◆ **1871: Robert Cunningham & Thomas Hankin.**

Contracted by the government to improve the trail from Gitenmaks to Babine Lake—the route of the miners.

◆ **1871: "Spokeshute"/ Port Essington.**

Cunningham and Hankin had a falling out with Woodcock and decided to locate elsewhere. Cunningham took out a pre-emption on the south side of the Skeena River near the mouth of the Ecstall River. This had been the fall campgrounds of the Tsimpsean Indians and was known as "Spokeshute." A trading post was built there and the name chosen for the new settlement was "Port Essington."

◆ **1871: Skeena Post.**

The Hudson's Bay Company bought land from Cunningham and erected a store called "Skeena Post," with Matthew Feak as Postmaster.

◆ **1876: First salmon cannery.**

At Woodcock's Landing by North Western Commercial Company. Changed hands four years later and the name was changed to Inverness.

◆ **1877: Skeena Post closed.**

Stores transferred to Port Simpson.

◆ **1887: Reverend Robert Tomlinson.**

Wintered at Kitwanga.

◆ **1888:**

Reverend Tomlinson established the "Holy City," called Meanskinisht (now Cedarvale). Jr. Chief Trader R.H. Hall recommended that steamers be used on the Skeena.

◆ **1889: First Skeena survey.**

The Hudson's Bay Company hired Captain George Odin to survey the river. He recommended the use of sternwheelers for navigation.

◆ **1890s: Canneries increased river traffic.**

Seven canneries in the Skeena estuary. Much river traffic. Native men caught the fish and the women worked in the canneries.

◆ **1891: *Caledonia I.***

The beginning of the sternwheeler era.

Skeena River Log

What's in a Name?

Remnants of mystery surround even the name of this mighty river. Of this much we are certain—the Tsimpsean people called their river "K'shian." According to legend, a certain giant who gathered water from the clouds that hovered over the mountain tops, to sprinkle on the earth below, one day accidentally overturned the container. The water that spilled down formed the Skeena River. The Indian word "K'shian" means "water from the clouds."

K'shian

"The Skeena was known to early traders, circa 1787, as Ayton's River, and is mentioned under this name in a long public letter describing the coast hereabouts, addressed to Captain George Dixon from Captain Charles Duncan, dated Islington, 17 January, 1791. Capt. Duncan, in the sloop *Princess Royal*, was at anchor at the entrance of Ayton's River in the summer of 1788." [1]

Ayton's River

An excerpt from the above-mentioned letter reads as follows: "On the first of June I got in amongst Princess Royal's Isles, and not finding anchorage, made fast to trees, head and stern; Boomed the vessel off from the rocks and on the 2nd of June, in the evening, anchored in the mouth of Ayton's River about 15 leagues north-east of where I had stopt the night before."

"Ayton's River (Skeena) named by George Duncan, June 2, 1788, at least he entered it that day." [2]

Ayton's River [Error in name—Charles, not George Duncan]

"Skeena River—First named Ayton's River by Captain Duncan of the *Princess Royal* in 1788. Later known either as Simpson's River or as Babine River." [3]

Simpson's or Babine River

1852: Skenar

"Gold was reported 'by Indians' to have been discovered up the Skenar River on 8th April last." [4]

Skeena (K'shian)

"On the authority of Dr. Ridley, late Bishop of Caledonia, this name is

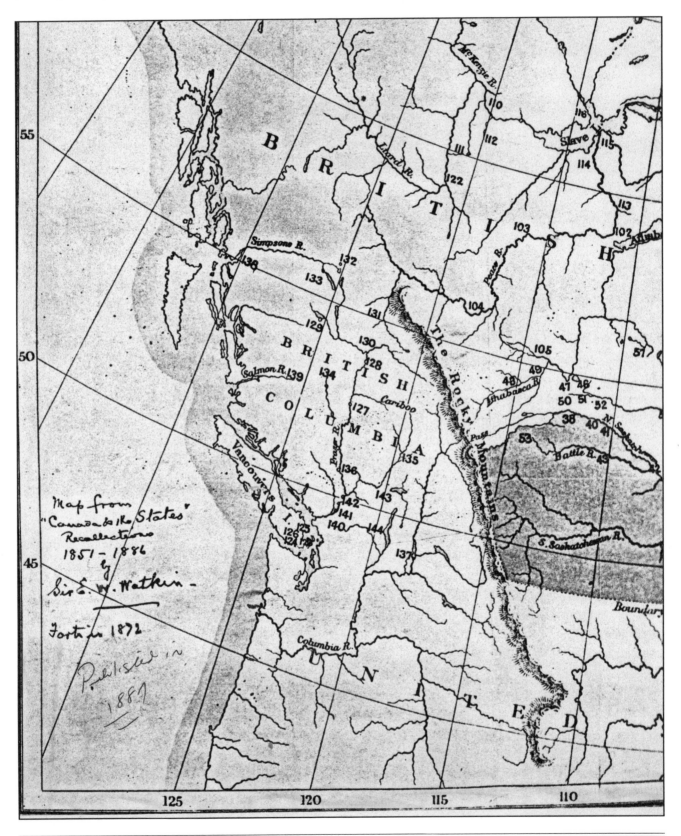

an adaptation of K'shian, the Tsimpsean name for the river, meaning a 'divide.' "[5]

"The original name of this river, as given it by the Indians, is 'Ikshean.' To this the name 'Skeena,' by which it is known to the whites, does not appear to bear any resemblance."

Ikshean

" 'K'shian' does not mean a 'divide' but a 'flowing out.' 'Iksh' as a prefix always implies 'out of.' Comparing the two terms we have 'Ikshean' made up of 'iksh,' 'out of,' and 'shean' or 'shyen' which means 'the clouds.' This indicates the clouds as the source of the river."[6]

"Water of Terrors."[7]

Skeena

"River of Mists"—BC government historical marker.

Skeena

What Do Early Maps Say?

◆ **Ayton's River:**
"We have not been able to find a map using that name."[8]

◆ **1834: Hudson's Bay Company map**
British North America—"By permission dedicated to the Honourable Hudson's Bay Company. Containing the latest information which their documents furnish. By their Obedient Servant, J. Arrowsmith."

The Skeena River is not marked on the above map. Simpson's River and Babine Lake are marked.

◆ **1862: Arrowsmith's map**
Arrowsmith's *Map of British Columbia and Vancouver Island* shows the Upper River as Simpson's or Babine.

◆ **1862: MacDonald's map**
"British Columbia" by MacDonald. Mouth of river is marked "Skina;" upper river "Simpson" or "Babine."

◆ **1865: Hudson's Bay Company map**
The river is not named.[9]

◆ **1867: Anderson's map**
Anderson's *Map of British Columbia* shows it as the "Skeena River."

◆ **1872: Hudson's Bay Company map**
This is a map showing their posts for that year. The river is marked "Simpson's River."

◆ **1877: Walbran's comment**
"This river (Skeena) has not yet been correctly surveyed, a sketch survey

Opposite: This map shows Hudson's Bay Company posts in 1872. The river is marked "Simpson's River." Courtesy HBC Archives.

only having been made as far as the Raspberry Islands in 1877, by Commander G.J. Hanmer and Officers of the H.M.S. *Daring*." [5]

◆ 1879–80 survey map

"Map of part of BC and N.W. Territory from the Pacific Ocean to Fort Edmonton." Drawn to illustrate the Report of George M. Dawson (Geological Survey of Canada). Marked "Skeena River" with a comment in brackets (K'shien of the Tsimshian Indians).

◆ 1911: Geographic Board Report

"Skeena" receives official sanction.

The name "Skeena River" was officially adopted by the Geographic Board of Canada and it is listed in the 10th Report of the Board, 1911. This report stated that the name was "not Skena." (See *Report of Geographic Board of Canada*, 1924. This is a consolidation of all previous reports.)

The Skeena Was a River! – The second largest all-Canadian river in BC

Source: Skeena Mountains

Delta: Pacific Ocean, 54th parallel

Length: 350 miles

Drainage: 15,000 square miles

Tributaries:
Bulkley ◆ Babine ◆ Sustut ◆ Kispiox ◆ Kleanza ◆ Zymoetz (Copper)
Kitsumkalum ◆ Lakelse ◆ Exstew ◆ Gitnadoix
Exchamsiks ◆ Ecstall ◆ and others

Lake System:
Bear ◆ Babine ◆ Morice ◆ Bulkley ◆ Kalum ◆ Lakelse ◆

Constant rise and fall in water level—in the Canyon, as much as 17 feet in 24 hours

Brown, dirty water

Swift, treacherous, but navigable

"Never gives up its dead."

◆

Many people have felt compelled to attempt to record in words their impressions of this river---her mystery, her haunting beauty, her deadly fascination and her vicious treachery.

The Indians called her "K'shian, water of the clouds." The river boatmen, less poetic, called her an unpredictable wench. By temperament she is nervous and unstable, impatient to leave her birthplace in the storm-shrouded rock spires of the Skeena Mountains, hurrying to tide-water with a determination that made her the West's fastest-flowing major waterway. Some sternwheeler skippers credited her with being among the toughest of North America's navigable rivers. Others disagreed, saying she wasn't among the toughest; she *was* the toughest! She could rise 17 feet in a day, fluctuate 60 feet between high and low water, puncture a sternwheeler's planking in a dozen rapid-torn canyons or rock-strewn rapids. "We don't navigate the river," one veteran skipper observed, "we juggle our way down."

◆ Art Downs

Essentially a mountain river, the Skeena's waters are swift-flowing and treacherous . . . Its tortuous upper reaches fall rapidly through the heavily forested mountain valleys. As the Sustut and Babine tributaries enter, the valley widens into bench land on either side. Nevertheless, the flow is still rapid and the riverbanks mostly steep. After the Bulkley enters the Skeena, the flow is widened and the velocity increased. Many mountain streams join the river below this point, and the Skeena hurls an impressive mass of tumultuous water through the rocky barrier of the Kitselas Canyon into the broad Kitsumkalum Valley.

After crossing this valley, the raging torrent becomes a fickle stream, meandering amongst islands and sandbars, unable to make up its mind which course to follow. But the towering mountains inexorably force its brown waters westward, and finally the ocean tide rushes up to meet them, adding a pinch of salt to the muddy brew.
. . . Such is the Skeena---a river with a dirty brown face and a violent disposition . . .

◆ R.G. Large

BC's Beautiful River

◆ Vernon Quinn

This author felt only the beauty of the Skeena, not its violence.

There is no other river in the world just like the Skeena. It rises in a jade lakelet and, gaining in size and impetus as it goes, dashes down from the mountains, racing through wild canyons or deep gorges. Many rivers join it, bringing always a burden of lake water. The long irregular 100-mile stretch of Babine Lake which is the delight of fisherman, camper and canoeist, flows out to the Skeena through Babine River. And a few miles below the Babine the broad, turbulent, pale-green Bulkley gives its all to the Skeena.

To this point, near the town of Hazelton, the Skeena has flowed south between the mountain ridges. Now it turns westward, but to reach the sea it must cut through the entire Coast Range. This it does by winding in and out among mountain spurs, accepting and widening natural gorges rather than cutting through rock and forming canyons. The result is some of the most exquisitely beautiful scenery in America, perhaps in the world. Each turn of the river, each unfolding of the hills, is like a delicate etching. There is none of the wild ruggedness, the tumultuous grandeur of the Rockies to be found here. But long after the magnificence of ice fields and glaciers is but a blurred memory, the haunting beauty of the Skeena remains, poignantly.

The hills, amethyst and lavender-grey, fold upon one another softly, running up from the water, reaching their points out so that the river, as smooth as a lake, must turn and wander round. Here and there, in the midst of the broad water, there are islands, covered with spruce and feathery willow, the shingle beaches strewn with driftwood. Where the river is more shallow, boulders lie in its bed and are showered as the water dashes against them. Smoothed by this constant beat of the river, and wet with spray, they glisten like lacquered stones, in red and yellow and bright heliotrope.

The Skeena is a river of many moods---her many facets not always reflecting light, joy and gaiety. She has her sombre moments too---even her deadly ones.

Another turn and the river is narrow and deep, swift-flowing but smooth, its glassy surface mirroring the cliffs and the leaning trees. Above moss-green rocks a fringe of poplars, windblown till their leaves show white, gleam like flecks of silver where they reflect in the opal-blue water.

Hills, misty, unreal, smoke-blue and green and amethyst, rise steeply from the edge of the water and beyond them, mountains, snow-splashed, hazy, exquisitely coloured, stand softly against the sky.

Comaham

One evening in the 1940s, while going out on the point of the river to fish, we stumbled over something. We began to dig among the ferns and found a monument that had fallen down. It was cut from pink and white marble, with three pedestal slabs and a tall pillar, on which was inscribed: "In memory of Chief Comaham and his daughter, drowned at Skeena River Aug. 15 1873."

There had been a wooden fence around it, which had rotted away in the 70 years the monument had been there. I was told the marble had probably been brought in from Victoria, and that would mean by boat as the railroad was not built then. One finds many Indian graves in this area marked with stone slabs, inscribed with a verse and a name.

◆ Mildred Lambly

Tribute to a Brave Man
◆ Ruth M. Hallock

It was a very warm day in mid-August. The year was 1873 and Comaham, together with his small family, was on the last leg of a long hard pull up the Skeena River from Port Simpson to the Indian village at the mouth of the Lakelse River.

Comaham was a big man and the muscles stood out on his back each time he pulled on the boat oars. He watched his children carefully, for like most children on a hot summer's day, they were restless and anxious to reach their destination.

There was no real sound in the air. The still heat of the day had silenced even the birds. Only the Skeena River, swollen and angry from an extra heavy run-off in the mountains, complained and grumbled ominously under Comaham's boat.

The brown-skinned man looked at his small daughter, now in her fourth summer. Her eyes were bright black and her hair, not yet thick enough for braiding, curled damply over her tiny ears.

She smiled at her father and moved quickly to touch his strong hand. Suddenly the boat heaved on a treacherous flood swell and the child lost her footing and plunged over the side into the churning muddy water.

Comaham did not hesitate. He leapt into the river after his small daughter, shouting to her not to fight the swift current. His shouts and the cries of his little girl soon became part of the river's roar and his wife and remaining children sobbed, first in anger and finally in sorrow.

The Indians searched long at the mouth of the Shames River and at length the Skeena gave up the body of Comaham—but his bright-eyed child was coveted forever by "the River of the Clouds."

Comaham was a head man in Port Simpson and he and his family were well known throughout the Indian tribes of the north coast and Skeena valley. A great funeral and burial ceremony was ordered, and stonecutter George Rudge of Port Simpson was commissioned by his people to create a lasting tribute to Comaham's memory.

Comaham was buried on the Old Telegraph Trail near the station cabin occupied by telegrapher S.W. Dobbie and his new bride.

The headstone still stands, weather-beaten but sturdy. The telegraph cabin is almost gone but the remnants remain to remind Mrs. S.W. Dobbie of Copper River, BC, of the tiny home she maintained as a young bride.

Thanks to Mrs. Dobbie, this small bit of Skeena River history has been revealed. Thanks to the late Comaham, many a father will look upon his small daughter with just a little more reverence in these days when time is so fleet and the loving touch of a father's strong hand is often rare.

Headstone, Old Telegraph Trail. Inscription: In memory of COMAHAM and his daughter Drowned at Skeena River Aug. 15, 1873
(33-C)

Canoes on the Skeena

For centuries the Skeena played the same important role to the natives along its shores that most great rivers do. It was a highway for travel, communication, war and trade, a source of food and at times a means of protection. To breast its turbulent waters, a sturdy craft was required as well as the courage and skill to operate it. Tribes along the coast were fortunate in being the not-too-distant neighbours of the Haidas of the Queen Charlotte Islands. These were the master canoe builders, and with them the Coast Indians bartered their goods for the canoes they so prized for up-river transportation.

Canoe Building
◆ A.P. Niblack (c. 1886)

The tools used in canoe construction are surprisingly simple. The principal one is a kind of adze. Logs for the canoe are usually obtained in the summer and roughly hewn into shape in odd hours about the summer camp—the finishing work being left until winter. The trees are generally selected near some watercourse. The log is trimmed where felled to rough dimensions, launched into the water, and towed to summer camp. Often by combined labour numerous logs are gotten out in this way at one time, made into a raft, and by means of sweeps and sails and working the tides, brought to the village or to the camp. Good canoe trees are sufficiently rare to make their selection difficult and expensive in both time and labour. The best wood is yellow cedar, found on the Queen Charlotte Islands and in spots around the southern Alaska boundary. The smaller canoes are made from Sitka spruce and the very largest from the giant cedar.

The tree is felled with an ax (formerly stone ones were used). The trimming and rough hewing is done by wedges and sledges. The rest of the work is done by patient cutting with an adze. The canoe, being roughly worked out, is widened in beam by steaming it with water. Hot stones are placed in the bottom and stretchers or thwarts of gradually increasing sizes are forced in as the wood expands. The long spur ends in large canoes are neatly scarfed on to the body with a dovetailed joint and finished down as part of the whole. The smoothing work on the outside is often done with a chisel, but usually the interior of the canoe is chipped out with an adze. To lessen the friction of the water, the exterior is smoothed with sandpaper, sandstone, or sharkskin. The conventional colours used now in painting are black

Materials:
  yellow cedar
  Sitka spruce
  red cedar

Tools:
  adze
  ax—stone ax
  wedges
  sledges
  chisel
  sandpaper, sandstone
  sharkskin

Canoe capacity:
  2 tons
  Crew of five men, paid $20 to
  $25 each, per trip.

Tsimshian cottonwood dugout canoe; Kispayaks village, upper Skeena.
(34) / National Museums of Canada 102799

outside and white inside with a red strip on the inside of the gunwale running quite around the canoe and upon the bow and stern spurs. The lines of these canoes are remarkably fine, and when of considerable size and intelligently handled they are remarkably good sea-boats. Trips are often made in them to Victoria, BC; and in the early summer in search of birds' eggs, the Kaigani visit the outlying islands of the Prince of Wales Archipelago, about 25 miles out to sea.
(From personal observations in connection with the survey 1885, 1886 and 1887. Collection in the U.S. National Museum.)

"Sailors" of the Skeena

◆ Wiggs O'Neill

Below: Kaigani Haida.
(34-C) / Nat. Mus. J6487

In the early days ... the Haida Indians of the Queen Charlotte Islands became so adept at canoe building that they sold their canoes to all the upper river Indians. For river work they made canoes with a carrying capacity of two tons, which for Skeena River travel were manned by a captain and a crew of four "sailors"— usually Indian men from Port Simpson or Port Essington, who worked hard at bucking the strong and dangerous currents of the Skeena.

For the trip from the coast to Hazelton these "sailors" received from $20 to $25 each, poling the canoe through shallow or calm water and forcing it upward by a towline in the more difficult places. Naturally a keen rivalry grew up as to which canoe would make the trip in the shortest time, with the Indians putting forth Herculean efforts as their frail craft entered the boiling waters of the Kitselas Canyon.

Port Simpson

◆ W.H. Collison

The Indians on the Nass River were more or less familiar with white men before many of the tribes around them. This was owing to the advent of the Hudson's Bay Company on the northwest coast. The Company selected a projecting point on tidewater, near the mouth of the river, and here in 1831 they erected a trading post. It was built like a fort, with a view to defense in case of attack, as the natives could not be trusted in those days.

But there was a power more to be dreaded than the Indians, which the Company's officers had not considered. It was the strong Nass winds, which sweep down the river day and night for nearly three months, when the cold is most intense, thus not only rendering their exposed position untenable, but preventing the Indians from approaching the fort during this time to trade. The river freezes down to within a few miles of this point, and remains in the grasp of the Ice King for several months. The ice is generally from two to four feet in thickness.

The generation of Indians who remembered the first advent of the "Omukshewas," or White Men, have almost all passed away. Many of them are buried right on the site where the fort formerly stood. This

Nass River Indians met white men early.

point, which was formerly known as "Fort Point," is now known as "Cemetery Point" and forms the "God's Acre" of the Kincolith Mission Station. The oldest chief on the river, who only died lately, aged 83 years, informed me that he remembered the coming of the white men. He was then a child of some five or six years, and was taking his first lessons with bow and arrow. Another veteran took much pleasure in reciting and singing the songs the Indians sang when one of the Company's ships was seen approaching at the mouth of the river:

> Ho! Ho! Ho! Angland's ship a-ho!
> Hip, hip, hurray!

Laklquaha-lamish
Rose Island
Port Simpson

In 1834 the Company moved the fort to a place thirty-seven miles farther south, on a spacious and well-sheltered harbour known amongst the Indians as "Laklquaha-lamish," or "Rose Island," but now more generally known as "Port Simpson." It was so named in memory of Captain Simpson, who died after establishing the Hudson's Bay Company's fort on the Nass, and whose remains were removed to the new site when it was established.

Old Port Simpson

◆ Marius Barbeau

Early trading posts

The two decades from 1830 to 1850 were of great importance in the activities of the Hudson's Bay Company on the North Pacific Coast. Six trading forts were established within the short space of twelve years—Nass at the mouth of the Nass River in 1831; McLoughlin on Milbanke Sound and Nisqually on Puget Sound in 1833; Simpson to replace Fort Nass, on Chatham Sound in 1834; Durham on Taku Inlet in 1840; and Victoria on Vancouver's Island in 1843. S.S. *Beaver*, in 1836, began its long service between these northern posts and Fort Vancouver on the Columbia. And James Douglas tried to expand into Alaska the Company's command of the fur trade.

Trading patterns on the Pacific Coast.

The whole northwest coast from Alaska to California at first had been taken possession of by the Russians from the north and the Spaniards from the south. Then the British, through the convention at Nootka in 1792 between the captains Vancouver and Quadra, had secured a vast strip of the coast. But the field for many years remained open to all. Only after the fusion of the North West Company and the Hudson's Bay, was a definite plan of coastal expansion adopted and pursued. The North West Company had been the overland pioneer with its explorers Mackenzie, Fraser, Thompson and later, with Dr. John McLoughlin. James Douglas, a native of Jamaica, whose mother was a Creole, also had been a Nor'wester; and like other Nor'westers he was

James Douglas

gifted with a pioneering sense. No sooner did he start work with the Hudson's Bay Company in the early thirties than he endeavoured on behalf of his concern to grasp a good share of the rich returns of the fur trade among the northwestern natives. He boldly ventured into Alaska on the *Dryad*, in 1840, planning to establish posts at the mouth of the Stikine River and on Taku Inlet; these would serve as outlets for trade with the interior. But he failed on the Stikine because of the Russians and their confederates, the Tlinkit, who were determined to guard their privileges—a monopoly already almost a century old.

The only success Douglas then achieved was in settling the boundaries between the Russian and British territories, which eventually became the border between Alaska and British Columbia. We read, in Douglas' journal for 1840–41, that "Tongass (now on the border) is to be held as neutral ground, where either party may touch and trade provisions, but neither are to purchase furs, and the Indians may carry their furs to the market that suits them best; the close proximity of that place to Fort Simpson renders such a precaution necessary for the protection of our trade;" and an equal tariff for the Russian and the British companies was agreed upon.

Excerpt from Douglas' Journal

On his way down from the north in 1840, Douglas stopped over at Fort Simpson (a short distance north of the present Prince Rupert) and had an opportunity to observe at first hand the new Hudson's Bay Company's centre of native barter and intertribal relations. Fort Simpson for many years was indeed the most important post on the sea between Fort Vancouver on the Columbia and Sitka in Alaska, where the Russian-American Company had its seat. Its function was not only to draw to itself a great deal of the benefit of the company, but to establish peace and order among warlike natives, long demoralized by contacts and encounters with predatory seamen, and now addicted to a slave trade of their own which made them constantly infringe upon one another's preserves.

The importance of Fort Simpson

The early annals of Fort Simpson show how arduous a task its factors—Chief Trader Aemilius Simpson, John Work and Peter Skene Ogden—had taken upon themselves. The establishment was many times beset with difficulties, and sometimes its safety was threatened when it was besieged by the natives.

Aemilius Simpson
John Work
Peter Skene Ogden

Originally known as Fort Nass, it was founded in 1831 near the mouth of the Nass River close to Portland Canal, at a place on tidewater now named Graveyard Point, previously known as Fort Point or Cemetery Point and, to the Indians, Suskanmilks.

Early names of the site

We may wonder why its founders had so unwisely selected this inhospitable shore which was rocky, almost devoid of fresh water, without a harbour, exposed to the strong winds of the Nass sweeping down the river for nearly three months in the year, where the cold in the winter prevented the Indians from approaching, and made it risky in other seasons for the coast Indians to venture forth in their canoes

A more undesirable location could scarcely have been found.

because of the treacherous disposition of the river natives. Perhaps it was because the point seemed sheltered, was close to the Russian frontier and less than a score of miles from Fishery Bay on the Nass where three nations—the Tsimsyan, the Tlinkit and the Haida—gathered in the spring for oolachen (candlefish) fishing and barter. Fishery Bay, with its rows of huts extending miles on both shores near the end of tidewater, stood at the head of the Grease Trails (so called because of oolachen or candlefish grease, a vital commodity) reaching out fanwise into the interior.

The last night at the old Fort: Dr. Tolmie's diary says: "Ft. Simpson on the Nass was finally abandoned 30th August, 1834, a Saturday night; and such a Saturday night the Indians never had before, as the Tyees (chiefs) of the Company had made them a parting present of a 25-gallon cask of rum, and with this aid to festivity, the Indians duly celebrated the event."

Legyarh

Intertribal jealousies and feuds, if not the climate, forced the white traders to move to a safer harbour, one to which their customers could resort at all times in the year without fear of murder or molestation. An excerpt from Tolmie's diary on the departure of the Company's personnel from the Nass, shows how precarious was the situation:

"No sleep could be obtained on the *Dryad* anchored a short distance from the shore, a drunken orgy of the wildest kind taking place (on the shore); firearms were discharged, and shrieks and yells filled the air. Among it all could be heard the ripping and hammering of timber, and when the short summer night was over, the destruction of the fort was nearly complete. On the tide suiting in the morning the *Dryad* sailed."

It seems that the removal was brought about, in 1834, by an alliance between Kennedy, the local factor, and Legyarh, virtually the head chief of the Tsimsyan and the powerful leader of all the Eagle clans; Kennedy's mate was Legyarh's daughter and Legyarh was glad to avail himself of this opportunity to enhance his already great prestige. Legyarh was no mean trader on his own account; he had relatives and friends at home and abroad, among the Tlinkit of Alaska and the Haidas of the Queen Charlotte Islands. And he was a famous warrior, whose frequent raids on the coast and up the Skeena brought him slaves and new wealth. The new fort was therefore established on Legyarh's own domain close to the sea in a sheltered harbour known under the Tsimsyan name of Larhkwaralamps—"place of wild roses."

The new location

The white men named it Fort (later Port) Simpson, after Aemilius Simpson, who had died at Fort Nass and whose body had been reinterred at the new post. From the moment of its removal, the fort became a thriving centre of business and frontier life on the Pacific Coast, into which we can give here only a few glimpses.

Tsimsyans settle at the new Fort

Nine or ten of the Tsimsyan tribes, about 2500 strong, gathered around the new fort and resided there part of the year in large square cedar-plank houses arranged in tribal clusters. During the fishing and hunting seasons they resorted in family groups to their territories and stations on the coast or on the Skeena River as far up as the canyon. But they were always on hand for the barter, the winter festivals, and whatever feuds happened to break out among rivals or enemies.

By means of a fair and shrewd diplomacy, the factors managed to weather the storms and to keep on good terms with their restless customers from various nations. After Kennedy's alliance with Legyarh's Eagle faction, another local head of the Company, Captain William McNeill (a native of Boston who had commanded the brig *Llama* and travelled back and forth from Honolulu to the Northwest Coast), likewise took an Indian mate who brought to him and the Company the support and the inner knowledge of a leading Wolf clan of the Nass River. So that now both the Eagles and the Wolves of the Tsimsyans and their allies abroad formed an implicit confederacy with the white traders. In 1835, the Company established a subsidiary station at Port Essington, known to the natives as Spukchu, at the mouth of the Skeena River. Although its whole personnel at times numbered less than twenty men, sheltered behind a palisade, a heavy gate, and protected by a few ineffective guns, it could always keep the colours flying and the prestige of the Company unimpaired.

Intermarriages strengthen the position of both white men and the company

Spukchu

Yet there were trying times and days of strife. For instance, in the manuscript journal of the Hudson's Bay Company at Fort Simpson for 1834–1837, we read that the Tsimsyans had fought with Tongass (Tlinkit) Indians in front of the fort; nine were killed, etc . . . ; that the factor had trouble on his hands because an employee, a Sandwich Islander, had kicked a native boy; that a group of Massett Haidas (from the Queen Charlotte Islands) had fought among themselves outside the gates, five being killed; that in 1836, there had been a battle between the fort and the Indians; that a mutiny had broken out among the very employees of the Company on the *Beaver*; that a local chief named CacKas[?], in a fit of anger had claimed the very land on which the fort stood and had wanted the white traders to "clear out"; that casualties were many around the trading post in the fights between the Tongass, the Stikine (both Tlinkit from the Russian territories), the Haida, the Nass River natives and the Tsimsyan. There were lesser troubles too between the first missionary, Duncan, the "pagans," and the clerks of the Company, whose standards of living could not be ironed out to everybody's satisfaction. Drunken orgies and smallpox among the tribes often were a cause of anxiety for the Company's staff, consisting of half-breeds, French-Canadians, Orkney men, and Sandwich Islanders, who always remained barricaded behind stout gates.

Problems at the fort

Once, about 1855, the Tsimsyans tried to burn the fort for some unknown reason. This time the fort retaliated with shots from the cannons in the corner bastions. But ammunition was scarce. The Indians still enjoy telling how the chief factor would pay a shilling for every cannon ball brought back to be fired again!

An account of this quarrel is found in Clah's (a Native convert's) journal, which I interpret in current idiom—his was broken, almost unintelligible, English:

One day I went, a naked little fellow, into the chief's house; he was

Legyarh, the big chief, Kennedy's father-in-law. There were two hundred Haida canoes on the beach, in three rows; they had come from Skidegate, to trade dried halibut and potatoes in the town.

The people, the day following their arrival, went to buy halibut and to sell oolachen grease in exchange. Among them—men, women and children—was Legyarh's daughter-in-law, a handsome young woman from an island below. A Haida woman, calling her, offered a bundle of dried halibut for the box of grease she was holding forth. But the halibut was not to her liking and she would not accept. Incensed, the Haida threw the bundle into the face of the Tsimsyan woman with a sneer.

Legyarh's daughter-in-law, smarting under the insult began to cry. She dropped her grease box and went to Legyarh's house, the Beaver-House of the Eagles on the Island.

"What makes my son's wife cry?" asked the chief.

"She has shamed me!" was her answer, and she pleaded: "Send two warriors, two strong men, and make her man a slave."

Legyarh did so and the husband of the Haida woman was brought back, a slave to Legyarh's daughter-in-law.

But the Haidas were a powerful warlike people; they would not accept humiliation even from their ally, the mighty Legyarh. Nobody knows who fired the first shot, but Legyarh's nephew, as he was crouching under his uncle's house, was shot through the eye by a Haida and Legyarh commanded: "All Tsimsyan kill all Haida!"

The fighting lasted two days and two nights, until Dr. Kennedy, who was married to Legyarh's daughter, shouted, "Stop!"

But they would not stop, so he began to fire the big guns. The beach was covered with dead Haidas. As nobody wanted the bodies to rot there, the fight died out in the end. The bodies were buried on the hillside, where the wild cherry trees now stand.

On the morrow, the Haidas said, "Better tell Legyarh's nephew to make peace." And they made peace. Everybody cried and shed many tears.

After a few days the islanders went away, bringing with them the woman who had insulted Legyarh's daughter and started all the trouble.

Upon reaching their home at Skidegate, the Haidas wanted to tear that woman to pieces, three men at each arm, at each leg. Her uncle came out of his house, crying "Stop it! Let her go!" and he was willing to pay her ransom. It took him many years as nearly two hundred had died.

Exaggerated as may be this naïve account, it gives an idea of what must have been the feelings of the trade pioneers within wooden walls—marooned, as it were, in the whirlpools of a wild frontier life.

The following description of Fort Simpson as it stood in 1859 is taken from a manuscript of the Bancroft Collection, entitled *Forts and Fort Life in New Caledonia under Hudson's Bay Company Regime* by Pyms Nevins Compton (Victoria, 1878):

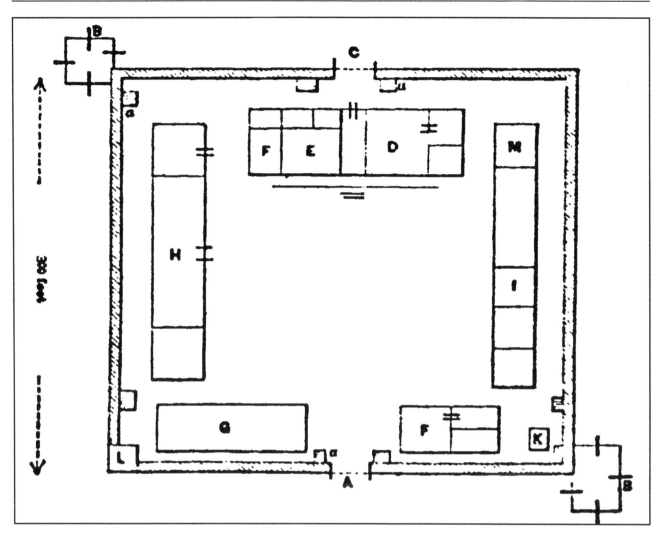

The fort was built on the same model as those of Rupert and Victoria; the only difference was in the size, that of Victoria being larger and with more buildings, a well and a garden. The houses and stores, two stories high, with shingle roofs, were built of logs ten to twelve inches square. The doors and sashes were painted and the walls whitewashed.

One of the most interesting features of the establishment, naturally, was the palisade. It was composed of "pickets and a bastion at each corner"—according to Compton's manuscript—or rather, as shown in the plan, at two corners diagonally opposite. In each bastion stood four guns, old eight pounders.

The gates were massive structures about six or seven inches thick, studded with large nails, to guard against their being cut down by the natives. There were small doors within so as to admit only one person at a time. A small box for the gate-keeper stood near the front gate.

The pickets surrounding the establishment were of cedar, about twenty-two feet long by nine to twelve inches thick; they were square laterally, to prevent bullets from passing between, sunk four feet deep in the ground, and attached to cross pieces, about four feet from the top,

Plan of Fort Simpson in 1859–66 by P.N. Compton, Victoria, 1878.
(From Bancroft's North West Coast)

A. *front entrance*
B. *bastions, 4 guns*
C. *back entrance*
D. *commanding officer's quarters*
E. *mess room*
F. *officers' quarters*
G. *trade shop*
H. *warehouse*
I. *men's houses*
K. *blacksmith shop*
L. *carpenter shop*
M. *kitchen*
a. *steps to gallery along palisade*

by means of wooden pegs or oblique notches. The ends of these cross pieces, about fifteen feet long, were mortised into stouter pickets called king posts.

An inside gallery ran around the whole enclosure of pickets at about four feet from the top, and afforded a capital promenade and a means of seeing everything. It was reached by a staircase giving separate entrance to the upper bastions, which were octagonal and loopholed for musketry.

A regular watch was kept all night in a small turret, surmounted by the flag staff, over the gate. Every half hour the call "All's well!" was repeated in nautical fashion.

Fort Simpson, in Compton's words, was "a typical fort, well kept, well built, and one of the finest on the coast." Captain McNeill was in charge at that time (1859) and the personnel consisted of thirteen other men—Orkneymen, French-Canadians and Norwegians. The steamer *Beaver*, replaced later by the *Labouchere*, served all the posts along the west coast.

Operations were carried on there by the Company until 1911, when the post was closed. Four years later, when the author was engaged in research among the local Indians, the two remaining buildings were burned down. In 1934, just a century after the establishment of the original fort on that site, the post was reopened. It is now the only Hudson's Bay post on the entire Pacific Coast, and serves the needs of a community composed of some fifty whites and six hundred natives and half-bloods.

And what of these early traders on the Skeena—how did they live and work and play? This article describes them well and leads them deftly from the pages of history onto the stage of reality.

Tsimshian Indians

◆ Vietta Worsley Baxter

The territory of the early Tsimshian Indians of BC's north coast extended along the Pacific from Metlakatla and Prince Rupert to Port Essington at the Skeena's mouth, then up Skeena to Hazelton. Before the coming of the white man, the Tsimshian lived a well-organized routine, governed by rigid laws of their own.

A slightly different dialect was spoken by each of the three tribal subdivisions at the villages at Skeena Mouth, midway on the Skeena at Kitsegleucas, and on the upper Skeena at Hazelton, Kish-ga-ges, and Kispiox.

Life was easier for the western Indian tribes than for their eastern brethren. The mild coastal climate provided cedar trees for houses, canoes, utensils and clothing. Food was plentiful in summer and by drying and smoking fish and some venison, they managed to get through the winter, except when the runs of fish occasionally failed, causing famine. Salmon was the staple diet, with cod, herring, halibut, sea and land mammals, berries, wild vegetables and greens, roots and oolichan oil as additional nutritious food. Berries mixed with oil were considered a delicacy.

They ate twice daily, usually roasted fish with oolichan oil and a dessert of berries and oolichan oil. While hunting, they ate only one meal, but at feasts there were many courses. Food was boiled with hot stones in a vessel or roasted on a spit.

Fish were taken by nets, spears, clubs and traps, the latter often resulting in bountiful catches. Every spring when the oolichan run

Totem pole at Kitwangar, BC.
(25-A) / BCARS 59323

began, the tribe went to the Nass River to catch their annual supply. The oolichan, or oil fish, provided oil for light and food. With dip nets each family raked them into their canoes, five to ten tons of fish per family every year. The oolichans were left in tight cedar boxes to decompose, after which the oil was pressed out and stored. This oil was highly prized by the interior Indians, who travelled annually over the "grease trail" from Babine Lake and other interior points to Kispiox for regular trading sessions.

In summer the Tsimshian lived in the middle and upper Skeena districts where they caught salmon and hunted deer and other animals. Often they killed animals individually with spears or bows and arrows, but in the fall rutting season they obtained deer by community drives with corral nets. In addition, the women and children picked and dried huge quantities of berries.

The mild climate allowed the Indians to dress lightly. Summer clothing consisted of a belt with a back and front hide strip. But in winter, they wore capes of deerhides, rabbits, or groundhogs plus cedar rain capes and hats of spruce roots. Foot gear was moccasins, stuffed with grass, and leggings. Chiefs wore better clothing than the commoners—a blanket in summer, furs or robes woven of mountain goat's wool and cedar bark in winter.

Crest designs of porcupine quills were lavished on hats and hide garments. All classes wore special ceremonial clothes, and tattoos, and nose, ear and lip ornaments were popular. Other items were carved headdresses and sea-lion bristles with ermine tails, as well as goat's wool leggings, decorated with three to four fringes and porcupine quills. But the decorative Chilkat blanket made of cedar bark and goat's wool, and worn by chiefs, was their most luxurious and beautiful garment.

In spring, summer and fall the Tsimshian lived a nomadic life, following the food supply, and living in temporary homes hastily fashioned from brush. Their winter homes were built in rows facing the sea, the chief's first with his totem pole standing in front. The large, square houses, of cedar with gabled roof, were rainproof. Inside, a recessed dirt floor with dirt platforms around the walls provided room for storage and grass beds. From six to fifteen families lived in one room. A fire lit on the centre dirt floor provided warmth, the smoke escaping from a square hole in the roof.

Each tribe was governed by a chief and several councillors, while society was regulated by strict laws obeyed implicitly by all. The penalty for breaking them was harsh, with the sentence for stealing being roasted to death. Needless to say there were very few thefts.

There were four social classes: chiefs, middle-class, commoners and slaves. Secret societies were the Dog-Eater, Cannibal, Destroyer and Fire-Thrower, into which chosen adolescent boys were initiated after study and rigorous physical discipline. Slaves were obtained from other conquered tribes and as a rule treated well. The chiefs and middle classes automatically belonged to the secret societies, but commoners had to save for years in order to give a potlatch, thus becoming eligible for a secret society.

Potlatches were gala affairs with feasting for several days and lavish gift-giving. Whole families worked for years to assist their elder in giving a potlatch and to erect his totem so as to share in his increased prestige. The cedar totem was carved with the family's crest or coat-of-arms, but it had no religious significance. Animals and humans were both depicted on the poles, each clan using its own crest—Eagle, Raven, Wolf or Bear.

After the feast, the potlatch host was penniless, but he knew his future was assured. Eventually, each guest must more than return the value of gifts received. The potlatch was thus a form of insurance, and also the only way a man could improve his social standing and that of his entire family.

Family life from birth to death was regulated by many taboos. The father's sisters must act as midwives at a birth and give the child gifts of cedar bark, to be doubly returned later. Groundhog skins were given at a birth announcement. Children were happy and seldom punished, but were trained in the clan's mores and manners. Usually, uncles and grandfathers taught these principles in the evening. No laziness was permitted. Boys were disciplined to cold bathing, followed by switching by their elders, a custom similar to Scandinavian and Finnish baths. At puberty they trained for the secret societies.

Girls were well-guarded and taught propriety. At thirteen they were required to live alone for ten days with no food or drink. Afterwards, a mat covered the girl's head for two weeks to ensure that she did not see any male during that period. At a subsequent date and feast, the girl's ears were pierced.

Taboos had to be observed in marriage, too. As a precaution against inbreeding, no one was allowed to marry within his own totem: Wolf, Raven, Bear or Eagle. Female property reverted from mother to daughter, while male property was inherited by a nephew on the female side, but children took on their mother's crests. Lineages were important, each family inheriting exclusive crests, songs, dances, names, stories, and privileges which no one else could use. Crests signified ancestors' adventures, including personified animal myths, all carved on totem poles and personal belongings.

In a marriage of the common class, the young man simply went to live with a girl in her parents' home. But in the ruling class, marriages were given careful thought by elders and a youth sometimes married his maternal uncle's daughter. The bride was taken to the groom's house and seated before a feast fire, during which she must not laugh.

In funeral ceremonies, sometimes cremation was practiced, but more often after the inner organs were burned, the body was placed in

Medicine man–Kitwangar
(25-A) / BCARS 51846

a cedar box in a tree, or the whole body might be placed in a burial tree in a cedar box. The body lay in state several days, surrounded by articles used in life—weapons, utensils and ornaments. Mourning was done by professional mourners, although the relatives cut their hair, blackened their faces and covered their heads with mats. Mourning lasted one year with re-marriage permitted after four years. A memorial service was held later when the family could afford to erect a memorial totem.

Tsimshian Indians believed in one God residing in the sky who watched over men in life and punished them in the afterlife—or rewarded them, whichever they deserved. Indian life had many rituals, including making sacrifices to the spirits of the first animal and fish during hunting and fishing. Taboos and rituals were also observed before canoe-making.

Old myths were told to the children, so everyone knew the fanciful stories of tribal ancestors, who were often depicted as birds or animals. Bodily cleanliness, fasting, and charity were favored; adultery, boasting and murder were discouraged.

Shamans, or medicine men, held their office by heredity and trained for it by fasting and bodily privation. They wore long, uncombed hair and aprons. The patient's family had to pay for their services or they risked illness and death. The Shaman's duties were to cure illness, caused by loss of soul, an evil spirit, or the spellcasting of an enemy.

In games, children copied the activities of their elders, thus preparing themselves for adult life. The adults loved gambling—sometimes even expensive canoes were won or lost—while the younger ones played more active games and sang and beat sticks on boards in a version of the "shell" game.

There were many inter-tribal wars, usually for revenge or some slur on the whole clan. Superior numbers, surprise attack and treachery tactics achieved most victories.

Weapons and tools—adzes, axes, chisels and war clubs—were mostly of stone; but the Tsimshian also had bows and arrows, harpoons, fish spears of shell or bone, and copper daggers. The Tsimshian produced many other articles. Canoes were made from cedar logs, while house fronts and corner poles, as well as ceremonial masks, staffs and charms were also carved from wood.

Totem poles, which originated about 100 years ago, were historical records of family accomplishment and prowess, depicted in symbolic carvings on cedar poles erected before a chief's home. To erect a totem pole, the clan had to give an expensive potlatch. However, after the Canadian government and the missionaries forbade pot-latches, the Indians did not bother to carve or erect any more poles. Only a few native artists continued and preserved the ancient skills. The abolition of potlatches contributed to the destruction of the whole Indian culture. But in the last few years, Indian art has come to be recognized for its true worth.

The Tsimshians still live along the coast at the mouths of the Nass and Skeena Rivers. About 90 percent are employed in the fishing industry and 10 percent in logging and longshoring. Many work in the coastal canneries during the salmon canning season, while others fish, although they have difficulty competing with the white man's modern, expensive boats and equipment. The Port Simpson band lives on the Tsimshian Reserve, and while the federal government provides good public schools on the reserve, students must leave to attend high school. This is a pity because although the Indians need understanding, friendship, and public acceptance, most of all they must have a full education and the opportunity to participate in contemporary life, while retaining pride and respect for their noble heritage.

William Downie

Major William Downie made a trip up the Skeena by canoe in 1859. Downie is said to have been shown a carving on a tree, which read: PIONEER HBC. Some say it was put there by John Work, one of the early factors at Port Simpson, but Work did not take over his post until 1835. It is therefore more likely to have been done by Donald Manson, who was sent up the Skeena by the Company in 1832, and ascended the river for 50 miles.

Downie's trip was remarkable for the speed with which it was done---just over two weeks---and the fact that he had no trouble with the hostile Indians. The information he gleaned from his travels was a help to those who came after.

The Diary of William Downie

I left Fort Simpson for the Skeena river on the 5th of August. From Fort Simpson to Port Essington is about forty miles. The salt water here appears a light blue colour, and runs inland about thirty miles; the coarse grained quartz of Fort Simpson is no longer seen here; granite appears. The banks of the river are low, with small hard wood, and cotton-trees on its margin, with some good-sized white oaks, the finest I have seen west of Fraser River.

Vessels drawing more than four feet of water cannot go more than twenty miles up the Skeena river, and it is very unlike the deep inlets to the southward. At our camp here some Indians visited us; they told us they were honest, but in the morning the absence of my coat rather negatived their statement. Next day we found the river shoal even for loaded canoes, as it had fallen much. I went up a small river at our next camp, called Scenatoys, and the Indians showed me some crystallized quartz, and to my surprise a small piece with gold in it, being the first I have seen in this part. The Indian took me to a granite slide, whence he asserted the piece of quartz in question had come from; I found some thin crusts of fine quartz, but nothing like a rich vein. Ten miles further I found more fine grained quartz, but no gold. I am of opinion, however, that good paying quartz will be found here.

From the small river just mentioned at the mouth of the Skeena or Port Essington, it is seventy-five miles; a little below it, an Indian trail leads to Fort Simpson; it is through a low pass, and the distance is not great.

From this, ten miles further up, is a small river called the Foes, on the south side; hence is an Indian trail to Kitlopes, on the Salmon River. The south branch of Salmon River is called Kittama.

By this time we were fairly over the coast range of mountains, and those ahead of us did not look very high. The current here was strong, and much labour required to get the canoe along, and we had to pull her up by a rope from the shore.

Gold is found here, a few specks to the pan, and the whole country looks like a gold country with fine bars and flats, and clay on the bars. The mountains look red, and slate and quartz can be seen.

Our next camp was at the village of Kitthalaska; and I started in a light canoe ahead of my party, as our canoe, by all accounts, could not get much further; I then determined to penetrate to Fort Fraser (supposed to mean establishment of H.B. Company).

The Indian who was with me informed me that a large stream called the Kitchumsala comes in from the north, the land on it is good, and well adapted for farming; the Indians grow plenty of potatoes here. To the south a small stream, called the Chimkootsh, enters, on the south-west of which is the Plumbago Mountain; I had some of it in my hand; it is as clear as polished silver, and runs in veins of quartz. Near this are the words "Pioneer H.B.C." on a tree nearly overgrown with the bark. The Indian told me this was cut by Mr. John Work, a long time ago. From here to the village of Kitcoonsa the land improves, the mountains recede from the river, and fine flats run away four or five miles back to the mountain sides, where the smoke is seen rising from the Indian huts; they are occupied in picking and drying berries for the winter. The Indians here are very kind to me, and wished me to build a house and live with them.

Above the village of Kitcoonsa the prospect of gold is less; below it, a man could make a dollar a day. As the season was so advanced I was not able to prospect the hills which look so well about here, and unless the Government take it in hand it will be a long time before the mineral resources of this part of British Columbia are known. I think this is the best looking mineral country I have seen in British Columbia.

From here to the village of Kitsogatala the river is rocky and dangerous, and our canoe was split from stem to stern.

Here we enter an extensive coal country, the seams being cut through by the river, and running up the banks on both sides, varying in thickness from three to thirty-five feet.

The veins are largest on the north-east side, and sandstone appears; it is soft, and gives easily to the pick.

The veins dip into the bank for a mile in length, and could be easily worked on the face by tunnels, and also by sinking shafts at the rear on the flats, as they run into banks of soft earth. I have seen no coal like this in all my travels in British Columbia or Vancouver Island. Here we had some danger from Indians, but a small present of tobacco, and putting aside all fear, or even appearance of it, succeeded in quieting them. I find it best to be cool and determined in the prospect of a fight.

The land around Naas Glee is first rate, and wild hay and long grass abounds. Potatoes are not grown here. There is no heavy pine timber in the neighbourhood, and the canoes are made of cottonwood.

Our course from Naas Glee to Fort Killamaurs, was N.E., and the distance about fifty miles. The land is good the whole way, with long grass on the benches near Fort Killamaurs. This is a very lovely place, and no sound to be heard save one—our voice. It seems a great pity to see this beautiful land, so well adapted for the wants of man, laying waste, when so many Englishmen and Scotchmen would be glad to come here and till the soil. Babine Lake is deep, and in some places five or six miles wide; there are islands and points of land to afford shelter from the storm, wherever the wind blows from.

At the head of Babine Lake there is a fine site for a town, and a good harbour could be made. A stream runs down here which would supply water for the town. This is what I call the head waters of Skeena River. There is plenty of water in the lake for steamers, and it is a hundred miles in length. From here to Stuart's Lake there is a portage over a good trail, and through the finest grove of cotton wood I have ever seen, to Stuart's Lake; the ground was thickly strewed with golden leaves, giving the scene an autumnal appearance, altogether different to what we expected to find in British Columbia.*

WILLIAM DOWNIE
To His Excellency, Governor Douglas, C.B., &c. &c.

* The harbour of Fort Simpson is a very safe, though not a perfect, harbour; the anchorage is good. It is apparently exposed to the west and south-west, but is protected from the swell by a reef, covered at high water and exposed at half tide. This harbour may be by and by of importance, especially if it shall be found necessary to open a road into the northern part of British Columbia, direct from the coast.—J.D.P.

The need to transport supplies and equipment for the Collins Overland Telegraph Company triggered the first attempt to navigate the Skeena River by sternwheeler. We are fortunate in having available the journal of Charles Morrison in which he recounts vividly his firsthand experiences with the Company.

Collins Overland Telegraph Company, 1866

◆ Charles Morrison (1920)

In May, 1866, I was working with a friend of mine, Arthur Bullock, who was doing a roaring business; but the hours were fearfully long—sixteen hours a day, and snatch a meal whenever possible. The strain overtaxed my health and body; being quite young I sought new pastures and entered the service of the Collins Overland Telegraph Company.

For several years unsuccessful attempts had been made to lay a telegraph cable across the Atlantic Ocean from Europe to North America; finally the Western Union Telegraph Company of New York conceived the idea of stringing a telegraph line across North America, through British Columbia from the southern portion, and north from Quesnel to the vicinity of the present town of Hazelton and on to Telegraph Creek on the Stikine River, thence through Russian Alaska, across the Bering Sea, through Asia, and finally to Paris, London and other European cities—a stupendous idea, and a still more stupendous undertaking.

The telegraph company was commencing work. The chief executives made a request to the British Columbia government: as they intended making a large expenditure in BC, that they be allowed to import from the United States all materials for the construction of the telegraph line, including provisions and medical supplies, all these items to be free of duty and other imposts. It had been reported in many quarters the Company intended to bring in cheap labour from San Francisco. It was also reported that this labour would be derived from an extremely low grade of the population, a class not desired in BC. Jobs were scarce and if the labour importation was allowed, it would deprive BC men of work.

The reply from the Government was wise; they would forego charges of duty and imposts on general construction supplies, but on the condition that the Company hire their labour in British Columbia, and whenever possible, that they employ as many Indians as possible. These terms were agreeable to both parties, and the great work, for great it was, began.

One large party travelled up the Fraser River to Quesnel, and were then to strike across country in a northwesterly direction to a point near the confluence of the Skeena and Bulkley Rivers. The Indian name of the latter river was "Watsonquah," but it was changed to the white name in honour of Colonel Charles S. Bulkley, who was in charge of the entire Collins project. The junction of these two rivers was in the direct proximity of old Hazelton and the village of Hagwilget, the latter being well populated in 1866; these natives were part of the Bulkley River Carrier Indians.

The other party was to start from New Westminster and follow the northwest coast of British Columbia in a northwesterly direction until they reached the mouth of the Skeena, between five and six hundred miles distant, the voyage to be made by sternwheeler. From the mouth of the river they would follow the Skeena until they reached the "Forks" of the Skeena and Bulkley rivers, where they would join with the overland party from Quesnel.

The northern coastal waters were very little known except to Hudson's Bay Company navigators and officials, and illicit whiskey traders on small schooners, men who plied their nefarious trade among the Indian inhabitants of the coast.

I joined the coastal party through their agent, Mr. Pitman, at their New Westminster headquarters. Other members of the party were: E. Conway, engineer in charge of all works; Charles Burrage, paymaster; Mr. Lugenbeel, chief bookkeeper; and our never-to-be-forgotten surgeon, Dr. George Chismore, my bosom friend who in later years became a leading surgeon in San Francisco. Directly in charge of the party was Captain James L. Butler, a splendid type for the job which he well proved as time went on; his accountant was R.W. Brown of New Westminster, formerly Colour-Sergeant to the London Irish Rifles; your humble servant—commissary clerk; and to round out the crew—forty construction and utility men; some were fine chaps, a few were rather tough, but all splendid workers. Writing this in 1920, I imagine I am the lone survivor of the party.

To transport men and supplies up the Skeena River to Mission Point (the junction of the Skeena and the Bulkley), between 160 and 180 miles, the company decided to use a sternwheel river boat.

The Sternwheeler *Mumford*

The proposed master of the vessel, Captain Tom Coffin, a fine white water man, had in 1864 investigated the turbulent waters of the Skeena in a small sternwheeler, the *Union*; incidentally the first steam-powered vessel ever to enter that river. Captain Coffin had drawn plans for a sternwheel boat of very light draft suitable for the rapid Skeena. These plans were submitted to the directors in New York. Quite naturally the directors had not the faintest conception of the build and other particulars of a British Columbia river boat. They would not accept under any conditions the plans tendered by the experienced Captain Coffin; instead they hired a New York marine architect to draft plans and design a sternwheel river boat for the swift waters of BC. The architect, of course, had no idea of the baffling, shallow, swift and treacherous Skeena. But he completed the plans and they were forwarded to the ship builders in Victoria. Captain Coffin saw at once they were not suitable, that he would never succeed in getting a vessel of that design up the Skeena. These opinions of the Captain were forwarded to New York, to which the answer came: "Build a boat according to the plans sent you!" The ultimatum was accepted. She was constructed according to the orders from headquarters, and proved a dismal failure in rapid and shallow waters. She was completed in detail at Victoria, and christened the *Mumford* after one of the directors in New York. Upon completion she left for New Westminster where she arrived on 2nd July, 1866. The loading of supplies etc. for the expedition was commenced immediately. It was here the writer joined her.

Mumford up the Coast

Captain Butler was anxious to get away on the 3rd July as the season was getting along. Besides he knew well the next day being the "glorious" Fourth of July, we would be unable to accomplish anything with his crew. So the loading went on apace, enabling us to sail the 3rd of July.

I might mention here we all had to sign very strict articles, which were no "paper" articles, for they were most strictly adhered to and carried out. We were not allowed to trade with the Indians or interfere with them in any manner whatsoever. The articles were identical for the Chief Engineer down to the cook. So behold us embarking on our voyage! Many of us—the writer included—had no knowledge of where the Skeena River was; I, for one, and many others had never heard of it.

The Voyage, Summer 1866

On July 3, 1866, the loading of men and supplies was completed; and that evening, under command of Captain Coffin, we set sail from New Westminster for, to most of us, parts unknown.

We had a fine trip up the coast; went through Seymour Narrows in flying style; called at Suquash, a coal mine below Fort Rupert, long since deserted. There was no Alert Bay Mission or cannery in those days; we then arrived at Fort Rupert, at that time a flourishing Hudson's Bay Company Post under the charge of Mr. Compton. We met him below the fort returning from a hunting trip and towed his large canoe up to Fort Rupert. Leaving the Fort in the evening, we crossed Queen Charlotte Sound during the night; there was very little swell, which was fortunate for us as sternwheelers are by no means adapted for sea work, and as Captain Butler quaintly remarked: "It was very like going to sea in a wheelbarrow!" We accomplished the crossing without incident, and after passing Bella Bella we luckily struck a calm streak in Milbanke Sound.

During the course of the voyage we were obliged to anchor several times to go ashore and cut wood as the steamer, heavily loaded as she was, had very little room for fuel. The weather was fine and the scenery grand, but packing cordwood on your shoulder over a rocky beach to the ship was not grand.

The food was good, but the vessel had only sleeping accommodation for the ship's company. We had to pick a soft plank at night on which to spread our blankets, which also were not grand. With so many mouths to feed our supply of fresh beef soon gave out, and we fell back on bacon, salt horse, salt pork, but as they were all excellent of their kind, we did not fare so badly. When we steamed through Grenville Channel, a deer was seen swimming across the channel. Captain Coffin shot it from the pilot house; it certainly proved a welcome addition to our fare; although there was one man who would not touch it, as he said venison was not fit food for white man but only fit for Indians to eat. We left him to enjoy his salt horse in peace.

At the north end of Grenville Channel we made a sharp turn to starboard, and perceived that the water was becoming muddy. We were informed we had entered the mouth of our goal, the Skeena River. The ocean tide when flooding backs up the river for nearly forty miles above the present Port Essington.

At the head of tidewater we encountered the full current of the river. Unable to make any headway, we tied up to the river bank. The men built a rough warehouse in which half the cargo was stored.

Final Attempt to Beat the Rapids

The *Mumford* made one more effort to surmount a riffle. Captain Coffin wedged the safety valve down. We had a line ahead fastened to a tree which was heaved on by a hand-power windlass. I was busy with a bucksaw, sawing short lengths of wood to feed the furnace. They heaved a five gallon tin of tar into the furnace, all the cook's slush and several sides of fat bacon. The steam gauge had gone to "no man's land." The line ahead parted and we gave up, dropped downstream several yards and tied up. The Chief Engineer knocked away the throttle lever, threw the fire overboard, and we were at peace.

The attempted ascent of the Skeena soon demonstrated the weaknesses of the *Mumford*. In spite of lightening the ship of more than half her cargo, we were unable to ascend further than the Kitsumkalum River. From there on the cargo for the upper river was trans-shipped to large Indian canoes. These canoes had a deadweight capacity of two tons and over.

So ended a coastal voyage by sternwheeler in July 1866. No beacons, lights, buoys or properly detailed charts.

Captain Butler proceeded downriver and up the coast to the Hudson's Bay Company Post at Fort Simpson (known now as Port Simpson), returning with a fleet of large canoes to freight our supplies up the river.

The *Mumford* went down coast to New Westminster for another load of supplies which she brought to the mouth of the Skeena, where it was picked up by freight canoes and transported to Mission Point at the junction of the Skeena and Bulkley Rivers.

Canoes & Freighting the Skeena River 1866

I made a couple of canoe trips as one of the crew, and I can truthfully state, if you wish to realize hard work, go freighting up the Skeena in a heavily laden canoe.

The *Mumford* with half a cargo made another futile attempt on the river and landed the supplies at a camp we named Mumford's Landing, below the mouth of the Kitsumkalum River.

Captain Butler loaded his flotilla of canoes for the upriver trip and left me alone at the warehouse to act as watchman. I was entirely alone for fourteen days. I had neither watch nor clock and it rained incessantly. I completely lost track of time. My camp outfit consisted of one tin plate, one coffee pot, knife, fork and spoon, a supply of matches, a hatchet and a six-shooter. Sounds a bit like Robinson Crusoe, doesn't it! Of course there were plenty of provisions in the warehouse, but alas! they had neglected to leave me that "all-in-all" of camp life—a frying pan; to remedy this omission I cut a cleft stick which nicely held a tin plate. It made a good substitute. At night I spread my blankets on the freight, and as the shanty had no door, I placed my camp outfit in the doorway so the entrance of an intruder would create a clatter and waken me. One night I was aroused by a noise like a man moving amongst the freight. I challenged—"Who is there?" No answer. Then I gave a warlike challenge—"Answer or I shoot!"—when behold, a large bush rat, the creator of the noise, bolted through the doorway; anticlimax—I rolled myself in my blankets and went to sleep feeling rather small after my martial ebullition.

The following day I was surprised at the return of all the Fort Simpson Indians with their canoes en route home. They had deserted Captain Butler and were bound for Fort Simpson. One of the young men insulted me in an unmentionable manner; I retaliated with a powerful application of my boot on that portion of his anatomy ordained by Providence to receive such a salute. My well directed blow lifted the young man about two feet off the ground. The Indians proceeded home, and I must say to their credit, they returned all the camp equipment before their departure. Their reason for this action: It appeared their leading man was awed by the magnitude of the work undertaken. Since he had decided that the whole concern was the private property of Captain Butler, and since he felt certain that no single man would have enough money to reimburse all the help hired, he reasoned that on completion of the work, the natives would be denied their due wages. Following this line of reasoning, he persuaded all members of the fleet to decamp rather than face further ruin.

This turn of events did not seem to bother Captain Butler, who definitely was not possessed of a panicky disposition. He left at once for the celebrated Church of England mission station Metlakatla which at that time, 1866, was the only and pioneer Christian mission on the Northwest coast, conducted by the celebrated William Duncan.

William Duncan was an outstanding missionary and also a keen man of business, with his eye on the main chance when it redounded to the success and good of the village. He operated a general store at his Mission, and realized immediately the immense advantage his village would enjoy by securing the canoe freighting for the Telegraph Company. He knew and understood the Indians as well as any Hudson's Bay Company Officer and spoke the Tsimsean language like a native. At the request of Captain Butler he assembled the people with their headman, Paul Legaic, one of the first converts, to explain particulars of the work. The people were agreeable, and a contract was speedily entered into with them to canoe freight up the Skeena River for the duration of the season. At the termination of the freighting, Captain Butler would meet them with a chest full of money and pay them in cash for their work. This arrangement was carried out to the satisfaction of both parties.

Captain Butler soon returned upriver with his fleet; and I, these Metlakatla men and a few Kitselas relatives worked faithfully throughout the season. The natives, in conjunction with our thirty-five white men laboured together very successfully. The white men, with one or two exceptions, were trained Columbia River boatmen, and took the lead on the trips upriver. Our head boat steerer was a man named Muller. A Prussian, Muller could neither read nor write, but what he did not know about river boating was not worth knowing. He was an all around good fellow and captained the largest canoe manned by whites. John Mitchell was in charge of the second canoe, an American and an honour to his country; Hicks, a fine type of young Englishman, captained the third canoe. These three vessels were very large cedar canoes purchased at Fort Simpson. Some of the men were as tough as they make them, but under a rough exterior, and sometimes awful language, there beat hearts of gold; they were all most kind to the "boy" as they were pleased to call me. Their memory is ever green to me.

The young gentleman who had shipped as our cook in Victoria rejoiced in the soubriquet of "Handcraft" Jaci, due to handling a vehicle of that description in Victoria. He had professed to Captain Butler a thorough knowledge of cooking. The Captain had advised him he required a capable man as the men would be working hard and must be well fed. Alas, when we arrived at the "Front" it was discovered his culinary knowledge was nil. His loaves of bread would have made perfect wadding for big guns; the rest of his cooking was in keeping. He was soon relieved; in exchange we got the coloured cook from the *Mumford*. This man was an expert in his department; the men would not permit him to do any work in the boats, they simply petted him. In return he served them the best meals possible under the circumstances and conditions.

First Passage of Historic Kitselas Canyon, 1866

Before making the first passage of historic Kitselas Canyon, we tied up in the evening just below the canyon. Captain Butler judged it wise to make camp and tackle the turbulent waters next day. Most of the men were pretty well fagged out from a long hard day.

Shortly after supper while enjoying our "Otium cum dig" (ease with dignity) and listening to what he called music from the concertina of our friend Muller, a small canoe arrived down the river containing an envoy from Kit-Horn, the Kitselas chief, with a message that if we attempted the passage of the canyon, the tribe would heave rocks upon us from above (the canyon had high box walls) and sink our canoes. They laboured under the delusion that we were a great trading company and would ruin their trade with the upriver Indians, the latter not being allowed to pass through the canyon to the coast. A gift of pig-tail tobacco was tendered and a fill up of bacon and beans; then the Captain informed the messenger we were not a trading company, but a working party, and far from interfering with their trade, would employ them and pay them for work they performed. Incidentally, the Captain ordered our arms chests to be opened, these contained a great display of Colt's repeating rifles, Sharp's carbines and revolvers. At the sight of this display the messenger's eyes widened in wonderment and fear. Captain Butler finally informed him emphatically he would go through the canyon in any case, also when he delivered a statement he would live up to every word of it!

Next morning we continued the journey and reached the canyon. In this period, the 1860s, both sides of the canyon were lined with large Indian houses populated with about five hundred inhabitants. The rock walls were lined with Indians far above us. They rushed down, but instead of smashing or sinking us they tacked on to our towlines and drew us through the canyon in triumph accompanied with much yelling and shouting. They were of great assistance to us because in the month of July the river was at a very high stage. It took the whole day to get the entire flotilla through. We were most thankful to camp that evening in a small and quiet bay at the head of the canyon. Following a hearty meal we all were soon asleep.

From this point I was placed in charge of a squadron of twenty-five Indian freight canoes. Rather an important charge for a young chap of twenty-two years. I endeavored to my utmost to merit the trust placed in me, and I believe I satisfied Captain Butler.

By this time I had got to really know our Chief. He expected every man to do his duty to the utmost. He never spared himself, was a fair and just man to both Indians and white men. As a consequence he was idolized by all.

I mentioned previously we were under the strictest orders not to interfere in any manner with the Indians. One of our men broke this rule and sneaked into a native village in the dead of night; he created a disturbance and was driven out.

Next morning, knowing nothing of the midnight episode, we started out with our canoes; when lo and behold, we perceived the rocks lined with Indians armed with flintlock muskets. Their spokesman demanded the man who had disturbed them during the night. Captain Butler ordered silence from his men, then asked the Indians to point out the offender, which they promptly did. The offender confessed his fault and Captain Butler discharged him at once. This prompt action satisfied the Indians. We were obliged to take the culprit along with us upriver so as we could return him to the coast by the first return canoe. Unfortunately he was one of our prize boatmen, and to him his greatest punishment was not being allowed to work. Each time he touched a paddle, pole or towline—came the sharp order from Captain Butler: "Drop that, you are not in the employ of the Company!" When we reached our destination, the offender approached Dr. Chismore, a close friend of the captain, and requested the doctor to intercede for him. Butler relented and the man was reinstated. From that time forward you could not have found a steadier or better behaved man.

Left in Charge of Mission Point Depot

I was behind the main fleet with my squadron and arrived at

Mission Point after the others had unloaded their canoes. A rough log building had been constructed for the freight and supplies.

By this time I had cut my foot badly on a sharp stone one evening just before retiring. I had nothing to cover it with except a woolen sock and heavy boot; the cut festered and became intensely painful. When I arrived at the end of my journey I was done in for lack of sleep. I shook hands with Captain Butler, who remarked, "What is the matter with you, my boy? You look like a ghost and as though you had nothing to eat for a week. Go to the cook and get filled up." I went over and managed to eat a bit; then the Captain summoned me and asked me if I would remain in charge of the freight depot; of course this meant being left alone. Other men who had been approached on the subject had flunked it because of the near proximity of the interior Indians who at that period were wild men. I replied I was quite willing to stay. His answer was, "That's the boy! When we go downriver tomorrow we shall leave you alone!"

When the men learned of my decision, their comforting re-marks were, "the Hagwilgets will capture you and eat you alive, then take the stores and supplies!" I thought differently because I had considerable experience before this with the Fraser River Indians. The entire party left early the next morning and I remained "solus."

My foot was still extremely painful, the gash being across the bottom directly under the ball of the foot. I got out my penknife, sharpened the small blade on a stone, took a bandage and salve from the medicine chest, limped down to the river and soaked my foot in the ice-cold water, then jabbed my knife into the swelling and cut it open; nearly a cupful of matter discharged and I obtained immediate relief. I applied salve, bandaged it up and experienced no more trouble. I continued to soak it in the river constantly. I knew nothing of germs, microbes or blood poisoning in those early days. These luxuries came with the advent of civilization.

Hagwilget Indian Braves

After the departure downriver of men, boats and canoes I was to be alone until their return in two or three weeks. Quite a responsi-bility for a lad of my age. Under my care and watching were many tons of provisions and general construction supplies.

I cooked my lone supper the first evening, and feeling tired I rolled into my blankets and dropped off to sleep in the open air as the weather was beautiful and warm. Next morning I rose early and walked down to the river for my daily cold bath.

I had just finished breakfast when down came about a hundred Hagwilget Indians to survey the white boy and his camp. They were a fierce-looking lot, not a pair of trousers among them, their faces painted red and black, and each carrying a Hudson's Bay Company flintlock musket and long knife. I think they were more curious than warlike. I sat on a stump smiling like a Cheshire cat with all of them staring at me. We could not converse as none knew the language of the other. Then I was struck with a bright idea. I noticed an old man who appeared to be their chief. I rose and approached him, cap in hand, made a most polite bow, extended my hand to him and we shook hands most cordially. I then took a very large United States Army kettle, of which we had many, placed a quantity of rice in it, filled it with water and placed it on my camp fire to boil. I then poured in a couple of pannikins of molasses and stirred it with a large stick; I distributed tin plates and iron spoons amongst them, then a large helping and they enjoyed what to them was a glorious feast. They were my solid friends from then on. Their fierceness after all seemed to have been on the surface. At the same time I could not help but credit myself with a bit of diplomacy.

I had a few visitors every day, all men with the exception of one woman, the wife of the chief. The other women of the tribe kept strictly away from the camp.

The fleet arrived again. Most of the white men were surprised to find me alive and looking so well and hearty. The canoes discharged cargo and returned down stream for another load.

I took a cold bath in the river every morning clad in nature's garb. The Indians including the wife of the old chief, were most interested in my performance; some attended daily to witness my morning ablutions. I imagine they seldom washed themselves and were astounded at seeing a man wash his body daily.

River and Overland Sections Join—1866

We had successfully got word to the overland working party that we had reached the confluence of the Skeena and Bulkley Rivers. The pleasant result was the arrival of three or four Indians with pack loads of fresh beef for us. To eat fresh meat again was a delightful change from our staple diet of beans and bacon. The land party drove a fine band of steers with them to ensure a supply of fresh meat.

One morning the old Chief accompanied by a number of his tribe came rushing along the trail shouting, "Man-o'-War, Man-o'-War!" I was very much puzzled by their outburst and wondered what they meant. The enigma was solved when a small pack train of four or five cayuse ponies appeared under the charge of a whiteman, with an order for provisions from the land party. These Indians had never seen a horse before but had heard of the terrible Man-of-War from the Coast Trader Indians. Today in the 1900s the same Indians own any number of horses, and from the children up are splendid riders.

Original Indian Bridge, Bulkley Canyon

Be it known, these Carrier Indians have no canoes, but are really wonderful bush travellers.

Previous to the arrival of white men, and with no expert advisors, they had constructed a wonderful bridge across the Bulkley River Canyon at Hagwilget. This bridge was built on the cantilever principle and was devised by employing their native ingenuity and natural skill. A bridge a hundred or more feet above a roaring canyon without a single nail or piece of iron composition, wood pegs instead of nails, and all the timbers fastened together with native rope made of twisted cedar withes. It was not, as some people have written, built principally by members of the white race. The bridge was there when we arrived, and it is my firm belief we were the first white men to see it. From our top men down all agreed it was a stupendous piece of workmanship. However, it was a trifle shaky and calculated to try the nerves of any individual crossing it for the first time.

Trial Trip by Canoe Through Bulkley Canyon

The Bulkley Canyon was judged impossible for navigation. No Indian had attempted to ascend it by either boat or canoe. Somehow, we had to transport equipment through the canyon to meet with the overland working parties, who were short of telegraph wire and insulators. How was this to be accomplished? Our coast canoe and freighting Indians positively refused to even attempt the trip. Captain Butler turned to me and asked if I would essay the passage in a small canoe to ascertain if it was possible to get a loaded canoe through. I managed to persuade three daredevil young Coast Indians to accompany me.

It was a formidable task. The canyon was narrow with almost perpendicular rock walls on either side, and the whole body of the Bulkley River roaring through the chasm. We towed almost continuously, using the most precarious footholds in the rock crevices and fissures. After most grueling and dangerous efforts we arrived at a small bay of comparatively still water above the bridge crossing. This was far enough for the purpose of our experiment. A hopeless job for a regular freight canoe. Following a rest we commenced our downriver race—and a race it was. It took us fully three quarters of a day to complete the upriver journey, and three quarters of an hour to make the down trip. I think we would have outrun a railway train. When we shot out of the mouth of the canyon we were greeted with a tremendous roar and chorus of yells from a party of spectator Indians. A few more minutes and we landed safely back where we started at Mission Point. We had the dubious honour of being the first canoe ever to ascend and return through the Bulkley River Canyon, Mission Point to Hagwilget and back. No D.S.O. for me and no decorations for the spunky crew.

Crossing Bulkley Canyon by Bridge

When the telegraph line was completed to the banks of the Bulkley River, the river had to be crossed by 105 white men, 200 pack animals, numerous Chinese cooks and Indians and a herd of beef cattle.

Old Indian bridge, Bulkley River,
Hazelton, BC.
(65-C) / Wrathall Coll.

To attempt to swim animals through the torrent was impossible. To solve the river crossing, Steve Decker, the general foreman, ordered up his gang of first-class bridgemen to build a bridge across the Bulkley Canyon. But a serious stumbling block arose; the Indians most strenuously objected to such a proceeding. One of the wise men of their tribe informed them that if the "whites" spanned the river with a bridge, no salmon would pass that imaginary line in the waters of the canyon. Our chief did not wish to clash with the natives in any manner, so a great conference and palaver ensued. After much talk, the Indians consented to allow Steve Decker to strengthen and repair their original bridge to make it passable for men, animals and supplies.

All hides of the cattle killed on the way from Quesnel had been transformed into rawhide ropes which Steve used to lash the bridge strongly. He laid a new floor on the old decking, and the passage was made safely by all concerned, although I am of the opinion that humans and animals alike were glad when the crossing was completed. A load and great strain was lifted from Steve Decker's mind.

Construction—Bulkley Crossing to Kispiox on Skeena River

The work went along swimmingly from the Bulkley River crossing to the Skeena River opposite the large and flourishing village of Kispiox. This was and still is (1920) the largest Indian village on the Skeena. In 1866 I imagine they numbered some 700 or 800 souls.

Amongst these people, as usual, was a learned Indian doctor or medicine man who, thinking very rightly that the advent of the white man would destroy his power over his people, informed them that if the telegraph wire crossed the Skeena River near the village no more salmon would ascend the river; furthermore all birds and animals crossing under or over the wire would instantly die. These predictions alarmed the people of Kispiox, who sent word to Mr. Conway that they would shoot the first white man to cross the river if he was in any way connected with the Telegraph Company.

This was a serious threat. Mr. Conway ordered all work stopped and every man armed. We possessed adequate supplies of arms and munitions to be used only in case of necessity or emergency. He concealed the white men in ambush along the Skeena bank opposite Kispiox village. Conway then came down to Mission Point for another council of war at which it was decided to send Mr. Burrage and young Morrison up to Kispiox to parley with the Indians. I cut up a quantity of pigtail tobacco into short lengths and placed it in a rice mat. Tobacco in the eyes and minds of the Indians was equal to fine jewelry. We then poled the small canoe approximately twelve miles from Mission Point to Kispiox. On arrival we were greeted by a horde of armed Indians, but with diplomacy and tact, Mr. Burrage managed to explain to them that our work would bring them cash money. He further announced that if the Chiefs would come forward he had a present of tobacco for each. Instantly a large section of the crowd became Chiefs. The tobacco bag was emptied and a general handshaking ensued. We returned to the camp, stowed the arms and munitions away; the men returned to their work from their points of ambush without the Indians ever knowing a man was under arms. The populace of Kispiox turned on their wise medicine man and chased him out of the village!

The work went along quietly and the telegraph line was completed to a point forty miles north of Kispiox village.

A telegrapher accompanied the project with his telegraph instrument and a portable battery, and when work finished at 6:00 p.m., he attached his instrument to the end of the wire. Presto! we had the latest news from New York. It still seems wonderful to me to this day!

One evening Mr. Conway called a halt, then turning to the listening crowd, announced "Boys, the Atlantic Cable has been successfully laid by the steamship *Great Eastern*. Messages are now crossing from London to New York via the Atlantic Ocean, so I expect our work is over!"

This news came to us towards the end of September 1866. Mr. Conway's prediction of the work being ended proved true. Shortly afterwards all construction was stopped and all hands, with the exception of a few, were ordered to the coast and thence to Victoria to be paid off. The depot at Mission Point was empty at this point, all the stores having been shipped to the end of the telegraph line.

To Wrangell in Russian America

When the entire operation ceased on the Skeena, orders came to Mission Point that R.A. Brown, Captain Butler's bookkeeper, and myself, the commissary clerk, were to engage a small canoe, go to the coast, and follow the coastline northwest to Wrangell in Russian America. There, we were to report to Captain Butler for further instructions.

The Collins Telegraph Company had shipped quantities of provisions up the coast to Wrangell, which at that time was merely a Stikine Indian village. About a quarter of a mile from the village was a large log building with a lean-to at the side: a former Hudson's Bay Company trading post, now used by the telegraph company to store provisions and supplies; the stock of telegraph wire was stacked on the beach. Altogether the company had enough materials on hand to construct five hundred miles of telegraph line.

Brown and I found that procuring a canoe at Mission Point was almost impossible. The Hagwilgets, being land or Carrier Indians, had none. There was one very large canoe at the depot, the last to arrive with a company load. This canoe would be returning to the village of Metlakatla; but it would have cost a small fortune to charter such a vessel as it required a crew of eight to ten men to navigate and handle her. At this juncture the owner spoke and it was then I had the pleasure and honour of meeting with the Tsimpsean Chief, the celebrated Paul Legaic. He was truly a great and fine man. He stepped forward and placed his canoe—a splendid craft—his crew and himself at our service free of charge.

Legaic was the chief man of William Duncan's celebrated mission of Metlakatla, and one of his very earliest converts at Fort Simpson. His kind offer was gladly accepted, and so R.A. Brown and Morrison embarked for the salt chuck.

The crew made a very comfortable place for us in the stern sheets, just forward of Legaic, our host and captain. A fine trip we had down the river, not stopping at all, but eating and catching what little sleep we could get in the canoe. How the crew managed I do not know; they seemed to me to belong to an order of sleepless beings. We passed what is now Port Essington, which at that time was only being used by the Indians as a last camp on their way back from Metlakatla and Fort Simpson after hunting and salmon drying upriver. We passed the present Inverness on a beautiful moonlit night, the sea smooth as glass, and were greeted with the same solitude. We, the passengers, became tired of sitting still and essayed paddling, but no—Legaic quietly took the paddles out of our hands and made us desist, saying, "I asked you to travel with me not to work!"

We arrived at Metlakatla at 5:30 on a beautiful morning; the village looked very pretty to us, quiet and peaceful. This was the pioneer Mission Station of the Anglican Church under the auspices of the Church Missionary Society of England; and in 1866, the only Christian mission on the Northwest Coast. It was ruled in a thoroughly autocratic manner by the celebrated William Duncan.

Upon our arrival at Metlakatla we were naturally tired and hungry from our long trip. However, we intended to procure a canoe and continue our journey to Fort Simpson, where we were certain of a hospitable reception by the Hudson's Bay Company officials.

We had previously been informed that Mr. Duncan disliked any white men landing at the village. On striking the beach Legaic invited us to his house for breakfast. We did not wish to embroil our friend in any trouble, and told him we would wait on the beach until he kindly procured us a canoe for Fort Simpson. The Chief drew himself up in a most dignified manner and said, "I ask you to come to my house, not to Mr. Duncan's. Come on!" We walked up to Legaic's house where we had the pleasure of meeting his wife and daughter. We were royally entertained—warm water, scented soap and clean towels for our ablutions—of which we were much in need! We then were seated at a beautifully laid table and a most sumptuous repast: salmon cutlets, venison steaks, splendid potatoes, tea, coffee, bread and butter, and withal two boys to wait upon us. Paul Legaic took the head of the table and fulfilled the duties of host to perfection.

After breakfast Legaic found a small canoe owned by Thomas Eaton. He, with two of his boys, transported us to Fort Simpson, fifteen miles distant.

Haida canoe, Masset, Graham Island, BC.
(34-C) / BCARS 46714

1866

1899

Canoes on the Skeena

Chief Trader William Manson and Thomas Hankin ascended the Skeena River by canoe, in September of 1866.

"In those days (1899) some of the Indians had what they called 'five ton' canoes and it was in one of those that we embarked. Our canoe had as other passengers an Indian family complete with two dogs. We had 1000 lbs. of ore in sacks which with the 23 people aboard gave the canoe a real payload."
— *G.V. Cowrie*

Ocean & River Canoes

♦ R.G. Large

Canoes were once the only means of transportation on the Skeena.

In the earliest days ... on the Skeena and in the adjoining waters, the canoe was the only method of transport.

The ocean-going canoe was made of cedar, hollowed out from one large tree trunk. Until the coming of the white man the only attempt to strengthen the hollow trunk was made by steaming the shell and inserting spreaders, and these were designed to improve the riding qualities of the hull rather than to make the structure any stronger. Under the stresses of heavy seas, the use of sail, or the pounding of fast running water, it was not uncommon for the cedar canoe to split, with disastrous results for the passengers. Possibly for this reason and because cedar was not as prevalent up the river, the river canoes were generally made of cottonwood. The trees being smaller, the resultant canoes were narrower, with less freeboard.

Cottonwood for river canoes

In spite of these limitations, the ocean-going canoes of the Haidas reached a high level of perfection. The cedars on the Queen Charlotte Islands attained an immense size and allowed for the construction of canoes up to seventy feet in length. The style varied with different tribes, but generally the bow and stern were built up to avoid broaching seas. As with the early sailing ships, native artists often decorated these raised bows and sterns with weird figureheads.

When the missionaries started using canoes for their trips around the coast, they taught the Indians to bend ribs or strakes into the canoes, to strengthen them and make them safer for ocean travel.

Missionaries used canoes

In travelling the Skeena, the coast Indians used their cedar canoes of smaller size for the river navigation, while the cottonwood canoes were employed by the upriver Indians. An average canoe would carry a crew of five, a helmsman in the stern and four paddlers, and would be capable of transporting several tons of freight as well as passengers. In negotiating the faster stretches sometimes it was necessary to "line" the canoe along the shore.

This form of travel was far from being comfortable. The trip was slow and often hazardous, and for long stretches of the river the banks did not lend themselves to suitable campsites. Lying exposed throughout a wet night on the bare rocks was poor preparation for the rigours of another day of struggle against the current.

Kitselas Canyon, 1913. Charles Durham with sweep, Nellie Durham standing.
(41-C)

Canoe Days

◆ Wiggs O'Neill

Hazelton---"The Forks"

Hankin was not the first!

When the Hudson's Bay Company established their trading post at Port Simpson in 1834, it became their headquarters and trading centre on the North Pacific Coast. They later established a post at Massett on the Queen Charlotte Islands and later opened a post at the junction of the Skeena and Bulkley Rivers—where Hazelton still stands today. In the old days before Hazelton got its present name it was always spoken of as "The Forks." The land where it stands was originally taken up by one Thomas Hankin, who probably was the first white man to come up the Skeena River. [Editor's note: as we know, Hankin was not the first!] He called it Hazelton, it is said, because of the quantity of hazelnuts growing there. He arrived in 1867. Shortly afterwards Mr. Hankin sold his store to a man named W.J. Walsh, who operated it for a time and in 1879 sold out to the Hudson's Bay Company, who have operated the post ever since.

Through Port Simpson and Massett they controlled the fur trade of the Queen Charlotte Islands, southeastern Alaska, the Nass River valley and the various islands and inlets adjacent to the mouth of the Skeena River. Hazelton was the trading centre of the Upper Skeena Valley and its hinterland, including the extensive Babine Lake country to the north, the Bulkley Valley and the Morice Lake country to the south. At this point transportation became a major problem. While the Hudson's Bay Company had their sailing ships and schooners on the coast, the main headquarters at Port Simpson and the Massett post could easily be supplied with trade goods from headquarters at Fort Victoria the same way, but the problem of supplying Hazelton was a very different proposition. As no roads or trails existed up the Skeena Valley, the Skeena River itself was the only alternative. And what a waterway! When one considers that the distance from Hazelton to salt water is 180 miles, and in this distance the old river drops 800 feet, one can visualize that on leaving tidewater, very swift water, numerous rapids, canyons and sharp bends had to be overcome before one reached Hazelton, where pack trains and trails could be used in summer and dog teams during the winter.

Trading problems with Hazelton

The old Company was always a resourceful organization and although at times slow to move, always came up with an answer. They organized canoe brigades. They were fortunate in one respect, having the master craftsmen in canoe building at their front door, the Haida Indians of the Queen Charlotte Islands. Owing to the mighty red cedar trees that grew on the island, they turned out wonderful big canoes, the average of which could easily carry two tons of freight and a crew of four or five, and still have ample freeboard. The Haidas bartered these canoes to the Tsimpsean tribes on the coast and the Nishga Indians of the Nass River for the famous oolichan grease and dried herring eggs and other mainland Indian products. While the Indian people of Port Simpson or Lac-Wel-Amse, as they called their village, were on salt water, nevertheless they were excellent river men, as all their trapping and hunting grounds extended up the Skeena as far as the Big Canyon at Kitselas. They also had hunting grounds up all the tributaries of the Skeena in that area so the company really had a pretty good setup to organize the canoe transportation system. Each canoe was manned by a captain, a bowman and two or three sailors, as they were called, although not much sailing was done.

Canoe brigades

The captain stood in the stern of the canoe on a slightly raised

Poling Skeena River rapids, one man in harness.
(18-A)

platform. He handled a huge oar, swiveled on a bracket attached to the stern of the canoe. On the inboard end of the oar or sweep there was a strong heavy peg sticking up which the captain grasped with both hands. He had such a leverage that he could swing the stern of the craft either way he wished and had perfect control at all times.

The bowman's duties were to pole the canoe upstream and keep the bow away from the shore. The two or three sailors had the big job of poling upstream and when the current got too strong they had to jump ashore with a long cotton line with a harness attached for each man, get into harness and really pull.

Canoe Captains:
Fred Alexcee
Charlie Price
Walter Wright

The freight was contracted out by the Company to deliver the two tons to Hazelton. The captain made twenty dollars for the trip and the rest of the crew made fifteen dollars per man. There was great rivalry among the crews as to who could make the fastest time. I remember the three most famous captains. A small, wiry man named Fred Alexcee was the most outstanding. Charlie Price, a huge fat fellow who must have weighed 300 pounds, also drew down the prize at times. Walter Wright, who hailed from the village of Kitselas, horned in occasionally to get in on the money. Most or nearly all the freight of course was on the upriver trips. About all they were offered for the return, or downriver trips, were bales of fur from the Company's posts, the odd gold shipment sent through the Company's hands from Manson Creek and the occasional prospector or trapper as a passenger. The Company also operated a free mail service through their private pouches.

The trip of the freight canoes upstream averaged about a week, but the return trip to the coast usually took no more than a day. Some gentle paddling, and the drop of 800 feet over 180 miles did the rest.

The fur room at Port Simpson

The fur was quite an item in those days. They used to say that the north country was built on fur, and it was very plentiful in those early days. At Port Simpson the Company had a big wooden fur press in the fur room. The bin was filled up with furs of all varieties using bear skins for the outer wrappings, and when filled up with various kinds of pelts the fur boss would go up the ladder and turn the big screw press until it would become quite a small heavy bale. This would be sewn up in burlap and labeled in stenciled letters:

HUDSON'S BAY COMPANY,
London, ENGLAND.
From: Port Simpson Post, British Columbia.

For a good many years the canoe brigades were the only means of travel and communication on the Skeena River.

◆

Dugout canoe on Lava Lake
(34-C) / Nat. Mus. 73008

The Canoe Brigades

◆ Reverend Thomas Crosby, D.D.

A Note on Paddles
by Sylvia Robertson ◆
Cedar or maple were chosen
with the same care, to carve
paddles. They were hand-cut in
the straight grain of the wood
and so were stronger than
factory-made paddles. The
coastal Indians would use a
pointed paddle-blade.

Along the Fraser, where they
were used like poles in hugging
the banks to fight the deadly
current, the blades were even
more pointed . . . A strong
paddle was essential in those
perilous waters.

We made a great number of trips up the Skeena with the Hudson's Bay boats or freight canoes to the Forks. These trips were made in company with perhaps twenty canoes loaded with freight, five men being in each canoe, and we had abundant chances to preach and hold services on the way. Every Saturday afternoon a good camp was chosen and all the boats unloaded so that the freight could be dried and any leaks or other damages to the canoe repaired. The whole Sabbath Day was spent in rest and religious services. We visited all the villages on our return trips. Later on, we made an evangelistic tour along the Skeena as far as Kishpiax, with from twenty to thirty warm-hearted Christian Indian evangelists, when it was a delight to see how the young men worked with paddles, oars, pole or tow line, singing on the way, "We work until we die" or "We'll work till Jesus comes."

Missionaries on the river

There were some very dangerous places on the Skeena River. The canyon in certain stages of the water, "Splashing Rapids," "Bees' Nest" and "Kitzegucla Canyon" were the worst.

Danger spots

Once I was at the foot of one of these rapids, on one of my trips in the Hudson's Bay Company's freight canoes. The men in the canoes had poled as far as they could up the "riffle" and, not being able to get a tow line ashore, let go the pole and every man paddled for life to reach the opposite shore. Arriving there, a man, ready at the bow with a rope, had to jump ashore as soon as the canoe touched and whip his rope around a stump to save her going down into the terrible whirlpools below. As each canoe was loaded with two and a half or three tons of freight and usually carried a crew of five men, the loss of life would have been appalling if by any chance the man who jumped ashore missed his fastening, for nothing could have prevented the canoes and their crews from being swept into the maelstrom below.

A near-tragedy

While my canoe was waiting in still water on the right-hand shore and we were watching to see how the others would manage, two canoes got over all right. The third, with an old Tongass Chief who did not know the river as captain, was not so successful. The men had to let go their poles and were paddling for their lives. Getting too much down into the wild water they would often miss their stroke, as the waves were so high and they were sometimes in the trough and sometimes on the crest. Suddenly we saw a man's hat in the stream. Paddling with great force on the top of a wave, he had missed his stroke, and had fallen into the water. The next moment came the shout, "Man overboard!" The old Captain was now landing on the point and could not possibly come down from where he was to rescue his man.

My Captain shouted, "All hands to your paddles; what do you say, shall we go and save the man?" The men shouted, "All right!" (Ahm, Ahm!) and out we plunged, every man pulling for his life right into the wild waters and into what seemed to be "the very jaws of death." Now came a shout by the Captain: "Back water, or we shall miss our man!" Just at that moment, amid the whirlpools and rushing waves, we saw our brother as he came up for what must have been the last time, for, as he said afterwards, he was blind and could not hear a word we said. A long pole was thrust against his breast and he seized it with a death grip. A strong young man held the pole and, with the assistance of another man who grasped him by the clothes, their sinking comrade was pulled into the canoe. As soon as we got him on board, we rolled him and lifted him up and down to get the water out of him. This took some time and when he began to revive I gave him some Jamaica ginger. By this time we had finished rubbing and working with him and were far down the river in calm water. During the day he seemed to be much better, but was dull for some days after.

This all happened in much less time than it takes to write it and I do not think any one of us would have been ready a few minutes before to make such a terrible venture for all the world.

Many a trip I made up that river. On a more recent one, a man was lost. I was travelling with the Upper Skeena people on their way from the salmon canneries. We had over one hundred people in the company. On Monday morning it was raining, but some started early. After a while my captain and party got out and, just as we were pushing from the shore, a shout came down the river, "Canoe upset!" Crossing the river, we met with evidence of it. We picked up a sack of flour, some mats and some clothing, floating down. Another shout came down the river: "MAN LOST!" I landed on the other shore and ran up over a bar

"MAN LOST!"

about two miles. There I found a poor blind man and his mother, sitting on the bank of the river, with part of the broken canoe lying on the beach. They were crying and told how it happened. A long tree was lying out from the shore on the surface of the water with its roots still fast. In trying to get past the outer end of it, their canoe sheered in, when the strong current pushed them under the log. The man at the stern was knocked off and he and part of his steering gear were carried away. He was seen no more. The other two caught hold of the tree, and thus got ashore.

I need not say that was a day of great sorrow among the party. All went ashore to camp. The friends of the lost man prepared a feast on the bar of the river, and called everyone to it. Here we had a good chance to preach to them and tell them to "prepare to meet their God." The same night a large party came up to the village of Kitsum-kalem, just across from us. I preached to them also. Next morning I headed a search party of two canoes. We went down the river about ten miles to look for the body of the lost man, but did not find it.

Kitsum-kalem

Port Essington

Port Essington in its heyday.
(26-A)

Robert Cunningham

◆ John W. Morison

My father, Charles Frederic Morison, first met Robert Cunningham in 1868 at the Hudson's Bay Company fort at Fort Simpson, where Cunningham was factor and/or officer in charge of the post. In the year 1869 my father was appointed to Fort Simpson as bookkeeper. In 1870 Cunningham applied to HBC headquarters for an increase in salary, which foolishly was refused him. Upon receipt of their decision he decided that entering business for himself would be far more profitable and immediately tendered his resignation. He left the HBC employ, and my father succeeded him as officer in charge.

Mr. Cunningham entered into partnership with Thomas Hankin and they started an independent trading post at the western mouth of the Skeena River slough called Woodcock Landing, subsequently named Inverness. Mr. Cunningham left this location in 1871 and established a trading post farther up the Skeena on land he acquired from the government. This place he named Port Essington. On this land, he set aside a portion for Indians who wished to reside there.

In later years Essington became the distributing point for northern BC. Later in the year in company with Thomas Hankin, a trading post was established near the junction of the Skeena and Bulkley Rivers. Mr. Hankin named the settlement Hazelton because of the profusion of wild hazel which covered the district. This trading post expanded into a large general merchandise store which flourished until the late Twenties, known under the trade name of R. Cunningham & Son Ltd. Mr. Hankin was then long since dead.

As time passed, Mr. Cunningham's keen business acumen resulted in progress and expansion. At Port Essington, besides his large two-storey general store, he erected a spacious and comfortable hotel, a large community hall, a salmon cannery considered very modern at that period, and a steam sawmill with a capacity of fifty thousand feet per day—in those days a huge output for that section of the country.

When Prince Rupert began to construct houses, dwellings and board sidewalks, the Cunningham mill supplied the lumber.

Other enterprises were three steam tugs, the largest of which, the well-powered and appointed SS *Chieftain*, plied the coast for many years. In conjunction with the cannery he installed the first freezer and cold storage plant in the north.

He constructed the passenger and freight carrying stern-wheeler *Hazelton*, which plied between Essington and the town of Hazelton. The latter had now become the distribution point for all the northern interior. The *Hazelton* was a fine swiftwater model designed by the late Captain J.H. Bonser, the skillful pioneer captain of the Skeena River. Two other operations were a salmon saltery and a dogfish oil refinery at Porcher Island.

It is impossible to hazard a guess as to what heights this great pioneer would have attained in the history of northern BC had he lived longer. Unfortunately, following a short illness, he died in Victoria, April 1905, at the age of 68.

My father describes him as an Irish gentleman of great physique, with a marvellous personality, generous to a fault, a true pioneer of the old stock, and one, if not the first, to develop the potentialities of northwestern British Columbia.

Robert Cunningham
(46-C) / VPL 1792

Cunningham, Port Essington, & the Skeena

◆ Phylis Bowman

Once the leading community of the north, this port is situated on a rocky point where the Ecstall River joins the Skeena River near its mouth. It grew rapidly as more and more settlers came to the new land in the north to try their luck as prospectors, fishermen, miners and traders, and used the mighty Skeena as the route to reach the rich resources of the interior of the province.

Just as the name "Dunsmuir" is synonymous with Victoria, the name "Cunningham" is used in conjunction with Port Essington. For it was a young, ambitious Irishman named Robert Cunningham who saw the potential of this port as a centre for the coastal trade to Skagway and the Klondike and as a natural jumping-off place for the traffic to the interior.

Cunningham came to the Pacific coast in 1862 to help Father William Duncan with his Anglican Mission at the Indian village of Metlakatla. After serving there for two years, he went to Port Simpson, the HBC's post 20 miles north of Metlakatla, to work for three years. In 1870 he applied to Victoria for land at the mouth of the Skeena River.

In the spring of the following year, the gold rush up the Skeena began and Cunningham built a large store on the north shore of the river with a partner, Thomas Hankin.

The store did a roaring business as miners flocked into the area, impatiently awaiting the spring thaw so that freighting could begin. As canoes were the main mode of transportation at that time, large numbers of Tsimpsean Indians joined the throngs, offering their canoes at $1.50 a day, and their services at $1.00 a day, plus food.

The large canoes, made of red cedar, were usually obtained by the Tsimpseans by trade with the Haida Indians of the Queen Charlotte Islands who were the foremost canoe men of the coast.

These canoes could carry about 4000 pounds and were manned by five men. As Cunningham and Hankin had the contract for the bulk of the shipping upriver to the Hazelton gold fields, they had two freight canoes on the river.

Wishing to expand, the resourceful Cunningham took out a pre-emption on the land across the Skeena at the junction of the two rivers.

This was the customary stopping-place for the Tsimpseans returning in the fall from their fishing and trapping expeditions up the Ecstall and was called "Spokeshute," which means the fall camp ground. The name "Ecstall" was derived from the Tsimpsean word "Hocstall" meaning "dirty water," and is pronounced "Oxstall."

On this site, Cunningham built a large trading post and called it Port Essington, the name which Captain Vancouver had originally given to the whole of the Skeena estuary, named after one of his officers.

Cunningham set aside a portion of his land and encouraged the Indians to settle there. Gradually a small settlement grew up around his trading post as he sold some of his land to settlers and employed them at his sawmill. Wishing to encourage trade with the Hudson's Bay Company, the wily Cunningham contrived a plan to attract the captain of the chief trading vessel, the *Otter*, as she passed Port Essington.

He gave his Indian helper orders to build several fires in the bush around the community, making it look as though there was a large Indian encampment, so the skipper came ashore to trade with them— and also with Cunningham.

In the summer of 1871, Chief Factor James Grahame of the Company went to Port Essington from Victoria aboard the *Otter* and bought three lots from Cunningham on which was built a small store. This establishment, known as "Skeena Post" and run by postmaster Matthew Feak, did not do well and the Company closed it in September 1877 and transferred its contents to their stores at Port Simpson.

Before any banks were in operation in the north, Cunningham and the Hudson's Bay Company issued their own currency in small denominations up to a dollar, which they used in trading. The Company's coins were made from copper and Cunningham's from brass. When this system was no longer used, the Company dumped its supply of coins in Port Simpson harbour. Some of the coins were saved and may be seen in the Museum of Northern British Columbia at Prince Rupert.

One of the largest industries around Port Essington was fishing. During these busy years, there were seven canneries built around the mouth of the Skeena, two of which were at Port Essington, one owned by Cunningham and the other by the Anglo-British Columbia Packing Company, known as Boston Cannery. At first salmon were caught by gillnetters and eventually by seining boats and trollers.

Indian village, Port Essington
(36-C)

Of all the different kinds of salmon running in the Skeena—the spring, the sockeye, the coho, the pink and the dog—the sockeye is foremost for canning.

In the early days, a great deal of the work in the canneries was done by hand, mostly by Indians and Chinese people, who were extremely adept at their work.

Cans were made at the canneries before the fishing season started and were punched out of sheet tin by manually operated machines and soldered. Cooking methods were also primitive—the filled cans were wheeled into large ovens, called retorts, where they were cooked by steam.

The air had to be released from the can by punching a hole in the top of it. The top was then re-soldered and the final cooking took place. The can was painted with a heavy coat of lacquer and labelled.

A Chinese could put labels on a can as fast as any machine—he would run the paste brush down a stack of labels and his hands would move unbelievably fast—catching the can with one hand and rolling it into the label which he held by the other, almost faster than the eye could follow.

Cunningham also built the first cold storage plant in the north, and it began operating in 1892.

As trade increased, Cunningham had several steam tugs, and his *Chieftain* was a familiar sight in northern waters for many years. As he had a branch store in Hazelton, in 1900 for the upriver trade he replaced the canoes with the sternwheeler *Monte Cristo*.

To cope with this improvement, his rivals in trade, the Hudson's

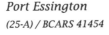

Port Essington
(25-A) / BCARS 41454

Bay Company added a ship, the *Strathcona*. Not to be outdone, Cunningham put on a new ship, *Hazelton*, in 1901, and it was the fastest on the river. In answer to this, the Company replaced their fleet with a larger vessel, *Mount Royal*, under the command of Captain Johnson.

East Dufferin Street, Port Essington (25-A) / BCARS 85743

Competition between the two ships was very great, and the skippers would go to any lengths to beat each other. In July, 1902, the *Hazelton* made the round trip from Port Essington to Hazelton in two days, seven hours and 55 minutes, counting all regular stopovers and the layover at Hazelton to unload freight.

Two days later, the Company's *Mount Royal* made the identical trip in two days, six hours and 15 minutes. Four days later, Cunningham's ship made the trip in 47 hours. The climax of this competition was reached one day when the two ships were racing up the river and Captain Johnson of the *Mount Royal* attempted to crowd the *Hazelton* into shallow water.

Bonser turned his ship, struck the *Mount Royal* amidships and pushed her right up onto the beach. It is said that Captain Johnson was so infuriated that he shot at Bonser with his rifle. That put an end to the frantic racing.

Another rival of Cunningham's was Peter Herman, a young German who came north in 1885 to work for Cunningham, and then branched out for himself. He built up several businesses for himself and was one of the founders of the Liberal Association in the north and

*Cunningham's Skeena River
Cannery*
(25-A) / BCARS 10779

was its president for several years. Eventually he ran for member of the Legislative Assembly but was defeated by Charles W.D. Clifford.

Since the river was closed to freight traffic in the winter, there were many community dances and activities during that period. The main planked road, Dufferin Street, was lined with stores and restaurants which stayed open until late in the evenings, and the three hotels, the Essington, the Caledonia and the Queens, did a roaring business in their liquor trade and at the poker and blackjack games in their back rooms.

The town was wide open then and street brawls and fights occurred frequently.

But during all this growth in the community, the Anglican and Methodist Churches had established missions there and had many church activities going on too. It is interesting to note that one of the missionaries who was greatly revered for his work up the Skeena and Naas Rivers, Robert Tomlinson, was married to a Victoria girl, Alice Woods.

It is estimated that in the passage of time, more than 3000 persons lived in Port Essington. Life was prosperous and a rich bounty of fish, game, timber and trapping provided a good life for the people of many nationalities who settled there—Japanese, German, Indian, Chinese, English and Finnish.

The port went downhill rapidly after the Grand Trunk Pacific Railway was completed along the north bank of the Skeena to Prince Rupert in April of 1914. The railway became the main means of transportation and the paddle-steamers gradually dwindled away. As Port Essington was on the opposite bank of the river to the railway, many of its residents moved to Prince Rupert or to southern British Columbia for jobs.

And now, Port Essington is a near-deserted overgrown shell of a town. Several disastrous fires have wiped out sections of the settlement, one of the largest being on July 4, 1961.

Twenty-five buildings were destroyed and 50 people were left homeless. Fanned by a strong wind, the flames wiped out the main thoroughfare along Dufferin Street, and the 3000-foot high column of smoke was clearly visible for 15 miles. Also lost in this fire were the church, the community hall, a hotel and the last large store. The historic school was not touched.

A last big fire in March of 1965 burned six of the remaining buildings, and these charred remains, along with the rotting piles of the once-industrious canneries and warehouses which line the shore, are the only relics left of this port, so well-known and busy during those prosperous freighting days.

Of the three pioneer communities in the north, Metlakatla is remembered for Father William Duncan and his devoted flock of converts who made the village the headquarters of the Christian Gospel on the Pacific coast; Port Simpson is remembered as being a big trading post for the Hudson's Bay Company.

But it is Port Essington that is remembered for its boom of prosperity, its winters of liquor, song and laughter, its many-nationed population and its rapid decline into oblivion and neglect. The mighty Skeena, with its treacherous undercurrents and strong tides, could no doubt tell many strange tales about this port. Today, only a few Indian families live there as well as some Finns, but the name of Robert Cunningham, who died in Victoria in April 1905, is still remembered and revered.

Skeena River Commercial Cannery at Port Essington, ca. 1915. Between the wharves a fishing fleet is being formed to be towed downriver. Several tow boats are involved, each belonging to different canneries. The cannery, on the right, has a new galvanized iron roof to lessen the fire hazard of cedar shingles. A corner of the Anglican church is at right. (25-A) / BCARS 78972

The Ghost that Guards the Skeena

◆ Gladys Blyth

At the junction of the Skeena and Ecstall Rivers 24 miles southeast of Prince Rupert is the pathetic remains of what was once Port Essington. Originally an important trade centre of more than 1200 people, it is now a summer home for a few fishermen.

The town's founder was Robert Cunningham. He was an Irishman with a pugilistic build, unbounded energy and drive and an inborn business sense. The birth and growth of the town of Port Essington was a major achievement in his versatile life.

He started his career in England when he joined the Church of England Missionary Society. He was immediately sent to assist William Duncan, a lay missionary who, with a band of Tsimpsean Indian converts, had founded Metlakatla, a community north of the mouth of the Skeena River.

At Metlakatla Cunningham married an Indian girl, and through her and her people he gained insights which would one day be invaluable in his dealings with the Indians. Here, too, he saw the region's potential in furs and mining. He quit the church and moved to Fort Simpson, the Hudson's Bay Company's stronghold on the northern coast of BC. Within four years he was in charge of the post. But he was ambitious, and the knowledge he gained at this level whetted his desire to strike out on his own.

Finally he left the HBC to join forces with Thomas Hankin, a man of similar experiences who owned land in Hazelton where he had once set up a post for the Hudson's Bay Company. In 1870 the two men jointly applied for a pre-emption on the south bank of the Skeena estuary. While waiting for their application to be processed they set up a post at Woodcock's Landing on Inverness Passage, the northern entrance to the Skeena. Here they were in a good position to trade with the hundreds of men who were surging into the Skeena, Babine and Omineca districts in search of gold, copper and coal.

The inland gateway to this vast unexplored area was Hazelton, 180 miles upstream at the junction of the Skeena and Bulkley Rivers. This little settlement became the jumping-off place for miners, fur-traders, and later on the speculators interested in the land wealth of the Bulkley Valley. Realizing the importance of Hazelton, Cunningham and Hankin established a branch store in the community. In

Fishing fleet winterized in Port Essington
(36-C)

forthcoming years this branch led to intense rivalry between Cunningham and the Hudson's Bay Company.

But this was in the future. In 1871 trouble with the owner of Woodcock's Landing over a land survey persuaded Cunningham and Hankin to move across the Skeena onto their own pre-emption. Here, on a commanding point of land nosing into the Skeena, they set down roots for a town. Out of the muskeg, solitude and isolation emerged Port Essington.

The new location was already a favourite camp of the Tsimpsean Indian nation who called it "Spokeshute." Shrewdly, Cunningham retained the allegiance of the Indian hunters and trappers by paying them fairly for their furs. Furthermore, he encouraged the chiefs of the Kitsumkalum and Kitselas tribes to move their people to a land reserve he provided for them at Port Essington.

To establish a trade link with Victoria the partners needed a shipping connection and they got this service in a novel manner. The Hudson's Bay ship *Otter* was the only steamer serving many of the lonely coastal points but she called only where freight warranted. When the steamer was sighted at the entrance of the Skeena, Cunningham encouraged James Robinson, an upriver Indian staying with him, to hang red flannel underwear and other garments among the trees and to build fires on the beach. This bold advertising convinced Captain Lewis of the *Otter* that Port Essington was indeed a thriving town.

To construct warehouses, stores, dwellings and a dock, Cunningham built a sawmill where rough lumber and shingles were produced for the townsite. Later a larger mill was necessary and with it Cunningham introduced steam logging to the north coast and established what would become a major industry. Among those who bought lots in the new community was the Hudson's Bay Company, who set up a trading post.

Before long, Cunningham's town rollicked under the impact of brightly lit bars that flourished seven days a week with all-night gambling and other types of frontier entertainment. True, there were Saturday night outdoor concerts from a bandstand on the beach in front of the Essington, Queens and Caledonia hotels but generally children were whisked off the streets and young people kept indoors or well-chaperoned. There was a brief respite when temperance meetings and the signing of pledge cards cooled the ribaldry. However, on the heels of this, a resurgence in liquor traffic occurred until the government stepped in and closed the liquor outlets. The town's founder lived in the spirit of it all, equally at home in a fervent discourse from the pulpit as he was embroiled in a sizzling poker game. Altogether Port Essington was a heady place that earned the dubious title "The Gates of Hell."

"Old Diamond C," as Cunningham was known, never

Working on the nets. L. to r. John Sandhals, Iva Sandhals (Husoy), Ed Wahl, Vidar Sandhals. (36-C)

Indian revival band at Port Essington salmon cannery, 1897.
(25-A) / BCARS 16645

overlooked a single lucrative source of development. He watched the growing interest in salmon fishing and canning in Alaska and on the Fraser River. The first cannery in the Canadian north was built at Inverness beside his own trading post at Woodcock's Landing on Inverness Passage in 1877. That season the plant produced 3000 cases of sockeye salmon which had an immediate market. Other canneries followed, some of them Cunningham's, and thus was established the fishing industry in northern waters.

About this time the Hudson's Bay Company left Port Essington and there was also a split between Cunningham and Hankin. With his major competitor gone and his partner out of the picture, Cunningham was sole master at Essington, and for a while, foremost trader on the Skeena. However, the HBC which had abandoned its earlier post at Hazelton, established a new one. Like Cunningham, they used Indian canoe brigades to freight supplies upstream 180 miles to Hazelton. This expansion launched a bitter struggle between the Bay and Cunningham for trade supremacy on the Skeena.

Both firms carried on trade through a system of bartering, since sufficient cash for exchange was not available. Cunningham copied the Bay by setting up his own banking system. But, instead of bank notes, he issued brass trading cheques shaped like round coins and made payable by R. Cunningham. The Indians soon preferred them to cash since they had little understanding of money. For years this private money was the medium of exchange in the entire Skeena area.

Of all Cunningham's enterprises, the competition with the

Hudson's Bay Company on the Skeena River most keenly interested him. The HBC gained a tremendous advantage when in 1891 they brought in a sternwheel steamer to replace the Indian canoe brigades hauling freight upstream to Hazelton. The vessel, the *Caledonia*, operated successfully until 1898 when she was replaced with a new one. Cunningham, meanwhile, became more annoyed every time he paid the Hudson's Bay Company what he considered an exorbitant rate to have his freight hauled. Equally annoying was the fact that the Bay didn't give exactly the best of service to a rival business.

In 1890 he thereupon went into the sternwheel business himself by purchasing the small *Monte Cristo*. He shook the Bay by hiring their best and most experienced skipper, J.H. Bonser. Then before the staid Company recovered, Cunningham sent Captain Bonser to Victoria to design and build a sternwheeler for the Skeena. She was the *Hazelton*, and she was ready by the spring of 1901. She quickly proved superior to the Hudson's Bay Company vessels, which now included the *Caledonia* and *Strathcona*. The *Hazelton* that season made 13 trips to Hazelton, steaming upstream in about 40 hours, back down in 10. The Bay couldn't compete, so they ordered a new vessel.

She was the *Mount Royal* and she was ready for the spring of 1902. An intense rivalry immediately sprang up. "Beat the other boat!" became the cry of the river. This rivalry almost ended in tragedy when

Dufferin Street, Port Essington, looking east toward B.A. Cannery. In the building on the right are a drugstore, general store and restaurant. Close to where the children are walking, a man was stabbed to death one night after a fracas in a nearby cafe. The two buildings at the end of the street on the right are the Queens and Caledonia hotels. (25-A) / BCARS 78976

This native woman, in all her Sunday dignity, was probably on her way to a service at the Salvation Army hall. The native people were attracted to the Salvation Army's flags, drums, tambourines, and street marches, although the Methodist mission was long-established. On the left is the bow of a dugout canoe. These craft were still occasionally used although by this time (c. 1910–14) they were largely displaced by gas boats.
(25-A) / BCARS 78982

the two vessels met at Hardscrabble Rapids and fought it out. (This incident is described in detail later.)

With trade stability on the river, Cunningham's town continued to flourish. Church organizations moved in and, assisted by their leaders, Cunningham encouraged such amenities as a hospital, schools and more new homes. From the four main twelve-foot board streets called Lawrence, Kitselas, Hazelton and Dufferin, the road was extended a mile south to the sawmill for the benefit of families living beyond the Indian village. Altogether there was an atmosphere of confidence and prosperity.

Contributing to the atmosphere was a new railway, the Grand Trunk Pacific, under construction from Winnipeg across central BC to the Pacific. The line was to parallel the Bulkley and Skeena Rivers and terminate at a new port called Prince Rupert. Unfortunately it was also to bypass Port Essington, leaving the community to slowly disintegrate into the pages of history. But Cunningham did not live to know the fate of his townsite. He died in Victoria in 1905 at the age of 68.

The prolific enterprises he had amassed in real estate, shipping, logging and general trade were left to his son, George, and the executors of his estate. One of the largest and best collections of Haida Indian argillite carvings was also left to the legacy of his family. Beyond this his name is perpetuated in a lake, a mountain and Cunningham Passage.

But the founder's death did not slow the growth of the town. Ironically, the railway that caused its death also stimulated its greatest prosperity. Land speculators, railway contractors, casual labourers, settlers and hundreds of other people jammed its waterfront. New sternwheelers appeared, with the railway construction company of Foley, Welch and Stewart alone operating a fleet of five. Port Essington became the focal point on a whitewater highway that was alive with shipping.

Upstream went everything from livestock to Fraser Valley hay, sowbelly for construction crews to a travelling carnival headed for the Klondike. Lumber, nails, sheets of glass, gumboots, canvas, paint, Dr. Shoop's Restorative, eggs, dress patterns, machinery and everything else for an awakening country were all included in cargoes. In June 1910, a news item in the Prince Rupert *Empire* noted: "Farm and other machinery for Hazelton and interior points now cover an acre of ground at Kitselas where the steamers on the lower river have unloaded it for transfer around the canyon. In the lot are 35 mowers, wagons, ploughs, rakes and cultivators. One threshing machine and several binders are ordered but it is not known if they are in transit. This will make two threshers for the Bulkley Valley."

River traffic swelled when settlers headed into the Bulkley. In the spring of 1910 alone more than 300 were reported to have made the trip, exclusive of the families of those who had gone in the year before. Many of these stopped over at Essington awaiting steamer connections. Every available house and shack was occupied. Tents were set up in the muskeg and on the beaches, and even upturned boats were used as shelters.

Then two years later the railway was finished. The little frontier town started an immediate decline. It became the victim of fierce storms and heavy snows, of epidemics of typhoid, diphtheria and smallpox, and of disastrous fires which wiped out most of its buildings.

Gone are the stores, docks, warehouses and businesses. They burned to mounds of bricks, twisted water pipes, heaps of melted liquor bottles and general debris. A few houses still stand like ageless monuments to the hand of man. Rotting hulls of boats dot the shore. The remains of the last of the river steamers, the *Inlander*, lie on the beach, the outlines of its rotted-out hull barely noticeable in the grass and brush. Only the metal parts testify that it even once existed. A church, in fair condition, waits as it was left. In its yard a ladder still stands against the branches of a dying apple tree. Even the large graveyard lies choked with the encroachment of nature and rotting board walks. Graves with marble stones and smaller graves with fading white fences lie tucked among the tangled brush.

The rubble and the awesome stillness create an ethereal sense of unreality. Port Essington is today only a ghost, a ghost standing guard at the mouth of the Skeena.

Sternwheelers lined up in Prince Rupert harbour, date March 1, year unknown. Left to right: Distributor, Skeena, Operator, Conveyor.

(13-A) / BCARS 82736

Port Essington

◆ Walter Wicks

Port Essington was the hub of trade and steamer traffic for many years on the lower Skeena. Four canneries operated there for several decades and it was looked upon as the centre of the salmon industry and upriver trading.

Although the Hudson's Bay Company headquarters was at Port Simpson, their sternwheelers always made Port Essington their port of call en route to Hazelton for upriver trading and passenger service. This riverboat traffic had been added to by Robert Cunningham's two boats, and two others operated by private businessmen.

With the coastal vessels from the south always making their calls at this port in connection with the salmon packing industry, the little town became a hub of activity. On Saturday nights, it was like a little city with all the accompaniment of different forms of vice. In its seasonal activity it could boast a population of 2000.

Women who loved lightly came with the railroad construction, settling in an area at the far end of town, down by the old mill stream. This, coupled with the two saloons that always seemed to be doing a thriving business, brought the road workers from the camps across the river to town on weekends.

The only two roads, or boardwalks, were the scenes of fighting and drunkenness when these railroad "stiffs" hit town. The Skookum House (town jail) was usually overflowing during their stay. It was easy for an innocent person to become involved in a fracas, as some of these workers would come out of a saloon with a few drinks under their belts, prepared to fight the whole town starting with the first passerby.

The south portion of the town, which was occupied by the Indians, had been donated for their use by Robert Cunningham, the town's founder. It was unlawful for anyone to supply liquor to Indians, but there were always some whites who would break this law to accommodate an Indian friend, especially if there was a possibility of making a double profit on the bottle. Many a white man was convicted and jailed for six months or more. This time was spent in some institution in Vancouver, some 600 miles south, because Port Essington had no accommodation for prisoners for such a length of time.

Port Essington had its share of old-time characters who, in one way or another, contributed to the town's development. Such a person was "Keyhole Johnny," an elderly, bewhiskered gentleman who was one of the town's two constables. "Keyhole Johnny" was credited with procuring a great deal of his evidence by looking through keyholes. If he deemed it the proper moment for an arrest, he would simply demand entrance without a search warrant or a warrant for arrest, and without a gun—just his reputation and his fierce-looking whiskers.

If a bottle of hootch could be confiscated as evidence in an Indian house, so much the easier for a conviction. If both Indian and white were present, they would be quickly tossed into the Skookum House, the Indian to sleep off his stupor, the white man to await trial on the more serious charge of supplying.

St. John's Anglican Church, Port Essington, 1909. This replaced the first Anglican church, which had burned down the year before, and was itself destroyed by fire the year after. The third Anglican church stood for fifty years until it too was consumed by the great fire of 1961.
(25-A) / BCARS 78967

One night, while walking along the wide boardwalk known as Dufferin Street, I met Flora, a native girl with whom I had attended the Metlakatla School. As we stood and conversed about our former school days, a young Indian, large of stature, walked up to me and became very abusive.

"You dirty white thief—who asked you here? Now, get going before I tear you apart! You whites are all thieves."

At this early stage of my life, I had noticed many Indians still held some animosity towards the whites. There were many in whose breasts rankled a deep dislike for those white-skinned people whom they looked upon as despoilers. It took only a few drinks of whiskey to display it.

Having so voiced objection to my presence in the company of one whom he considered his girl friend, and as he was somewhat intoxicated, I stepped out of the way. The girl tried to quiet him but he would have none of it and made a lunge at me. I had always remembered my stepfather's advice never to allow anyone to step on my toes, so I used a trick I had learned from an old-timer. I suddenly butted him with my head in the solar plexus. That did it, for he crumpled up like a dishrag on the boardwalk.

A group of people had gathered, when I heard the girl exclaim, "Get out quick—here comes Keyhole!"

My feet became a great deal faster than my head had been as I disappeared down the walk into the distance. No one seemed to have recognized me and if that constable was looking for a young white man, he was wasting his time. I was soon to my gas boat with the engine wide open, heading downriver with the tide, to my cabin on the Inverness Slough, some 16 miles away. While the Indian was probably nursing his tummy and sleeping off his drunk in jail, I was snugly rolled up in my blankets in my "Home, Sweet Home."

Because of insufficient protection of the salmon travelling to upriver spawning grounds throughout the years, the geographical fishing limits were placed several miles farther downstream to allow for better escapement of fish, placing Port Essington high and dry, so to speak, above the fishing grounds. This, coupled with the completed railroad into the interior, which liquidated riverboat traffic, made Port Essington practically a ghost town in later years. What thrilling tales that Old Skeena could tell if all its river characters were gathered to relate their experiences on its waters through the passing years.

*Skeena River Commercial
Cannery, Port Essington*
(25-A) / BCARS 51445

Living Without Frills

◆ Walter Wicks

The coming of the long winter months at the cannery always brought up the question of procuring the prime essentials of life, meat and fish. We could do without money for long spells in the winter, but a person can become very tired of constantly depending on canned goods, regardless of their fancy labels, so my brother Paul and I did our best to procure these essentials from Mother Nature rather than from the cannery store. Wild meat and marine food was salted, smoked and canned.

Late summer, directly after the salmon season was over, was the time to take to the woods for berries to be preserved in the form of jams and jellies or packed in sugar. There were red huckleberries, wild currants, salal berries, two varieties of blueberries, high bush salmonberries and cranberries from the muskeg swamp.

Fresh milk was something we could not enjoy for lack of a grazing area in a coastal mountain country such as ours. Thus, we used condensed milk which we sometimes put on our bread as a spread. Fresh vegetables and fruits also were non-existent during the long winter months, these being practically unknown during this stage of our lives, for the only fruit was canned or dried, bought from the cannery store, such as dried prunes and apples packed in 10-pound boxes, also candy in bulk in 25-pound wooden buckets and hard round sea biscuits, shipped in 25-pound boxes.

We had wood stoves to keep us warm and the light of coal oil lamps to read and eat by. Mother would roast green bean coffee in flat tin pans in the oven and we boys would then grind it in a small coffee grinder, held between the knees. Today these are listed as antiques, but I believe we had better coffee than the prepared product sold in round cans today.

Beans, baked in gallon crocks, were one of our reliable foods, and homemade bread, baked in the stove for which we were continually cutting wood.

Mother would knit sweaters and long stockings for all of us, and then there was her ever-present chore of washing the family clothes on a scrubbing board and drying it around the stove.

The cannery water supply would be cut off during the winter months at the mountain dam, when all pipes, boilers and other equipment was drained. We then depended on a small mountain stream to which was connected an open flume. In freezing weather we chopped ice from this flume, trying to continue our water supply, failing that, to simply pack the water from the ice hole until the barrels were full. Did we think it was a hard life? No, it was just our everyday living.

In the winter months fresh eggs were rather difficult to procure because of our isolation, and only from an occasional steamer's call might we be able to get any. These we would pack in dry salt, which was our only method of preserving them for a limited time.

Our parents relied upon their limited knowledge of our afflictions and treated them to the best of their abilities. The common cold, with which man is so often afflicted, could not be taken care of by simply driving down to the doctor for a shot of penicillin or some prescription from the nearby drug store. Hot baths in a wooden tub, mustard plasters and hot rum were our stock in trade for such ailments.

For want of a medical man at the right time, a broken hand or finger might heal somewhat crooked, or a case of appendicitis, as we now know it, could prove fatal. If information was asked regarding the whereabouts of some person, the answer might be that he had died of a terrible pain in the stomach region.

Crude surgery often had to be resorted to. One day a Japanese woodcutter came running to tell us that one of their men had cut himself severely. My parents hurried over to the Japanese's house to see what could be done, but one look at the injured man made them realize that, with their limited knowledge of surgery, they were helpless. At dinner call, the man had stuck his double-bit axe into a wood block and, in foolishly stepping over it, his foot slipped, causing him to come down on the sharp edge in a sliding position, cutting his buttock wide open.

The lack of a doctor in the area demanded a quick decision. Our father sent us boys three miles up river to the Cassiar cannery to locate a man who had removed two frozen fingers during the Yukon Gold Rush days. From what we could learn, this man had never seen the inside of a medical school, but upon examining the patient, he asked Mother for a small darning needle, some linen twine, bandages and carbolic acid or whiskey, then instructed the injured man's companions to fill him up with as much saki as he could hold.

No adhesive bandages, iodine or proper antiseptics were at hand with the exception of some carbolic acid, found in the cannery store. In fact, there was not a first-aid kit on the place. Mother supplied the linen twine, darning needle and some ripped-up bed sheets for bandages. The makeshift doctor put a light curve in the needle by bending it over a candle flame, then returned to the patient with my parents following along to give what help they could.

As Mother told us later, the patient may as well have been dead for all the fuss he put up, for his countrymen had filled him with hot sake, an Oriental alcoholic beverage distilled from fermented rice.

With plenty of stitch marks to show for his ordeal, he recovered and called on Mother to thank her for the aid given, bowing repeatedly and in pidgin English saying, "Tank you, Missy Wicky, tank you."

Such a primitive way of life is a far cry from our modern way of living.

The King of the Skeena's Last Voyage

◆ Edward E. Prince

The noblest rivers in all the world are in our fair Dominion, and in many respects the noblest of all Canadian rivers is the majestic and mysterious Skeena. It owes its supremacy not to its length, for it is only a little over 330 miles long, nor to its width, for it is barely three miles wide where it debouches into the Pacific; but it has an imposing and royal mien, and its stupendous environment of forbidding mountains, with the vastness and volume of its swift waters, makes it well-nigh unique.

To the traveller, on the voyage up from the Gulf, the mighty St. Lawrence appears more like an arm of the sea than a river, 15 to 70 miles in width, and the glaciated Laurentian Heights on either bank intensify the impression. The colossal Mackenzie, 2500 miles long, and its delta, over 50 miles in width, convey no single impression; while the great Saskatchewan, as it sweeps into Lake Winnipeg, after its long course of 1200 miles, yields mainly a sense of greatness lost in loneliness—its low wooded banks and waste of silent waters below the Grand Rapids increasing the aspect of melancholy. The Fraser, most famous of salmon streams, dissipates its yellow flood in gravel shallows, between low reedy sandbanks, destitute of all picturesqueness, and calm after its tempestuous rush through 300 miles of wild craggy canyons. But the Skeena moves like a proud queen between her giant guard of frowning heights, whose scarred precipices shelter green glaciers and shining fields of snow, and whose foothills are studded with stupendous poplars, pines and larch.

"Sublimity," in truth, is the only term applicable to the Skeena, amidst her impressive scenic environment. Through what a colossal portal the salmon-laden stream pours into the sea! From far-off Babine Lake, 2500 feet above sea level, the emerald Skeena speeds through the frightful Kitselas Canyon, where more than one Hudson's Bay sternwheeler has been dashed to fragments; past Hazelton, for a hundred years a solitary trading post, by many a strange Indian village, and by the little-traversed Kispiox, the fruitful Bulkley, and the Kitsumkalum, Kultwa, and Lakelse Valleys, the adjacent overhanging mountains, for over half of the Skeena's 335 miles, threatening to close their jaws upon the fleeing terrified stream.

Here on Christmas Day, 64 years ago, Robert Cunningham came to teach the Tsimpseans the white man's faith. A tall stalwart Irishman, with clear blue eyes, a ruddy beaming countenance, a shrill cheery voice and irrepressible energy, he rapidly realized that there were earthly as well as heavenly treasures to challenge his powers. The vast timber and mineral resources of the Skeena, the little-developed fur trade, the boundless salmon supply, overmastered him. Laying aside the preacher's sombre garb, he became a pioneer in commerce, a builder of towns, the father of the Indian tribes—the veritable King of the Skeena.

He was a son of Tyrone, born at Tullyvalley on New Year's Day, 1837, and his first years when he was a preacher were spent with William Duncan, the famous missionary to the Pacific Indians. A few years later he became an officer of the Hudson's Bay Company; but in 1869 he opened a store of his own, in partnership with Thomas Hankin, a young Englishman, and soon did a large trade at Woodcock's Landing, now known as Inverness, North Passage, Skeena River. Across the wide river was Spok-sut, a great resort for the Indian Tribes, and better known by the name which George Vancouver bestowed, in honour of his friend Admiral Sir William Essington of the Royal Navy. Thither Robert Cunningham moved, and two years later pre-empted the whole townsite.

His energy and enterprise made Port Essington a centre of North Pacific commerce. Lumber mills, salmon canneries, fur marts, hotels and stores arose, and Robert Cunningham was master of all. He was the Skeena's lumberman, salmon canner, fur trader, hotel proprietor, banker, house-builder, church leader, and friend of all, white and red alike. Whatever his faults, he was supremely a man of his word. He never deceived an Indian, or, for that matter, a white man. Men of twenty different tribes came to have infinite trust in Robert Cunningham. Many an Indian from the remote "Stick" country, above the canyons, brought his fox skins, his mink and bear, from the coast his sea-otter and fur seal, and throwing them down on the floor of Cunningham's store would ask to know their value.

"They're worth so many dollars—a hundred dollars, or a hundred and fifty," the Tyhee white man would say. "Do you want money or flour, or other goods?"

"No, Mr. Cunningham, I'm off to the Fraser to fish and cannot wait. Pay me sometime—not now," was the reply of the Siwash.

Metal tokens, stamped with various values, were sometimes given to the Indian hunter, but the supply of these often ran out, and tearing off a card or a corner of strong wrapping paper from a bale of cotton or cloth, Robert Cunningham would write on it the value and date. Seizing this eagerly, the Indian would hurry down the beach to his canoe, pushing the precious piece of paper inside his marmot vest. Such fragments of card or paper were often not brought back for months, or even years. Sometimes they were soiled and begrimed, worn to tatters, and quite illegible when brought back, but no Indian ever questioned that it would be redeemed or ever doubted Robert

Cunningham's word. However greasy and blackened through contact with the Indian's skin for a summer or longer, these "promises to pay" were held to be as good as Bank of England notes. No Indian, on the other hand, ever tried deception in the historic general store at Port Essington, and Robert Cunningham's word was as good as his bond.

A striking example of the confidence of the Indian may be quoted. In the early 1860s a huge project was partially carried out for the construction of a telegraph line to Europe through the Rockies and across the Bering Strait. The Collins Overland Telegraph Company spent upwards of $3,000,000 on the scheme, and employed a large body of Indians to carry great supplies of wire up the canyons. When the completion of the second Atlantic submarine cable was announced, the work on the Skeena was abandoned. To this day vast quantities of valuable wire lie in the forest jungles of the upper Skeena. Payment to the Indians was arranged by means of new dollar bills from Ottawa. But, to the surprise of the wage-clerk, the Indians refused to accept them.

"Those no good maybe—we won't take them," they said.

"But these notes are from the Government, and that picture on them is the Governor-General," declared the clerk.

"Maybe that's so—Indian doesn't know. Likely no good. Indian won't take them," they repeated, "but we'll take Mr. Cunningham's money."

The telegraph contractors had no alternative but to get supplies of brass tokens from Robert Cunninghan. These were paid to them instead of Canadian government money, and the Indians were then perfectly satisfied. Such was their faith in the King of the Skeena.

The British Columbia coast is dotted with Indian villages, each consisting of a few wooden houses supported on massive piles over-hanging the water, occasionally beautified with lofty totem poles, grotesquely carved and often gorgeously decorated, as at Alert Bay or Oweekano Lake. So diverse are the local dialects that almost each community speaks a distinct tongue, so distinct indeed that the Indians of one village could not converse with those of another village, were it not that there is a widespread use of "Chinook"—the jargon of the trading posts.

To Robert Cunningham a mastery of Chinook was not suffi-cient. With characteristic determination he learned the native lan-guages, and was able to speak nearly a score of Siwash tongues, even the little-known tongues of the "Stick" Indians, in the upper regions far from the sea. At marriage-feasts, native baptisms and funerals, and even at Potlatches and Tyhee celebrations or chieftain's festivals, visiting Indians speaking in their own strange tongues would ask Robert Cunningham to interpret their orations to the "other brothers." When Sticks and Haidas and Kitimats, Nootkas and Nawhittis, met Naas and Skeena Tsimpseans on convivial or ceremonial occasions, Robert

Cunningham could always be relied upon to tell the local tribes what their brothers from afar had said.

In the spring of 1905 a serious illness assailed him. His ruddy, almost rustic countenance became pallid, and his tall erect figure somewhat bent, although his fresh, shrill loud voice lost none of its force. He was persuaded to make the trip, nearly five hundred miles, to Victoria for medical treatment. He was fond of Indian foods, especially the rich, evil-smelling oolachan oil, an open cask of which scented the air near the large public hall at Port Essington, and he could never pass it without dipping in a finger and tasting the savoury, or rather the emphatically unsavoury, liquid, declaring, "I swear to my God that's good." Every morning for many weeks, when I sat down to breakfast with Robert Cunningham in his hotel, a large dish, piled high with five or six inches of boiled oolachan, was placed opposite him, and I was invited to try them. The fish are small, about the size of smelt, and similar in shape and silvery appearance, but I felt a slight repugnance at my first mouthful. They had a slight flavour of whale oil, but the meat was delicate and white. I soon learned to enjoy them thoroughly, and a large dishful soon disappeared when the "chief" and I combined our efforts! Salmon, the chief dish of the Skeena, bacon, eggs in all styles, and other hotel dainties, were religiously ignored when oolachan were procurable. To swallow the first oyster on the shell is repulsive to most people, but repugnance usually soon gives place to eager desire. It is precisely so with the rich and nutritious oolachans. This is often called the "candlefish" and it abounds at certain seasons in the Naas and other north Pacific rivers. It is so rich in oil that the Indians are accustomed to apply a light to the tail of the fried fish, and use it as a torch. Hence the name is very appropriate.

After he had been under surgical treatment for some time in the Victoria city hospital, and forbidden to move about, he contrived one day to evade the vigilance of his nurse, and wandered into busy Government Street. It was a sunny April morning, and all the rank and fashion of the very aristocratic Pacific capital crowded this main thoroughfare. Robert Cunningham's tall figure and uncouth bearing drew much attention, above all when he happened to espy a friend on the opposite side of the street.

"Oolachan—a dish of oolachan, my good friend," he yelled in shrill Celtic tones! The fashionable ladies and their faultlessly attired escorts gave ample sea-room to the wild Irishman from the north—the King of the Skeena—as he uttered this unfamiliar morning salutation. Robert Cunningham's evasion of hospital rules cost him his life. His body, a few days later, was conveyed north to his beloved Skeena, where practically his whole life had been spent, and where he had reigned as king.

Great preparations were in progress for an impressive funeral at Metlakatla, a short distance from the mouth of the Skeena, where a fine church, almost of cathedral dimensions, had been built in 1862. Adjacent to this is a spacious consecrated cemetery, situated upon a rocky eminence overlooking the group of native houses, the original houses of Spok-sut. The Bishop of Caledonia had arrived in time for the funeral, and a considerable number of clergy, Hudson's Bay Company officers, and old Cassiar pioneers, and an imposing procession was being arranged. But it was not to be. The mist hung low over the broad waters of the majestic Skeena, and over the extensive Metlakatla lagoons, on the funeral morning. Like noiseless shadows hundreds of Indians, in their graceful high-prowed canoes, came gliding with ghostly stealth from every village along the coast. They had come with their "klootchmen" (wives), children and dogs, from distant Indian settlements, paddling all night, or in some cases for several nights. How the news had travelled so quickly, the white men had to confess they could not understand. Never had such a vast fleet of these wonderful Pacific canoes assembled on the British Columbia seaboard before. Under the bright April sun the veil of mist melted away; and as the body of Robert Cunningham was borne from the big white steamer to the church, the canoes with their picturesque crews clad in precious Tlinkit blankets and other quaint guise closed in, in a great semi-circle and silently moved inshore. The canoes were then drawn up side by side in a long black crescent upon the beach, and the Indians gathered round the corpse. There were Indians from the Naas, the upper and lower Skeena, Port Simpson, Kitimat, Bella Coola and Alert Bay, tall Haidas from the Queen Charlottes, and others even from Mission on the Fraser, as well as from Namu and Nootka, and Quatsino, Kyuoquot and Sooke. When the clergy and the group of white residents prepared to move, in solemn order, to the church, the Indians raised a loud protest.

"No! we will not have this funeral! Robert Cunningham was one of us!" they cried, "We will bury him. He shall not rest with your fathers, but amongst our own Tyhees, amongst our own departed chiefs."

It was like a rumble of thunder in the still air, for the Indians' voices are sonorous and deep. It betokened storm. There was no alternative. These dark-skinned aborigines meant what they said: "He was one of us—he shall sleep with our departed chiefs."

The high-prowed canoes—large cedar dugouts, recalling in elegant design the famous gondolas of Venice (gracefully curving out of the water at stern and bows), were soon gliding in long lines out to the open sea. On one of the largest of these lay the body of Robert Cunningham, the coffin covered with the Union Jack, and surrounded by wampum and strings of Haikwa or tusk shells, blue and yellow shawls, coronets of cedar fibre and all the other strange artistry of the tribes—Tsimpseans, Haidas, Kitkatlas, Nitinats and many more distant peoples. Slowly the thin dark line moved out.

How silent the mirror-like water, and its colossal amphitheatre

of mountains and towering forest trees! How noiseless the long procession of shadowy canoes! Suddenly there burst forth the thunderous
drumming of Indian musicians, beating on old-time instruments—the
hollowed trunks of cedars, characteristic of Siwash harmony—while
the noble sonorous chanting of the men's voices rose, wave on wave
of sound, like a swelling Gregorian chant of mediaeval monks. Nearly
two thousand Indians joined in the sad chorus, but there was no vulgar
crash of sound, only a rumbling murmur of farewell, like a dying roll
of thunder amongst the mountains. So slowly did the ghostly procession move down the smooth glassy tide that the April sun began to
sink behind the far-off ranges of Queen Charlotte Islands, and the white
summits of the Coast Rockies were suffused with crimson, and chrome,
and violet. Still the solemn chorus rose and fell on the evening air.
About the foothills, in the yawning gorges, and over the dark forest the
gloom was gathering before the floating funeral bier of the King of the
Skeena was lost in the blue evening mist. Into the shadowy mist the
weird procession of canoes passed, while the distant chanting and the
solemn booming of the Indian drums died away in the night. Such was
the last voyage of the King of the Skeena!

> Far away a sad mysterious music
> Wailing from the mountains and the shore
> Burdened with a dark majestic secret,
> Softly soaring heavenward evermore.

A "majestic secret," indeed, for only the Siwash Indian knows
the place where the King of the Skeena sleeps!

Salmon Fishing

Fisheries Commissioner's Report (1902)

Of the provincial northern coast salmon waters the most important and extensive is the Skeena River. It is second only to the Fraser. Canning began there in 1877 with a total pack of 3000 cases. In 1887, with five canneries running, the pack was 58,592, and ten years later there were eight canneries operated, with a total pack of 65,905. The pack reached its highest limit in 1902 with 154,875 cases . . .

The fishing grounds of the Skeena district extended from a point on the river some twelve miles above the village of Port Essington to Chatham Sound. From Port Essington to De Horsey Island the river may be described as an estuary. The tides rise to a height of twenty feet. At low water the greater portion of the extensive sand flats of this basin are exposed. The main channel runs along the north shore. At De Horsey Island the waters divide and pass through either the North Skeena Passage or the Southern Passage. The North Passage is very narrow throughout its length of six miles, and terminates north of Smith Island. The South Passage, which is the main entrance, passes to the south of De Horsey Island, and to the north and south of Kennedy Island. The channel north of Kennedy Island terminates in Malacca Passage, as the southern end of Chatham Sound is called. The fishing in the Sound is largely confined to the waters south of Rachael Island, but in some seasons is extended out towards Brown Passage, through which the sockeye appear to enter from the open sea, though a portion of the run is known to come in through Edye Passage, to the north of Porcher Island. The first catches are usually made in the vicinity of Rachael Island. As the season progresses the water is covered with boats, from Port Essington to the Sound. Previous to the introduction of the Columbia River pattern of boats the fishing was confined largely to the inside channels. With the advent of the round-bottom boats and the increasing demand for salmon, the men have advanced further out to meet the incoming fish, so that the season is longer and appears to start earlier than formerly. Fishing in the inside channels is regulated by the tides. The nets are cast at high tide, and drift out with the ebb. When the "drift" has been covered, or the "snagging grounds" reached, the nets are hauled in and the boats return to the home station on the flood tide. The canners maintain receiving stations at many points, where the fishermen deliver fish to be transferred to the cannery by tugs and steamers which ply back and forth. By this method each cannery has boats fishing upon every drift of the extensive fishing grounds. For outside fishing brisk westerly winds, which bring clear skies, are most desired. On bright, clear days the fish travel closer to the surface and are more easily caught by the nets. Once the fish pass into the shallow, inside channels, where the discoloured water of the river conceals the nets, the effect of weather conditions is not so marked as it is farther out. Previous to 1897 the boats used on the Skeena were of the flat-bottom variety, at which time the round-bottom model known as "Columbia Riverboats" were introduced, whose superiority for the outside fishing was at once demonstrated, resulting in their general adoption since 1899. Most of the boats and nets used are the property of the canneries, and are rented to the fishermen on the customary one-third basis. Where fishermen provide their own boats, they are allowed two dollars per week as rental. In cases where fishermen own both boat and net they are paid nine cents each for sockeye, and twenty-seven cents each for spring salmon, instead of the usual prices of seven cents and twenty-five cents paid for fish caught by cannery boats and nets. The nets used for catching sockeye are the regulation machine-made web-net, made of six or eight strand thread of 5 ¾-inch meshes, and from 40 to 60 meshes deep, and 200 fathoms long. These nets last from one to four years. In this vicinity a greater loss is occasioned by snags than in any other section of the province. The canners usually charge to profit and loss 35% per annum of their value, to cover the season's losses.

Fishing for sockeye begins in the latter part of June, and ends about the middle of August. The main part of the run is looked for early in July.

There do not appear to be any marked periodic fluctuations in the run of sockeye in the Skeena. They are considered better fish than those taken in Rivers Inlet, as they contain more oil and are of a better colour, though they do not bring quite as good a price in the market as the Fraser River fish.

The spring or quinnat salmon run begins in May and ends about the first week in July. Like in the Fraser River, these fish vary considerably in colour. The white and pale pink-tinted fish predominate, which lessens the value of these fish. Some of the canners use seven and a half-inch to ten-inch mesh nets (called "spring salmon" nets) in May and June and the early part of July, for the purpose of taking the early run of these fish. This part of the run is stated to more nearly approach the standard red colour. The canners do not accept the white-coloured spring fish. When offered for delivery to the cannery, the receiving clerk slashes the fish near the head and tail to examine its colour, and if it be white the fish is rejected. The proportion of white-flesh fish is stated to be about one-third of those taken, and one-third is said to be pink, while the remaining one-third is the desirable deep red colour of the first quality.

The coho salmon runs in August and September and the dog salmon in September, October and November. Up to the present time little effort has been made to catch large numbers of either of these fish, but with the increasing demand for these grades their value may be more fully recognized, as the runs of both varieties is stated to be large.

The Skeena River is, after the Fraser, the largest in the Province. It carries to the sea the waters of an extensive mountainous area, on the coast slope of which the rain and snowfall is over 100 inches a year. Its principal source is at Babine Lake. It is believed at one time to have drained Stuart, Tecla and Quesnel Lakes, whose waters now flow into the Fraser River. From Port Essington, at its mouth, to the little settlement of Hazelton, a distance of 180 miles, the river is navigable by powerful stern-wheel steamboats during the greater part of the summer. Some 90 miles above the mouth of the river it rushes with great force through a narrow canyon, which renders navigation impossible during the season of extreme high water. During the winter months the river is frozen over and the greater portion of the watershed is buried under snow and ice. South of Hazelton the valley of the Skeena varies in width from one to four miles. Precipitous mountains of considerable elevation rise on either side, the summits of some of which are perpetually covered with ice and snow, and the lower elevations with a dense and exceedingly valuable growth of timber.

Respectfully submitted,
John Pease Babcock,
Fisheries Commissioner.
Victoria, December 1, 1902

Windsor Cannery Aberdeen, Skeena

◆ Alfred Carmichael

(A season in a salmon cannery, 1891)

The canning season proper begins when fishing begins, on the 15th of June. Up to that date everything is being made ready. In Victoria during the winter, the cannery manager contracts with a Chinese firm to make the cans and handle the salmon, which includes cleaning, filling, soldering, testing, boiling, labelling and casing the cans. The company supplies the tools. When fishing starts, the "boss-Chinaman" hires Indians to clean the fish and fill the cans.

By late March or early April, the river is clear of ice and the manager, boss-fisherman and Chinamen arrive. From then on the Chinese are kept busy making cans. Nets are made and old nets mended by Indian women, working under a white net-boss. When fishing commences, the net-boss becomes the boss-fisherman.

The boiler, retort, baths and cannery fittings are seen after by an under-manager, who must be a very competent man, capable of turning his hand to anything—for if something goes wrong with the boiler or retort, the whole season might be wasted.

The main building has five parts. First the cleaning house, with two double cleaning tables, two washing tanks, two drainers and two cutting machines. The salmon's tails, heads and digestive organs slide down a chute cut in the centre of each table, straight down into the river which flows under the cannery.

In the second room, at three filling tables 40 workers fill the cans with salmon. At the end of the filling tables on three large benches, Indian women polish the cans to remove leftover grease.

Along one side of the third room, the soldering department, is a long bench where the sides of the cans are soldered and leaky cans are fixed, using a stove, three soldering irons, two cans of flux, a scrape awl and a tool called a body seamer. In the middle of the room are the soldering machines. Here the lids are soldered on, and the cans roll down an inclined chute to the fourth room—the bath room.

In the bath room are three testers, six boiler baths and a retort. These are heated with steam from the large boiler. The baths are just large wooden tanks made to fit the coolers.

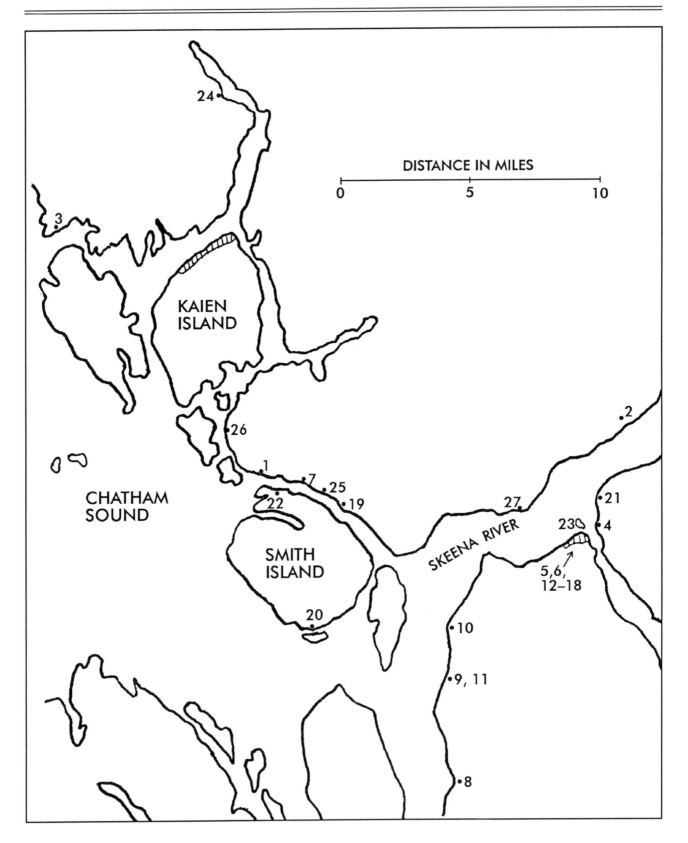

Operating canneries, Skeena River, 1877–1920. Many canneries had several names, many of them local and never written down, but canneries using the same building for their plants at different times under different official names are treated as separate canneries.

Opposite: Operating Canneries, Skeena River, 1877–1920

1877	Inverness (1)	1901	Ladysmith (15)
1878	Windsor/Aberdeen (2)	1901	Skeena River Commercial
1882	Metlakatla (3)		or Skeena
1883	Balmoral (4)	1902	Pearce (17)
1883	British America (5)	1902	Turnball's (18)
1883	Skeena /Cunningham's (6)	1903	Cassiar (19)
1889	North Pacific (7)	1903	Oceanic (20)
1890	Standard (8)	1904	Alexandria (21)
1892	Royal Canadian (9)	1906	Dominion (22)
1895	Carlisle (10)	1906	Village Island (23)
1898	Claxton (11)	1913	Tuck's Inlet (24)
1899	Anglo–Alliance (12)	1916	Sunnyside (25)
1899	Globe (13)	1918	Port Edward (26)
1901	Herman's (14)	1920	Haysport (27)

The fifth department is a large loft where the coolers are kept until the cans are perfectly cold, and where the finished cans are stored.

By the first of June, twenty white fishermen have come up from Victoria for six weeks of camping and fishing. Thirty-six Japanese are making boxes, tables and stools for the three camps. Each camp has a camp-boss who counts the fish every tide and credits them to the men. He must also mend snagged nets and generally see after things.

It is a curious sight to see twenty Indians coming to work in the morning flourishing their long knives. If you pass by they might make a pretend thrust at you, watching your face to see if you are frightened.

A Company steamer tows scowloads of fish from the camps to the cannery. Forty-five boats are the total number licensed. To each boat there are two men, a fisher and a puller. The latter is hired by the former for either wages or halves. The fisher makes a contract with the manager. This year (1891) 25¢ was paid for a spring salmon and 6¢ for a sockeye, regardless of weight: a 10-pound spring would fetch 25¢, and so would one weighing 80 pounds.

Salmon species are spring (red and white), sockeye, steelhead, coho, humpback, and dog. The white springs are discarded because the London market will not believe they are genuine salmon, even though they are sweeter and much more delicate than the reds, and many consider them superior in flavour. It is a great pity when the men catch mostly whites in a tide, and do not get a cent for them.

The springs arrive from early June to early July, when the sockeye arrive. The sockeye are pretty silver salmon, weighing about 25 pounds. The flesh is a very bright colour and splendid for canning. In a good season these fish are very numerous, boats last year catching an average of 200 every tide. Steelheads are a fine looking fish but of no use in canning owing to their light colour. The Indians smoke them for winter use. Cohos are only taken when other salmon are very scarce.

The scourge of the rivers are the humpback, arriving at the end of July in such millions that every other kind of salmon is crushed out of the river. All nets have to be taken up or the humpbacks will destroy them. As the season progresses their humps get larger. The hump is a dark brown colour, while the breast is a reddish, yellowish, greenish, washed-out-looking colour horrid to the eye. Toward the end of the season they get very lazy and it is easy to catch them by their tails. I have seen nets so full of these fish that they had to be towed ashore.

At the first cleaning table the salmon loses its head, tail and internal organs. In the first washing tank it is given a great scraping and scrubbing and all fins etc. are cut off. Then in a second tank it is washed again. Water is constantly kept running through the wash troughs. A cutter picks the salmon out of the drainer and places one salmon if spring, and two if sockeye, lengthways onto the cutting machine. The turn of a lever cuts the salmon into the desired lengths, then a chopper cuts them into the desired widths. The salmon now slide down an inclined chute or drainer into buckets where one Indian is constantly kept busy filling the buckets and another takes them to the fillers who, if they do their job properly, put into each can one piece of back and one piece of breast. Each filler has a ticket. For every tray of cans she fills a Chinaman puts a hole in the ticket. A tray holds 12 cans if flat and 24 if tall. Three cents a dozen is the rate at which they are paid. A good filler can do 12 in four minutes. We had generally 26 filling at an average rate of 65 cases an hour. When a tray is full it is taken to the weighing and cleaning table where an Indian woman weighs it and passes it to the cleaners who are Indian children, six in all. Each child rubs the can with a piece of net and passes it on to the next. A Chinese worker puts on the lid and the can goes through the soldering machine. There is a small hole in the centre of the lid; without it, the air inside could burst the can open under the pressure of passing through this machine. The cans now roll down a chute to the bath room where Chinamen solder up the holes in the centres of the lids and place the cans in coolers. Each cooler is hooked onto a crane, and lowered the first tester until water covers the tops of the cans. The steam is turned on until the water reaches the boiling point. Leaking cans are carefully picked out and sent to the leak-stoppers. The cooler is then taken from the tester and lowered into a boiler bath. When all three boiler baths are filled, the steam is turned on and the bath boils for one and a quarter hours. Then the steam is turned off, the boiler-bath emptied, and each can is struck a sharp rap with a mallet, to tell by the sound which cans have burst. A hole is then pricked in the top of each can. The juice and steam often spurt up twelve feet, then the tops of the cans are brushed with a small broom, the holes are re-soldered and the cans again tested with mallets.

The coolers are now piled seven high on trucks. When three trucks are loaded they are run into the retort, the door is closed and the steam turned on. A thermometer at the far end of the retort helps a superintendent keep the temperature at 240° F. After two hours and five minutes the steam valve is opened, and when the pressure falls to zero the door is lifted and the trucks pulled out onto a turntable. Three Indians, contracted for $90 to wash the season's output, lift each cooler, dip it into a caustic soda bath to remove all the grease from the cans, then rinse it in a clean water bath. The coolers are then put on trucks and taken to the loft to cool. After a day in the loft, the cans are sounded with small steel rods and the good cans are piled to await casing. When fishing ends, half of the Chinese start making boxes out of lumber from the cannery's Rivers Inlet mill. The remaining Chinese lacquer, label and case the cans. The ends of each can are dipped in lacquer to prevent rusting, and then labelled. The cans are again sounded, leaky ones taken away, and the good ones cased.

After all the salmon is shipped the boats are drawn up and washed, then stowed away in the cannery.

Excerpt from Minority Report of Fisheries Commission (1908)

We desire again to call your attention to the danger which threatens the salmon fisheries of the northern district of the province . . .

Many new canneries have been constructed there in the last few years and the number of licensed boats increased. The Commissioners realized this danger two years ago, and in the Interim Report of December 7, 1905, recommended that a limit be placed on the number of canneries and the number of boats licensed in this district. There are no international complications affecting the salmon fisheries of the northern districts of the province. The situation there is entirely within the control of the government. If these valuable salmon-producing rivers are depleted the responsibility will rest upon it alone . . .

Up to a few years ago the sockeye salmon canned on the Skeena and Rivers Inlet was small in proportion to the amount produced by the Fraser River but during the last two seasons the pack on these rivers has exceeded that packed on the Fraser. The pack of sockeye this year at both Rivers Inlet and the Skeena greatly exceeded that packed on the Fraser. The latter having been the greatest salmon-producing river in the world, has now fallen to third place in the rivers of the province. Excessive fishing, which depleted the Fraser, now threatens the extinction of the salmon of the Skeena and Rivers Inlet.

We strongly urge as a remedial measure that no additional canneries be permitted in the northern district, and that the number of fishing boats licensed at Rivers Inlet be limited to 550, those at the Skeena River to 800 boats and those at the Nass River to 200 boats.

Campbell Sweeny
John Pease Babcock
Members of the Commission.

The Sternwheeler Era

S.S. Mount Royal
(25-A) / BCARS 29415

The Country of the Skeena

◆ J. Herrick McGregor (c.1902–03)

The Skeena (from Scheean, the river) long solely travelled by Indian canoes, was in 1866 ascended as far as Kitsumkalum, some 45 miles above tidewater, by the steamer *Mumford*, with supplies for the great overland telegraph line, and 15 years later so good an authority as the late Dr. Dawson gave it as his opinion that this marked the limit of possible navigation.

An old settler on the Skeena, however, who was on the steamer at the time, tells me that the *Mumford* would have had no difficulty in reaching the Forks at Hazelton, and that her reason for turning back when she did was in order to make a trip up the Stikine with wire and provisions for Telegraph Creek.

At all events the navigation of the river for about 200 miles has been successfully accomplished by the Hudson Bay Company, and the Cunninghams of Port Essington, for some twelve years past, and the

◆ Facts About Sternwheelers ◆

Used more in BC than anywhere else in North America—*why?*
1. Flat bottom—rode water like a duck.
2. Shallow draft—6 to 8 inches of water was sometimes enough.
3. Wooden construction—buoyant.
4. Easy to repair.
5. Easy docking—no wharf needed.
6. With paddlewheel astern, could pass through narrower channels.

Appearance

Varied from the packing crate variety to floating "wedding cakes."
Average size—125 ft. x 30 ft. Blunt bow, no keel.
Kingposts—mastlike uprights to which iron braces (hog-rods or chains) were attached to prevent sagging at bow and stern.
Hogposts—Uprights on either side of the kingposts. Attached to bow and stern.
Turnbuckles—on the hogchains to adjust bow or stern if sagging or sway-backing occurred.
Decks—Larger boats had three—main, cabin and texas decks.

Crew

Varied according to size of boat and era. Averaged 12–17.
Captain—the "Last Word"
Mate
Carpenter—always busy
Purser
Engineer(s), firemen, wood passers
Stewards
Cook(s)
Freight clerk
Deckhands

Noisy

Paddlewheel slapping water, steam screeching from stack, deep-toned whistle, catcalling of crew members.

◆

last season saw no less than four steamers plying her waters at one time.

About four years after the fall through of the old telegraph scheme, a considerable rush of gold seekers opened up the Omineca placer camp. Caucasian travellers were more common on the river and the vested interests of those Indian tribes who, at Kitselas and other points, levied tribute on passing commerce, suffered a shock from which they have never recovered.

Shortly after this, preliminary surveys were carried up the river with a view to making Port Simpson the western terminus of what is now the CPR, and if I am not in error it was rather against Mr. Sandford Fleming's recommendations that the railway was ultimately carried through the lower latitudes and down the valleys of the Thompson and Fraser. This survey, like the preliminary operations of the telegraph company, was abandoned, fell into oblivion and appeared to have been so much waste effort. It is encouraging, therefore, to note that last summer not only saw the great telegraph line in actual operation, with a branch extension from Hazelton to Port Simpson, but also beheld again a party of railroad locators working from Kitimat Arm, by way of Lakelse Lake to the Skeena, and up towards the Forks under the management of Mr. J.H. Gray, who first became acquainted with the possibilities of the region on the old survey above mentioned.

About the time the Kitimat company secured their charter an attempt was made by Victoria parties, on behalf of American mining capitalists, to secure 30,000 acres of land as a bonus for building a wagon road through the Kitimat and Skeena Valleys to Hazelton. That they failed to obtain the required assistance was perhaps unfortunate—certainly not conducive to the rapid occupation of these valleys, as the capitalists in question had planned a very interesting scheme of colonization and mineral development.

However, since the ultimate destiny of the Skeena watershed rests entirely on its exploitation as a railway route, the delay in establishing settlers will count for little if the present charter holders are able either to carry out construction say as far as the coal beds tributary to the Bulkley—or to make terms with the builders of that through line which alone can fully rouse to prosperity the great central portion of British Columbia.

The Skeena, *the* Operator *and the* Conveyor *docked at Prince Rupert.*
(4-B)

Pioneer Pilots of the Skeena

◆ Mrs. M.W. Boss

The Skeena River, a veritable mountain torrent, with a drop of five feet to the mile and a run of 180 miles, afforded no small problems to these skillful skippers. They had to contend with rapids, sandbars (ever shifting), whirlpools, driftwood, uncharted channels, canyons, high water and low water, and at times, strong headwinds. Consequently it was necessary to "line" over the difficult places.

For many years Fort Simpson was the distributing point for the Hudson's Bay Company's steamers—a run of fifty miles by sea to Port Essington (Spoke-shoot) and from there it took an average trip of three days to Hazelton depending on the stage of the water. There was no night travelling and the ship tied up each evening at a cordwood pile to "wood up" for an early start next morning. In the early days some of the first boats were obliged to wait a week or so for the river to rise, so while waiting the passengers fished and enjoyed an outing ashore. During these delays the usual betting ensued as to when the ship's whistle would give the "all clear." On the other hand the down trip was done in less than a day, depending on the "skook-um-chuck" (tide).

Many years ago I had my first introduction to the then "Old *Caledonia*" at Fort Simpson. The captain, J.H. Bonser and family of Portland, Oregon, were aboard and had just completed a successful run on both the Skeena and the Stikine rivers.

That fall of 1890 my stepfather, the late J.M.L. Alexander, who had been cattle ranching on the Queen Charlotte Islands for two years, had chartered the Georgetown Sawmill steamer *Nell*, under Captain Madden, to transfer his family and a herd of 19 fine steers to the mainland. The cattle were dumped off at Elizabeth Island and we proceeded to Fort Simpson, where lying at the wharf was the little *Caledonia* all gleaming in a coat of fresh white paint with its bright red paddlewheel. A pleasing sight to us children after the dark and heavy-looking sea craft of the coast! Perhaps many old timers will remember Mr. Pat Hickey who was a veteran engineer of the Kootenays and then chief of the *Caledonia*. In fact, he spent many years on the Hudson's Bay Company boats. The purser was Anthony C. Mouat of Victoria and his brother, William Mouat, was second engineer. Otherwise the crew included a mate, steward, watchman, cabin boys, Indian pilot, deckhands and woodpassers. In a few days the *Caledonia* would be hauled out on the ways for the winter months.

There was much talk then of a trans-Canada railway coming into either Fort Simpson or Kitimaat, hence there was a regular land boom. My stepfather, Messrs. Charlie Clifford, R.H. Hall and other Hudson's Bay factors staked townsites at both sites, but were doomed to disappointment and our cattle went wild. As we all know, 17 years later the Grand Trunk Pacific chose Kaien Island for its terminal.

S.S. Caledonia
(25-A) / BCARS 29418

Riverboats
on the Skeena

◆ Mrs. C.G. Stevens (1936)

A relic of the early life of the Hudson's Bay Company lies in Prince Rupert harbour, British Columbia. This is what remains of the riverboat, *Hazelton*, a sternwheel steamer. This old boat could tell many interesting and romantic stories of early adventures along the Skeena River. The hull of the old *Port Simpson*, sister ship to the *Hazelton*, also lies near Prince Rupert on Digby Island.

In the early days the Hudson's Bay Company found it very difficult and expensive to supply their interior posts from Port Simpson, which at that time was the headquarters and main distributing point for New Caledonia, as the northern district of British Columbia was then called. All goods had to be taken in by canoe up the Skeena River and all raw furs brought out the same way. This not only was a very dangerous means of transportation, owing to the treacherous river and the hostile Indians encountered along the way, but was expensive and wasted a great deal of time. About the year 1889, on the recommendation of Mr. John Flewin, who was then government agent of the district, Mr. R.H. Hall, chief factor of Port Simpson trading post, decided to investigate the possibilities of running a sternwheel steamer on the Skeena River as a means of lessening this expense as well as reducing the hazards of distributing supplies to the interior.

As a result, Captain George Oden of New Westminster, a well-known river steamboat man, investigated the possibility of negotiating the treacherous Kitselas Canyon on the Skeena River. Under his instructions the first Hudson's Bay Company sternwheel river steamer was built in New Westminster in 1890. This boat, the *Caledonia*, was about 100 feet in length. Captain Oden successfully negotiated the Skeena River to Hazelton with her in 1891, and then carried on a successful trade up and down the river till the spring of 1898, when the boat was towed back to Victoria and her engines transferred to a new, larger *Caledonia*. This new steamer plied the Skeena for a number of years and also made an annual trip up the Stikine River. Captain Oden was succeeded by Captain Bonser, a capable, well-known river man.

Because of both the Yukon gold rush and all the fish canneries that were opening along the northwestern coast, the Hudson's Bay Company needed more boats to handle the rush of river business. The steamer *Strathcona* was built in Victoria and launched in 1900, where it worked in conjunction with the *Caledonia* until 1902, when they were joined by the much larger and more beautiful *Mount Royal*. This later boat was also built in Victoria by Mr. Alex Watson, one of the finest ship builders known.

Other companies joined the river trade, and in 1900 the steamer *Hazelton* was one of the first boats to be built in Victoria. It was built for Mr. George Cunningham of Port Essington, who operated it on the Skeena River until selling it to the Hudson's Bay Company about 1903. The *Hazelton* then ran with the *Mount Royal*, and the two smaller boats were laid off. The *Mount Royal* was unfortunate in bridging the canyon at Kitselas in July, 1907. It turned over and drowned several of the crew, including the purser. The old *Caledonia* was brought into service

S.S. Hazelton
(25-A) / BCARS 4940

again for the rest of that year and then the large new steamer *Port Simpson* took the place of the *Mount Royal* in 1908. This boat was also built in Victoria by Mr. Watson.

There was constant rivalry among the different captains and companies on the river as to who could make the best trips. Great difficulties had to be overcome all the way. The Skeena River was very treacherous at any time, and with the continually shifting sandbars, difficult turns, narrow canyons and rushing waters, the captains and their crews always had to be on their toes. In spite of these difficulties, boats would try to outwit each other, play tricks—anything to delay the other captain's schedule. For instance: picking up extra supplies of wood along the way so that the ship behind would not be able to get her fuel. This all added to the excitement and pleasure of the passengers, and as the same captain was seldom on the same boat two years in a row it made it all the more interesting, as the captains were well known by everyone who travelled the river. Even among the Hudson's Bay Company's own captains there was great rivalry, especially between Captain Johnson of the *Mount Royal* and Captain Bonser of the *Hazelton*. They even went so far one time as to stage a small naval battle and fired shots at each other, but no damage was done. They also tried to ram their boats once in the middle of the river. Their rivalry ran beyond a joke several times, but it certainly held the interest of their passengers. The captains on the various steamers were also always trying to see who could make the fastest trip up the river to Hazelton and back. Captain Johnson made one trip in fifty-six hours with the *Mount Royal*, and a little later the same season Captain Gardner made it in forty-seven hours with the *Hazelton*.

S.S. Mount Royal
(26-C)

Kitselas Canyon was the most difficult section of the Skeena River. After the loss of the *Mount Royal*, when the water was particularly high the Hudson's Bay Company would usually keep one of their steamers above the canyon and the other below and portage all freight across from one vessel to the other. They usually kept the *Hazelton* on the upper part of the river, as it was the smaller boat and more easily handled. The waters of the Skeena would rise very quickly and at Hazelton it would often rise seventeen feet at the wharf in one day. Right in the Kitselas Canyon there was a rise of sixty feet in the high water season, so it can be readily understood the captains of these riverboats had no easy tasks.

In the early days the Hudson's Bay Company riverboats made their regular trips from Port Simpson up the Skeena whenever enough freight and passengers warranted them doing so. However, as there was a great deal of rough water between Port Essington and Port Simpson, the boats soon made their headquarters at Port Essington and travelled regularly between there and Hazelton, generally about once a week. Their first trips of the year, always very exciting, were usually made about the beginning of May. Trips earlier in the season had to be made by canoe. It was a great thrill to the people of the interior to get their first supply of fresh fruit, mail, etc. after being shut in since the last trip of the season, which was generally made about the end of October. At the end of the season, with the exception of the *Mount Royal*, which returned to Victoria every fall, the boats all went back to Port Simpson, where they were pulled ashore till the next spring.

The *Hazelton* and the *Port Simpson* were the only two Hudson's Bay Company steamers that ran on the rivers after 1908. They both carried sixty to eighty cabin passengers and from sixty to one hundred tons of freight, the *Port Simpson* being considerably the larger boat. It would usually take them three or four days to go up the Skeena to Hazelton and about one or two to come back. These steamers also made at least two trips up the Stikine River as well as numerous side trips to different canneries. In 1908 they also began excursions to Prince Rupert and around Kaien Island.

The steamer *Hazelton* was engaged in river trading until about 1911, and the *Port Simpson* for a year longer, until the completion of the Grand Trunk Railway in 1912. After lying idle at Port Simpson, the hull of the *Port Simpson* was finally sold to M.M. Stephens of Prince Rupert in about 1915, and now lies as a wreck near the city. We understand that the Hudson's Bay Company transferred the engines of these two boats into transport boats built for the Mackenzie River. The hull of the *Hazelton* was sold to the Prince Rupert Yacht Club in 1912 and used for a clubhouse until it was finally abandoned in 1924. It now lies in Prince Rupert harbour, a vivid reminder of romantic bygone days along the northern British Columbia coast.

Up the Skeena River to the Home of the Tsimshians

George A. Dorsey, Ph.D.

Chief----Hazelton Indian village
(25-A) / BCARS 15456

(From a lecture delivered at the Field Columbian Museum, November 13, 1897)

In a recent number of the *Monthly* I described some of the incidents of a visit to the Haida and Tlingit villages about Dixon's Entrance; now I am to speak of the Tsimshian villages on the Skeena River. The Tsimshian Indians are one of the five great stocks which make up the aboriginal population of the coast of British Columbia and southern Alaska. They are shut in by the Tlingits on the north and by the Kwatiutls on the south, while on the head waters of the Nass and Skeena Rivers they come in contact with the great Tinneh or Athabascan stock. The Tsimshians are probably the most progressive of all the coast Indians, and are one of a few stocks on the American continent which are holding their own in point of numbers.

Desiring to visit those villages which are least contaminated by modern influence, we ascended the Skeena River to the village of Kitanmaksh or Hazelton. The Skeena is the historic river of British Columbia; its name means "Water of Terrors." Nearly every rock, every bend, every canyon is the scene of some mythical tale. The scene of the birth of the Tsimshian nation lies in its valley; the rock is still revered upon which rested the Tsimshian ark after the flood, and the "Dum-lak-an," the "new home and place of dispersal," is still a mecca to which pilgrimages are made. In the modern development of the Omineca and Cariboo gold fields the Skeena has been the highway to the sea. For hundreds of years canoes have been paddled up and down its waters; it has been the highway for intertribal trade from time immemorial, and when the Hudson's Bay Company's post was established at Hazelton, and merchandise began to pour into the upper country in a steady stream, the Tsimshians with their canoes enjoyed for a long time a monopoly of the carrying trade. Gradually, as they learned the ways and methods of the white man, the price per ton of freight from the coast to Hazelton began steadily to rise, until in 1891 the tariff of sixty dollars a ton was declared ruinous by the company, and they decided to build their own steamer with which to carry their freight up the river.

Port Essington is the chief port of the mouth of the Skeena, and in Essington we found ourselves on the twenty-third day of July. The *Caledonia* was up the river on her third trip, but was expected back any hour, but so delightfully uncertain is the river voyage that, as we were informed, "there was no telling when she would be down—in fact, she might be caught above the canyon and wouldn't be down for weeks."

The town of Essington dates back to 1835, when the Hudson's Bay Company established a post there. Its only rival for pre-eminence on the coast is Port Simpson. The town in summer is completely given over to fishing, the salmon cannery of Cunningham & Son being one of the largest on the coast, and the river for twenty miles is dotted with canneries. In one day, while we were in Essington, the catch of salmon on the river was 92,000 fish. In addition to the cannery the town boasts a good hotel and a Salvation Army. An Indian Salvation Army is worth going miles to see, for the Indian is a natural-born salvationist; the Army permits him to make all the noise he chooses, sing as loudly as he pleases, and, best of all, he is entitled to make a speech every time it comes his turn.

In the afternoon, about four o'clock, on the day after our arrival, a long, shrill blast of the whistle aroused the entire town, for the *Caledonia* was in sight. Down we went to the wharf, and the entire town followed. What a motley crew you will find on one of these British Columbia wharves! What colouring, what a Babel of tongues—Tlingits from Alaska, Haidas from the Queen Charlotte Islands, Tsimshians from the Skeena, Kwatiutls from Vancouver, Chinamen, Japanese, Greeks, Scandinavians, Englishmen, and Yankees; men, women, children, dogs, and from two to six woolly bear cubs. The *Caledonia* is the exclusive property of the Hudson's Bay Company; she is not a common carrier, and does not encourage either passengers or freight, as the tariff rates prove. There is a feverish haste and hustle about the movements of the steamer which are fairly contagious. She makes her first trip early in the spring, as soon as the ice has left the rivers, on the Stikine; then it is a wild, eager ambition of the company to have her make four trips up the Skeena before the river closes up in the fall.

We had as passengers two prospectors from Spokane, a mining expert from Victoria, a native evangelist from Essington, and about fifty Indians, mostly women and children, each one with a varied assortment of boxes, bales, bundles, and dogs; the crew numbered twenty, and we had about one hundred tons of freight on board.

From Essington to Hazelton is one hundred and fifty-two miles, a panorama of unending and unbroken beauty; never monotonous, always interesting, it presents a river voyage which is probably not equaled, certainly not excelled, by any other river voyage of the same length on the American continent or in the world. We began the voyage on Sunday morning, we tied up in front of Hazelton on Saturday night. To recount in detail the haps and mishaps of each day's progress would take more time than I can command. In one day we made forty-eight miles, on another day we made one hundred yards, on another day we didn't make a foot. With plenty of water under her keel the *Caledonia* could run twenty miles an hour; she could cut her way through a sand bar at the rate of a yard or so an hour; and at either rate of progress she burned each hour from one and a half to two cords of wood.

For the first ten miles the scenery does not differ materially from that which we are accustomed to in the inland sea from Victoria to Alaska. Then we enter fresh water and for the next forty miles steam through one long mountainous gorge, for here the river has cut completely through the Cascade Range. The mountains begin at the water's edge and rise almost perpendicularly to heights of from three to four thousand feet. Their lower limits are covered with dense green forests, which seem to grow out of the solid rock. The summits are

Totem pole—Hazelton Indian village, c. 1909
(25-A) / BCARS 19143

smooth and glistening, and often covered with snow and ice. Here and there we can trace some tiny rivulet issuing from an ice bed high up among the clouds, and every portion of its course can be traced down the steep mountain wall until it gives one final and headlong plunge into the river. At times these streams, taking their rise in some extensive glacier, are of considerable magnitude, and fairly roar as they leap and hurl themselves downward from their dizzy height. Here we learned a curious fact about the river: in summer it falls when it rains, and rises when the sun shines, so rapidly do the pent-up snows of winter disappear and rush down the mountain sides under the heat of the spring sun.

Until noon of the second day we had been making good time, but now the fun began, for we had left deep water and had arrived at the first flight of the eight-hundred-foot stairway which the *Caledonia* had to climb ere Hazelton could be reached. The river had been gradually

S.S. Inlander *heading at full steam up Kitselas Canyon* (26-A)

widening as one island after another had been passed, until now it was nearly half a mile wide and flowed through four channels. The captain attempted one channel, but we couldn't gain an inch, and in drifting back again down the rapids the current carried the boat against the rocks and, with a crash and a lurch, but minus some woodwork, she was in the stream again. Then two other channels were tried, but without avail, although the wheel was throwing water and gravel over the pilot house. The fourth channel was next tried, but the current was too strong. Then we "lined her out," and this novel method of getting a huge steamboat up a stream soon became only too commonplace. The method of procedure is this: The boat is forced against a sand bar and allowed to rest while men go forward in a skiff with a long four-inch cable, which is made fast to a tree on the bank or to a "dead man," a long spar buried deep in the earth of a sand bar and heaped over with boulders. When all is ready, the boat is attached to the capstan and the wheel begins to revolve. It is tedious work and often provoking, as when the cable parts, or the "dead man" gives up his hold, and the whole work must be done over again. The boat quivers from stem to stern, and the wheel, with all possible steam on, is simply one revolving ball of water. We fairly hold our breath as we listen to the dull vibrations of the boat, the rumbling of the capstan, and the grating sound of the keel of the steamer as she is being dragged through the rapids over the bar; but above all can be heard the voice of Captain Bonser as he shouts to his Indian pilot, "Go head capstan," or "Stop steamboat," "Stop capstan," "Go head steamboat," "Go head capstan!" In four hours we have made fifty yards, but we are in open water again and the boat settles down to its regular chug, chug, chug.

Eighty miles from Essington the Skeena in its flight to the sea makes its first plunge into the Cascade Mountains, and its entrance is indescribably grand. No pen or brush can do justice to the beauties of the Kitselas Canyon. At its mouth we are in a broad, deep basin, as if the river had felt depressed as it passed through the quarter-mile narrow gorge and had here spread itself out to breathe and rest before it started anew its downward journey to the sea. It was late in the afternoon, and the western sun threw long shadows of the lofty sky-crowned perpendicular walls of the left-hand side of the canyon over against the rocky islets and ragged, rock-bound eastern shore. Once we have entered, there is no faltering; "lining it out" is impossible here, and on and on the boat labours and climbs, twisting and turning through the narrow, tortuous channel. A quick eye and a steady nerve must command the wheel now, for a turn too much or too little would be fatal. One instinctively feels that the "Water of Terrors" is the proper name for this river, and with that feeling comes the other—that it was never intended for navigation.

After four hours' grinding over sand bars and pounding against rocks we tied up for repairs. One of the boilers had sprung a leak which could be neglected no longer. The delay of thirty-six hours was not without compensation, for the country about was open, and proved a relief after the long ride through the high-walled river from the sea to the canyon. The banks were low or moderately high and of gravel or sand bluffs and we could look off over a landscape broken here and there by solitary peaks or clustered mountains, their summits always covered with ice and snow. To the far east were the pure white peaks of the Five Virgins, their summits glistening under the bright sun. Even the character of the vegetation had changed, and the dense forests of sombre firs, spruces, and cedars of the lower river had given way to great cottonwoods and underbrush of hazel and alder.

In the afternoon we climbed a bluff near the river, from which we could look off over a country that was wild and extremely picturesque. To one side of us could be seen a great mountain, its summit covered by a mighty glacier whose blue-white ice gleamed and glistened in the sun. And there was no mistaking the power of the sun that day; its warm rays being especially welcome after some weeks of the cold, depressing gloom and fog of the coast.

We were now really in the country of the Tsimshians, and every few hours we drew up in front of some quiet, peaceful village, its almost deserted cottages guarded by the totem poles of former days. In succession we passed Meamskinesht, Kitwangah and Kitzegukla, with now and then a small salmon fishing station. The villages proved disappointing both in their smallness and modernness, and none of them seemed worthy of any extended visit. From time to time we passed great black patches in the forest, the result of extensive fires, sure signs that the rainy coast was far away.

On Friday night we tied up to the bank within five miles of our

Medicine man—Hazelton
(25-A) / BCARS 15469

destination, but we had yet to pass Macintosh's Bar. That was accomplished on the following day, after eleven hours' hard work and by five o'clock we had reached the "Forks," or the junction of the Skeena and Bulkley Rivers. Our course was to the left, up the Skeena for half a mile, and in a few moments more we tied up in front of the stockade post of the Hudson's Bay Company; we had reached Hazelton. The region about us was "Dum-lak-an,"—"what will be a good place," the home of the Tsimshians.

Before 1870 the town was farther down the river, on the flat at the junction of the Bulkley and Skeena Rivers. It has had additions to its population from Kis-pi-yeoux, and from villages down the river. There are also to be numbered among the inhabitants the Indian agent, Mr. Loring, the Hudson's Bay representative, Mr. Sargent and his assistants, and Mr. Fields, the missionary. The Indian population numbers about 275. The town occupies a low, uneven plain, which, beginning at the water's edge, extends back for a quarter of a mile, where it is hemmed in by a high bluff on the face of the second river terrace. There are but few of the old houses left and still fewer totem poles, and they are without particular interest. Most prominent in the village is the warlike stockade of the company's post, with its two bastions at opposite corners, and the blockhouse in the centre of the enclosure, now hidden by the store which stands in front of it. The stockade was put up in 1891, when an Indian uprising was feared throughout the length of the river.

Wherever you find a trading post and a missionary you can not hope to find people who retain much of their native life or who are of great value to anthropology. But still Hazelton was sufficiently primitive to be of interest in many respects. In matters of dress the Indians are almost on a footing with the whites, but they still make a curious garment for winter's use which is worn by nearly all of the interior tribes. This is a blanket made out of long, narrow strips of rabbit hide, and is warm, heavy and extremely durable. We were fortunate enough to find a woman who was engaged in making one of these curious garments on a most rude and primitive loom. Other garments are still occasionally made of Indian hemp, which grows wild and in abundance. This is beaten and pounded and then spun into fine thread, and woven into the desired form.

In former days the Indians used large quantities of the wool of the mountain sheep in making the beautiful clilcat blankets that formed an important part of the chief's costume, but now the Indians buy most of their wool. Its chief uses are for sashes and belts, which are still worn and made after the fashion of former days. Of other garments of daily use, except moccasins, there is nothing remaining. There are a few remnants of ceremonial costumes still in existence, and by a bit of good fortune we were enabled to secure the complete paraphernalia of a shaman, or Indian doctor, who had only recently renounced his native practices and joined Mr. Field's band of Christians. In the outfit thus acquired were rattles, charms, blankets, masks, and headdresses of various kinds. From another individual we secured the complete costume of a member of the fraternity, or secret society, of Dog Eaters. The Tsimshians have four such societies, and the Dog Eaters stand third in rank, being surpassed only by the Man Eaters or Cannibal Society. The chief object of this outfit, apart from the white and red cedar bark rings, was a long club, one side of which was ornamented by a fringe of red cedar tassels. Of interest also was the curious cap made of plaited bands of red cedar bark, and so ornamented as to represent the head of the owl. Another object secured from a shaman was a peculiar bow and arrow. These were purely ceremonials, and were only used in the dances of the secret societies. By an ingenious device the point of the arrow could be opened out, and in this position represented the open jaws of a serpent. On the bow

The little houses over the graves in an Indian cemetery might contain any property of the deceased, from corsets to sewing machines.
(16-B)

were two fins, that could be lowered or raised at will by means of cords, which represented the finback whale. The bow itself is of light soft wood, and is bent by means of a string passing around the operator's body, the two ends of the bow being fastened to the body of the bow by leather hinges.

In all the ceremonies, both religious and civil, an important part of the costume is the mask. These are generally of wood, and portray all manner of real and fanciful personages. Some of them are wonders of in-

genuity, being so constructed that the eyes, mouth, and often the ears can be moved at the will of the wearer. Some of them are even double, and so arranged that by drawing open the outer mask, an inner one of an entirely different character can be revealed. For some time the museum has possessed one of the rarest masks ever to be brought out of the Tsimshian country. It is finely carved of bone, and its teeth and tusks are those of animals.

Hazelton is of much interest to the observer of the human countenance, for while the residents of the town are Tsimshians, there is a village nearby on the Bulkley River, the people of which belong to the great Tinneh or Athabascan stock, which extends from the Arctic Circle on the north to the territories of Arizona and New Mexico on the south, where it is represented by the Apaches. In some respects the differences between the Tsimshians and Tinnehs, or Howgelgaits, as this branch is called, are quite marked, and these differences stand out in great relief because more or less of the population of Howgelgait spend a part of their time in Hazelton, and so one sees representatives of the two stocks in close contact. The Tsimshians, like the Haidas, are great canoe people, and are rather short-legged, with great development of the chest and shoulders. Like the Haidas, also, they have strong, long arms, which bespeak familiarity with the paddle. The Howgelgaits, on the other hand, are a pure mountaineer people, and are tall, robust and finely proportioned. Their hair is black, coarse and abundant. The eyebrows are thick and remarkably wide at the outer side. This same peculiarity may be observed in the masks of this tribe. The beard is sparse, but it must be remembered that the hair is generally pulled out as it appears, particularly on the cheeks, while the mustache and the chin tuft are allowed to grow. Among the Tsimshians the face is wide and the cheek bones are prominent. The nose is narrow, with a depressed root. Neither the Tsimshians nor Tinneh practice artificial deformation of the head. With the Tinneh, or more exactly the Howgelgaits, the forehead is broad and less receding than is usual with the American aborigines. The face is full and broad and the cheek bones prominent, but the nose, unlike that of the Tsimshians, is well formed and generally aquiline, although occasionally it is thick and flattish. Their lips are also thick and the chin is more prominent than is usual among the Tsimshians. The eyes are large and of a deep black colour; the jaws are generally very heavy and massive.

Of traces of the ancient prevalent fashion in deformity we saw very little. One old woman still retained the labret, but it was only a shadow of the former labrets in size. Although the long, finely polished bone ornament which the men formerly wore in a hole through the septum of the nose has entirely disappeared, we saw a few old men in whom the pierced septum was still plainly visible. With the Howgelgaits it was formerly the custom to load down the ears with highly polished bits of abalone shells, which were suspended by means of brass rings inserted into holes one above the other on the outer margin of the ear, extending from the lobe around the entire helix.

Hazelton's "City of the Dead" stands on a high bluff overlooking the town and valley, and commands a view off over the broken forest-clad country which is as beautiful as well could be. A trail winds along the face of the bluff until the crest of the plateau is reached, where it divides into a right and left path leading through the main street of the silent city. The sight is strangely odd and picturesque. Over each grave has been erected a neat frame house, often of considerable dimensions. All are painted with bright colours, and the effect is decidedly "mixed." In one of the houses, which was substantially built and neatly carpeted, I saw through a glass window two chairs, a washstand with full assortment of toilet articles, and an umbrella, while at the rear of the house stood a table on which was spread a neat cloth, and on the table was a lamp. On the floor was a new pair of shoes. Over the table hung a large crayon portrait of the departed occupant of the grave beneath.

In another house I saw chests of clothing, and suspended from a cord were garments of various kinds, including a complete costume of the fraternity of the Dog Eaters. These five-feet-deep graves covered by little houses are not the usual manner of burial with the Tsimshians, for until a very few years ago the dead were cremated. Even today in the neighbouring villages of Kispiyeoux the dead are buried in shallow graves just in front of the house.

Of the many charming spots about Hazelton which are well worthy of a visit, we had time for only one—a horseback ride to the Howgelgait Canyon. The ride was most enjoyable in every respect. The road leads from the town up over the plateau through the burying ground, and then on through a partly cleared forest of cottonwoods and maples. Then we plunge into a two-mile-long lane, the trail scarcely wide enough to admit of the passing of a horse, through a dense grove of hazel bushes, laden to their tips with unripe nuts still protected by their green fuzzy envelopes; and now we know whence came the name "Hazelton." Suddenly the grove terminates, and after dismounting and walking forward a few steps we came to the face of the canyon.

What a sight! On the opposite cliff, but on a higher level, stands the old deserted village of Howgelgait, with its great empty houses and skeleton totem poles. At our feet, down a sheer precipice almost a thousand feet below, the Bulkley River, set on edge, rushes and roars and foams through the rocky gorge to join the Skeena a mile away. Just by the mouth of the canyon, at the edge of the great whirlpool, and on a gravelly beach, stands the present town of Howgelgait. Hearing shouts, we looked closer, and far down we saw men moving about, their forms dwarfed to almost spiderlike dimensions. They were building a swinging bridge over the river, and the timbers already in place looked like the meshes of a spider's web.

Looking up the canyon, we could see from the opposite wall near the water's edge, and far below us, a rude scaffolding suspended by bark ropes over the river, and from this Indians were lowering their nets and drawing up salmon. One man after another would leave for his home, his back bending under the weight of many fish, his place to be taken by another, who began casting his nets. These rude scaffoldings here and all along the rivers are occupied by busy fishermen throughout the summer, for salmon is chief of the winter's food supply of these people. In one house we saw over a thousand salmon hung up to dry for use during the winter months.

We left the canyon for the ride back to Hazelton with keen regret, for no more fascinating spot did we find on our entire journey than right here. On the way we encountered a woman of the Carrier tribe of the Tinnehs from Fraser's Lake, who was returning from Hazelton laden with provisions and cheap calicoes.

We had scarcely entered Hazelton when the tinkling of the bell of the "lead horse" announced the arrival of the pack train.

Second only in importance to the arrival of the *Caledonia* to the people of Hazelton is the arrival of the pack train, for it brings the news of the far interior. But of much greater importance and value is the cargo of furs which are brought out on every trip in exchange for supplies which are taken in. On that day there were fifty-seven mules, each laden with two bales of furs weighing two hundred and fifty pounds, and including beaver, mink, otter, sable, and bear, all destined for the Hudson's Bay Company's house in London, there to be auctioned off in lots to the highest bidder, and then to be distributed to all parts of the civilized world.

Within less than an hour's time the precious furs were aboard, and we bade farewell to Hazelton. The *Caledonia* dropped back, was slowly turned around by the current, and with its steady chug, chug, we began our journey down the river, the power of the boat aided by the swiftly flowing water. If the slow, laboured journey up river was a revelation with its worries and anxieties, what can be said of the journey down river, with its kaleidoscopic panorama of sand bars, Indian villages, far-away snowy mountains, dense forests of mighty cottonwoods, lofty heights which tower above us clad to their very summits with eternal green, mountain streams, and innumerable waterfalls and cascades! And what shall one say of that memorable ride through the canyon, the wheel reversed and throwing water over the pilot house, the boat rocking and swaying to and fro! Before we were fairly aware of the fact we were out into that great, deep, silent basin again and off on the home stretch. Apart from taking on wood and stopping at one or two Indian villages, a delay of a few hours was made to permit some mining engineers to examine a mine. They had just come up from the coast and brought with them news of the gold excitement in the Yukon Valley, and now for the first time we heard that magic word "Klondike," which was soon to electrify the world and put the gold fields of California, South Africa, and Australia to shame.

At nine o'clock we were in Essington once more. "Klondike, Klondike!" on every side. The whole country seemed to have gone daft. One steamer after another went racing by the mouth of the Skeena on the way to Dyea and the Skagway Trail. But our fortunes lay in the other direction, and that night we were aboard the *Islander*, bound for Victoria and the south.

Hazelton—waiting for the boat.
(65-C)

Up the Skeena in 1899

◆ Wiggs O'Neill

The Hudson's Bay Company sternwheel steamboat, the *Caledonia*, was being outfitted at Port Simpson for its first trip of the season, late in April, up the Skeena River to Hazelton. Passengers had been arriving by the coast steamers to catch the first boat up the river to their respective destinations. As the *Caledonia* was the only boat on the river they could not afford to miss the first trip, so the only hotel in the town was full up for days before, and the sleepy little village was much more lively than usual. I had speared a job as waiter on the boat, which was a promotion as I had only been pantry man on the fall trip of the previous year.

The night before we sailed Mrs. Harding, the local school teacher, put on a school concert, to show off some of her talented pupils and to gather funds for school sports, as she was sure of a full house. My stepfather, Mr. Alexander, acted as chairman to add a little dignity to the occasion, as he was the local magistrate. The concert proved quite a success financially as well as being greatly enjoyed by the visitors.

We left early next morning on the first leg of our journey with a full complement of passengers and headed for the mouth of the Skeena River. Our first stop was at Inverness Cannery at the mouth of the North Arm of the Skeena, to pick up our freight cargo for upriver. The Hudson's Bay used to have all the freight landed there to avoid the rough water which was often encountered in crossing from Port Simpson to the river's mouth.

There were some very notable people on our passenger list. The Singlehurst party were bound for the Kitselas Canyon to open up the mining properties on Singlehurst Mountain. Mr. Singlehurst was an American big shot, related to the Gould family of New York. He wore yellow leggings and put on plenty of dog. There was an old Mr. Booth, a coloured gentleman and his small party bound for Lorne Creek, where he had placer claims. There was Jimmy Wells, who would be well remembered later around Kitselas and Usk. Jimmy had some native blood in him and was well educated. He was bound for Manson Creek in the Omineca Country, where he had been appointed mining recorder. There was a Colonel Moore from Catalina Island, California, with a big party. He was also bound for Manson Creek where he had placer holdings.

Also on board was a Colonel Beach of the Kildare Mining Company from Ottawa with a big party. He also held placer ground in the Manson Creek country. There was a big party of Chinamen aboard going into the Omineca diggings. On board was a Mr. Valleau, who I remember had a huge mustache; he was on his way to Hazelton to open the first provincial government office in the Interior. He was Government Agent and Gold Commissioner. There was a Mr. McGregor, a lawyer from Victoria on some mission for the government. There were a couple of fine looking big young men named Musgrave from Victoria who were surveyors also bound for Hazelton. There was a young man by the name of Billy Steele from Victoria who was going to Manson Creek. It might be noted here that Billy Steele spent his whole life in that country and only a year or two ago was brought out to Vanderhoof in bad shape and died there in the hospital. R.H. Hall, the general manager of the Hudson's Bay Company for BC, stationed at Victoria, was also on board as a member of Colonel Moore's party. You will notice that most of these people hailed from Victoria, but you must remember that Vancouver was only small potatoes at that period. Victoria was the Big Town of British Columbia.

This happened before the telegraph line was built, and of course Marconi had not yet invented the radio, so the first news the people on the Skeena had that the steamboat was approaching was when they heard the deep whistle way down the river, or the puff of the exhaust from her smokestack or the flapping of her paddle wheel as it churned up the waters of the Old Skeena.

To my surprise the steward appointed me waiter at the captain's table, where all the big shots were assembled. At luncheon coming out from Port Simpson to Inverness, the captain had stayed at his wheel as the sea was a little choppy. He had given his seat at the head of the table to Mr. R.H. Hall, the manager of the Company, who was a big man and very strong on the bull. Conversation got underway on various topics. Colonel Moore from Los Angeles mentioned the concert put on the night before, and said it was a very creditable effort and a fine show of talent for such a small community. Everyone agreed, although one gentleman remarked, "That Mr. Alexander, the Chairman, is a big man, isn't he!" Mr. Hall, the Bay manager, spoke up and said, "Yes, a big tub of guts."

I blew my top as the Mr. Alexander in question was my stepfather, and remarked to Mr. Hall that he was a big fat slob himself. He got purple with rage and was ready to kill the embryo waiter, but the humorous side of the situation, the lowly waiter taking a fall out of the general manager of the Company of Adventurers trading into Hudson's Bay struck the passengers and they all roared with laughter. Mr. Hall had a decision to make, so he cooled down and just told me that I was too damned cheeky. Mr. Singlehurst asked me to bring him a serviette and I said, "What is that?" and he said, "Well a napkin, damn it!" and Hall gave me a glare.

Next meal at dinner we had canned peaches for dessert. One passenger, a Mr. Davidson, who hailed from Ottawa, and was some onions in his own estimation, continuously extolling the wonders of Ontario, remarked that the fruit from Ontario had a flavour all its own. As soon as he had tasted the peaches on the table he knew they were Ontario peaches. I slipped back to the pantry and got the empty peach can, stood across from him and showed him the label and remarked, "Ah, Mr. Smarty, Cuttings Packing Company, California." Colonel Moore from California laughed so hard at the discomfiture of poor Davidson that he nearly had a fit. R.H. Hall called the steward and had me removed and demoted to the big long table where the common man had his grub, and another boy was promoted to my job. By the attitude of the big shot passengers I really think they missed me, and were sorry I had gone; they lacked entertainment. They showed it by giving me quite a few tips although I was not at their table. I might mention that you can see I was learning the waiter business fast, as I was already looking for the tips. The next scrape I got into was when I nicknamed the purser "Buttons." The purser, Mr. Crickmay, was very strong on gold braid and brass buttons. After addressing him one day as Buttons, he resented it very much and right there I knew I had cooked my goose with him.

The water was very low in the river and still big cakes of ice could be seen on the river bars, so our progress was very slow, feeling our way up the channels. When we got to Thornhill's Landing at the Little Canyon, which was at the south end of the present Terrace bridge, the Captain decided to lay up and wait for the water to rise. Time was dragging on our hands, so the passengers organized a mock trial. Mr. Hall was named Judge, three fellows named prosecuting attorneys and three named for the defence, among them Mr. McGregor, who was a real lawyer. Billy Steele was the prisoner and was charged with stealing the Hanging Wall off Captain Bonser's mineral claim. I was called as a witness for the prosecution; some smart Joe placed some rocks in Billy Steele's bed, and as his bed was on my side of the ship I had to make his bed and of course found the Evidence. The trial was well conducted and created a lot of fun for the passengers and crew. Billy was acquitted, through lack of evidence. In summing up the Judge said the only thing he could find against the prisoner was his name: "Steele."

After lying at Thornhill's for about a week, Copper River started to spurt real water and there was a sharp rise in the river, so we pulled out. After passing the Copper, the river was still very low, but after lining a few places we finally reached the Kitselas Canyon. At Kitselas we got rid of the Singlehurst party as that was their destination. Among the members of his party was a young man named Harry Stevens from Vancouver, who afterwards became a cabinet minister in the R.B. Bennett Government at Ottawa. He is still going strong and has been very active, chiefly in Board of Trade work in Vancouver, for many years.

I might mention that at this period there was no Terrace, as George Little was still in the Yukon mushing dogs, and had not arrived on the Skeena. After laying at Kitselas Landing for a few days, the water showed improvement so we pulled out and proceeded through the Canyon without incident. At this stage of water the Canyon was very easy to navigate, quite different to when the gauge at the landing showed three or four feet and the river was angry. By this time I had become quite proficient at the art of waiting table, got so I could carry five or six cups of coffee on my arm and was quite proud of my ability. But one day when my arm was loaded up the ship bumped up against a bar in landing and put both the coffee and me out of balance and I spilled a cup of hot coffee down a passenger's back. He was a brick. He sat still and endured it until I got things under control. I was lucky in picking the right man as it happened. He had been laid up for a couple of days with a bad attack of quinsey and I had doctored him with one of my mother's home remedies, a gargle of vinegar and pepper in hot water. So it paid off and I was in luck for once.

Our next stop, other than stopping for cordwood for the boilers, was at Lorne Creek, where the old coloured gentleman, Mr. Booth, and his party left us to get going on his placer diggings. The water was still low and our progress was slow. We finally arrived at Meanskinisht, or the "Holy City" as everybody called it. It is now called Cedarvale. The village was founded by the Reverend Robert Tomlinson, an early missionary, years before. Mrs. Walter Moberly, his youngest daughter, still lives there and grows strawberries. Mr. Tomlinson, the founder, was a fine old gentleman, always treated the steamboat crew well. His restrictions were that the boat could not land there on Sunday and that there could be no drinking or smoking while the boat was there. The Captain saw to it that orders were strictly obeyed.

We unloaded freight for Mr. Tomlinson and proceeded on to the Anglican Church village of Kitwanga, where we unloaded a goodly jag of freight. I might say we also landed mail at all these points, too, most of which was a good eight months old. Our next port of call was the Methodist village of Kitsegeucla, now known as Skeena Crossing. There was no settlement from there on to our destination—Hazelton, and some of the most difficult spots to navigate for a riverboat are in this area. This must have been an extremely late spring as it was getting well on to the end of May and the river was still extremely low. If I remember correctly it was near the end of the month when we reached Hazelton, having been twenty-seven days en route. It stands as a record even today as being the hardest and longest voyage ever made up the Skeena by riverboat. Our Captain, the veteran J.H. Bonser; our Chief Engineer was Mr. Daley; our Purser, E.J. Crickmay and our Steward, a Mr. Shaw. The rest of the crew didn't count much, including the embryo waiter. When we landed at Hazelton the whole town—whites, Indians and dogs—were all down to meet us. When the ship blew her whistle everyone waved and cheered, and the dogs sat on their hind ends and howled. The arrival of the boat meant fresh provisions, including fruit and case eggs and a fresh supply of new stocks for the Hudson's Bay store stone cellar. Dick Sargent was the HBC manager at the time and Dick led the parade across the gangplank to shake hands with everybody. There was one hotel there at the time and as he had been out of saleable beverage for some time, Mr. Olsen, the proprietor, was glad to see the boat.

After staying in port a couple of days unloading cargo etc., and taking on passengers for the Outside, we swung out into the stream and headed downriver. After twenty-seven days' push upstream we were back at our starting point, Inverness Cannery, in ten hours. Like the Chinaman's description of a toboggan ride, "Gee whiz, walkie milee," in reverse.

I had become quite proficient as a waiter before this trip ended and was thinking seriously of making it a career, but this dream was shattered on arriving back in salt water. Buttons the purser fired me, saying I was too damn cheeky to be a shipmate with him. That ended my dream of becoming a topnotch waiter. I never tried it again.

There are many names given to different hazardous places on the river which were most appropriate: Hardscrabble Rapids, Sheep's

Rapids, Devil's Elbow, Kloochman's Canyon, Whirligig, Beaver Dam and Hornets' Nest are but a few that I can recall.

Every steamboat captain who ran the Skeena in later years all sang the same tune. They named the Old Skeena the toughest river to navigate in North America. The riverboats held sway on the Skeena for twenty-two years. The last boat on the Skeena, the *Inlander*, finished up in September of 1912, when the Grand Trunk Pacific took over and put the steamboats out of business.

The river steamer days were grand and exciting days, not to be forgotten by those of us who lived them . . .

Name	Year	Owner	Captain	Remarks	Disposition
UNION	1864	Captain T. Coffin	Coffin	This 60-foot sternwheeler carried 4 passengers and 20 tons of freight. Chartered by Collins Overland Telegraph Co. to check river for transporting construction supplies inland. Sailed up Skeena 90 miles.	Unknown. Unsuccessful venture.
MUMFORD	1866	Collins Overland Telegraph	Coffin	Carried materials and supplies up the Skeena 2 or 3 times, as far up as 110 miles (Kitsumgalum River, possibly Kitselas Canyon).	Unknown. When the Overland Telegraph line was abandoned, there were no more sternwheelers on the Skeena for several years.
CALEDONIA I	1891	Hudson's Bay Co.	G. Odin Sr., F. Odin Jr., J.W. Troupe, J.H. Bonser	The only commercial boat on the river at this time, the stubby *Caledonia I* was about 100 feet long with a top speed of 16 mph. On her first trip she reached Hazelton in 9 days. At Captain Bonser's recommendation, in 1895 she wintered in Port Simpson and had 30 feet added to her middle to improve her handling and cargo capacity. For seven years she made three or four cargo trips to Hazelton every year.	Machinery went into *Caledonia II*. Hull lay on beach at Port Simpson until blown adrift and smashed on rocks.

The Operator, *damaged by a falling tree.*
(41-A) / BCARS 88164

Name	Year	Owner	Captain	Remarks	Disposition
CALEDONIA II	1898	Hudson's Bay Co.	J.H. Bonser, S.B. Johnson	Sold to a Prince Rupert syndicate. Renamed *Northwestern*. Wrecked at Mile 44 out of Prince Rupert.	Machinery salvaged and put into the *Omineca*. Hull lost in 1907.
STRATHCONA	1900	Hudson's Bay Co.	Odin, Masters, Smith	Made only one trip up the Skeena. Sold to a Vancouver Syndicate in 1900 and operated on Howe Sound.	Unknown.
MONTE CRISTO	1900	R. Cunningham & Son	Bonser	Cunningham hired Bonser, an HBC skipper, to buy a river steamer and operate it on the Skeena. The *Monte Cristo* was originally built for the Stikine, and after a couple of trips up the Skeena with Cunningham's freight, she was chartered by the Dominion government and taken to the Stikine.	Freighted construction supplies to Telegraph Creek for Yukon Telegraph Line. Rotted on ways at Port Essington. Machinery sold as junk.
HAZELTON	1901	Cunningham	Bonser	Bonser's pride and joy, the *Hazelton* was a fine trim boat for the Skeena. The HBC offered Cunningham $2500 a year for 3 years to keep the *Hazelton* on the ways in exchange for contracting all Cunningham's freight for his store in Hazelton. Captain Bonser left the Skeena for the upper Fraser River.	Dismantled in 1912. Machinery shipped to the Peace River and installed in a new boat. Hull sold to Prince Rupert Yacht Club and used as a clubhouse.
MOUNT ROYAL	1902	Hudson's Bay Company	Johnson	The Hudson's Bay Company's answer to the *Hazelton*, and a far more luxurious ship. Captains as well as companies were rivals and many races and incidents took place between the two ships.	Wrecked in Kitselas Canyon in 1907. Six lives lost.
CASCA	---	Mr. P. Hickey	Masters	Made one trip to Hazelton with full cargo.	Went to Vancouver. No further knowledge.
PHEASANT	1906	Vancouver firm	Magar & Watson, Bonser	Nicknamed "*Chicken*." Not a successful season; underpowered. In 1906 got contract to blow out rocks from "Beaver Dam" and "Hornets Nest." Stayed upriver too long.	Wrecked on the rocks at Redrock Canyon near present Skeena Crossing Bridge. Total loss.

Name	Year	Owner	Captain	Remarks	Disposition
CRAIGFLOWER	1908	Roy Troupe	Troupe	Nicknamed *"Cauliflower."* A miniature excursion boat from Victoria. Got as far as Kitseguecla rapids and gave up.	Returned to Victoria.
NORTHWEST	1907	North Coast Land Company	Bonser	An American company, with a store and hotel at Telkwa, bought this boat to ensure a steady source of supplies. Carried liquor for hotels in Port Essington and Hazelton.	Struck a snag and sank en route upriver in 1907. No loss of life.
PORT SIMPSON	1908	Hudson's Bay Company	Johnson, Jackman	The finest ever to operate on the Skeena, for model, speed and appointments. Left the Skeena in 1912 and was on the ways at Port Simpson until 1916.	Served on Stikine briefly, then dismantled. Machinery installed in new ship on Mackenzie River. Hull abandoned on Digby Island.

The Northwest *on the rocks, 1907.*
(46-C) / VPL 767

Name	Year	Owner	Captain	Remarks	Disposition
DISTRIBUTOR	1908	G.T.P. Railway, Foley, Welch & Stewart	Johnson, Doderick	Similar to *Port Simpson* but without elaborate passenger accommodations.	Machinery stripped in Vancouver, shipped north and installed in a new *Distributor* on the Mackenzie River.
OPERATOR	Unkn.	Foley, Welch & Stewart	Meyers	The *Operator* and the *Conveyor* were both freight boats. Taken to Vancouver, their machinery was sent to Tête Jaune Cache via Edmonton for use in new boats of same name on the upper Fraser.	Later on ways at Prince George. Machinery sold to sawmills. Hulls rotted.
CONVEYOR	"	"	Douglas	"	"
OMINECA	"	"	Shannon	Powered by the original *Caledonia's* engines.	Unknown.
SKEENA	1908	P. Burns & Co.	Magar	Supplied meat to construction camps. Operated mostly on lower river.	Left river in 1911. Taken south.
INLANDER	1910	Inlander Company	Bucey, Bonser	Homely but efficient. The last boat to come on the Skeena. Also made the final trip by sternwheeler on the river in 1912.	Left to rot on Cunningham Ways at Port Essington.

S.S. Operator *on the Skeena*
(25-A) / BCARS 52078

Highlights and Handicaps

View from the deck of a riverboat running the Big Canyon.
(17-A)

Running Risky Part Of The Big Canyon. Kitselas. B.C.

The Hole-in-the-Wall

This name was given to the first gap in the long chain of mountains along the Skeena, near the present Exchamsiks River bridge.

In 1948 a BC Provincial policeman, on patrol from Prince Rupert, visited Terrace and heard the following story:

I remember sitting up late one night having a coffee with an elderly native trapper in the police office. He was in jail for some minor misdemeanor. He mentioned he had been caught trapping beaver out of season on the Exchamsiks River, at the terrible Hole-in-the-Wall. I was curious right away as I had been by it several times in the patrol car and I asked him why he used that description.

"I heard it from my grandfather, who told me that because of the big salmon runs in from the Skeena, there was once a village at the mouth of the Exchamsiks River. The Exchamsiks flows through the Hole because it is the only way through the wall of mountains for miles along the Skeena.

"There was much raiding and fighting amongst the river tribes at that time. The sea warriors, the Massett Haidas, also raided us for women and slaves. Our clan posted lookouts, and when raiding parties came, we sent our women, children and old people up the Exchamsiks and through the Hole to open country. Our young men battled to protect our village from destruction. If they were lucky, many prisoners would be taken, and when our people returned there was great rejoicing. The prisoners were dragged to the high cliffs of the Hole-in-the-Wall and pushed over to be dashed to death on the rocks below."

He called it haunted, as he had heard the wailing of the dead as he camped there on moonless nights. You may say it was the wind in the cottonwoods and the talking of the water, but I know differently.

Hardscrabble Rapids

Near Usk, this is another part of the river where vessels often get mauled badly. The river here is about 300 feet wide, and it looks perfectly safe to steam straight ahead. Not a trace of froth gives warning of any danger. Suddenly the steamer changes its course and draws perilously near the rock cliff on one bank. Why? Right across that waterway but a few inches below its surface, so calm and still, runs a solid bar which can only be avoided through a very narrow twisting passage at one end. It is just wide enough to carry the steamer, and no more. But the captain cannot steam right ahead since there is no space in which to swing around. He drives the craft's nose into the cauldron, and just manages to squeeze his stern into the same enclosure. He then backs gently until only inches separate the revolving stern wheels from the foot of the cliff, crawls forward a foot or so, backs again the same distance, and so on for a few minutes, the bow being brought round a trifle with each manoeuvre, until at last there is a straight drive ahead. [2]

The Devil's Elbow

Near Lorne Creek, where the river flows straight into a rocky bluff and turns sharp at right angles. A real devil of a place to get round; had always to be lined. [5]

The Dugout

Another sharp turn like the Devil's Elbow—no rocky wall staring you in the face but bad enough. The Dugout called for extreme care and was nearly always lined. [5]

The Inlander *lining Sheep's Rapids, 20 miles below Hazelton, August 1911.*
(60-C)

Kloochman's Canyon

A very short canyon with rock walls; not very dangerous. Named for the ladies. [5]

The Whirligig

Here cross currents shook the sternwheeler like gravel in a prospector's pan. [4]

Sheep's Rapids

A section of the river where white water resembled galloping sheep. Lining was necessary. [4]

Kitseguecla Rapids

Where the Kitsequecla River comes into the Skeena. Not dangerous, but tricky. [5]

The Hornets' Nest

The worst place in the upper stretch of the river. Certainly no nest of yellowjackets was ever readier to let drive fierce jabs and stings against an interloper than are the rocks here. The surface is merely an expanse of short, choppy, milky waves tumbling and fussing in all directions. Progress is slow, the steamer passing through weird contortions to steer clear of this, that and something else. It is fortunate for the passengers that these boats are of shallow draught, for often it is only a matter of an inch or two between a granite tooth and the bottom of the boat, especially late in the year when the water is very low. It took more than an hour to thread the Hornets' Nest. [2]

The Beaver Dam

A row of big boulders spanned the river from bank to bank. There was one place where two of them were far enough apart to let a boat through. This passage had to be hit right on the nose. [5]

Editorial, *Omineca Herald*, July 25, 1908:

"A great deal is heard about the terrors and dangers of the Skeena River. On the coast the stories are more frequent and much worse. The accidents of last year have been magnified until prospective newcomers have been led to believe they are taking their lives in their hands to make a trip up the Skeena River on a steamboat. Most of these stories have their origin in the minds of some people endeavouring to make heroes of themselves for having made a very ordinary trip up and down a river, which, admitted to be not of the best for purposes of navigation, has been much maligned. There is one bad spot on the river. This is the canyon at Kitselas, through which steamers can be taken only at favourable stages of water. There is a wagon road around the canyon

Quotable Quotes from a variety of sources . . .

"Lying at the wharf was the little Caledonia (1890) all gleaming in a coat of fresh white paint and bright red paddlewheel. A pleasing sight . . . " [1]

"Going upstream, the furnaces demolish five cords of wood an hour, while downstream two cords less suffice for the same time." [2]

"In the summer of 1908 the Caledonia demonstrated the fearful punishment that a sternwheeler could absorb and survive. She gashed a 30-foot-long hole in her hull on a rock downstream from Port Essington in an area of the river known as the Skeena Boneyard. She was pulled off this obstacle but in backing up struck another submerged rock. Water poured in, extinguishing her fire, and she sank, leaving only her upperworks and pilothouse above the water. She was raised and beached at Port Essington and three weeks later was back in service." [4]

a mile in length and very level. Most of the freight brought up the river this season has been transferred around the canyon by means of this road. On the first trip of the *Port Simpson* this spring, half the passengers were worked into a state of terror by the fearsome tales of the canyon before they had gone half way to it. The men who told the wildest stories stayed on the boat. Some of them even remained asleep while the boat was going through.

"The Skeena River has been navigated for 17 years and during that time no passenger on any steamboat has been lost. This is a fact that should be remembered. There may be delays—often vexatious and expensive—but we cannot see where the danger comes in.

"There have been people drowned from canoes but it is not necessary to come to the Skeena River for that to happen. As an instance of how far perverted imagination can go, it was reported in Vancouver last winter that the wagon road around the canyon went over a mountain a mile high, whose precipitous sides were nearly impossible of ascent."

"In navigating the rivers not all the danger was from hidden rocks and foaming white water—pilots also had to watch the shoreline—witness the severe damage to the Operator *from a falling tree."*[1]

"When a Captain was asked, 'What happens if you lose the boat?' he replied: 'They just give us another in double-quick time. We have no Board of Trade inquiries here. What's the use? No one has a chart of the river; it never runs two days alike; captains are few and far between. If you lose the boat it's just hard luck. That's all there is to it.' "[2]

S.S. Port Simpson *at Port Essington (photo by P.E. Fisher) (25-A) / BCARS 29363*

Kitselas

Postcard of the town of Kitselas
in its heyday.
(12-A) / BCARS 76170

Will Robinson's
Men of Medeek
◆ Wilson Duff

A fitting introduction to the
history of Kitselas is Wilson
Duff's book review of Men of
Medeek by the late Will Robinson.
"Mr. Duff is Curator of
Anthropology at the Provincial
Museum of British Columbia. He
has published numerous papers
on the subjects relating to the
British Columbia Indians."
The Omineca Herald
January 16, 1963

"Getting Men of Medeek
published required a devotion to
local history comparable to that
shown by Will Robinson in
getting it written down. In Stan
Rough and his associates the
Skeena area has such devotees;
to finance the book's publication
they simply reached into their
own pockets. The result does
them great credit."

The Tsimshian Indians of the Skeena River place great importance on their family histories, and preserve them in the form of long epic narratives, memorized by a few chosen members of each generation. *Men of Medeek*, the traditional history of the Grizzly Bear People of Kitselas, is one of the most complete of these yet recorded, and ethnologically one of the most important.

The narrative was recorded in 1936 by the late Will Robinson of Terrace, in the course of many sittings with the late Walter Wright, Chief Neas-D-Hok of the Kitselas. In preparing it for publication, Robinson paraphrased it into more literary English and set it out in short single-thought paragraphs and 46 brief, single-episode chapters. The result, as intended, succeeds in recapturing the dignity of style and episodic rhythm of the original Indian narrative. Indian names are rendered less accurately than one might wish; however a map is provided which locates all the places referred to in the text. If the manner of presentation is Robinson's, the story itself, in its sequence and details, is Wright's. The reviewer has a copy of the same story, recorded 10 years earlier from the same informant by William Beynon, which is virtually identical.

The Kitselas (People of the Canyon) are one of the 26 Tsimshian-speaking tribes of the northwest coast Indians, and formerly occupied a pair of villages on the canyon 80 miles up the Skeena, a central location between the coastal Tsimshian and the Gitksan farther up the river. The tribe consisted of family groups representing each of the four Tsimshian clans. *Men of Medeek* is the history of one of the clans, of which Medeek, the Grizzly Bear, is the principal crest. Versions of the same story are owned by related families in the other Tsimshian tribes.

The narrative begins at Tum-L-Hama or Temlaham, the traditional homeland farther up the Ksan (Skeena) near the present Hazelton. Here, as ages pass, the prosperity and happiness of the people are disturbed only when they become forgetful and violate natural laws by mistreating animals. Two such violations bring on devastating encounters with the mountain goat people and with Medeek, a supernatural

Corner post of old Indian lodge at Kitselas.
(41-A) / BCARS 88155

grizzly, and both of these are perpetuated as crests. Another violation results in a famine, and the people are forced to seek new hunting grounds. They migrate down river, and after uneasy alliances and vengeful wars with the earlier inhabitants, take control of the canyon and make it their new home. Now in contact with coastal people, they become seafarers, and raid coastal villages to the south. Some of them find the coast to their liking and settle at Kitkatla, accepting an invitation to become chiefs there. More ages pass; more wars of revenge; newcomers join them from Kitimaat and from down the river. There is an encounter with the beaver people. The tribe grows, splits into two, and moves from site to site, as it progresses into recent times.

In its blending of myth with historical fact, and of the supernatural world with local geography, this is a classic example of history as the Indians know it. With this new insight into how their Indian predecessors viewed it, readers familiar with this beautiful part of the country form new associations for old landmarks. To the ethnologist the main importance of *Men of Medeek* lies in what it reveals about the persistent movement of people down the rivers to the sea coast in this area in prehistoric times. Here, heavily veiled in myth, is important information on the prehistory of the Tsimshian.

S.S. Inlander *in Kitselas Canyon.*
(12-A) / BCARS 76178

"Some of the mining outfits around Kitselas used a route via Kitimat to bring in supplies during the winter. In fact, the first trail was cleared in 1898 by a New York syndicate who were developing a mining property on O.K. Mountain."[6]

"Originally the farthest up river outpost and first class trapping area of the Tsimshian, Kitselas became a Hudson's Bay halfway house and steamboat landing between Port Essington at the mouth of the Skeena and Old Hazelton. The railway era transformed Kitselas into a thriving community and construction headquarters. First small tents, then larger tents and finally well-made buildings appeared along graveled streets. The hotel, bar and dining room were without equal except perhaps in Prince Rupert. There were also restaurants, stores and offices, two Justices of the Peace and the inevitable Provincial Constable."

Gateway to the Past
◆ Ed Kenney (1972)

Four hundred yards on the north or upriver side of Kleanza Creek on Highway 16 are two roads; one heads up the mountain to the ski-hill and the present; the other heads towards the river, Kitselas Canyon and the past.

From the beginning of time until about 1912, Kitselas Canyon was the most important site on the Skeena River. It was here that the mighty tribe of the Canyon Tsimshians, the Kitselas, held sway. Nothing passed up or down the river without their permission. They exacted their toll on all trade items moving to the sea or hinterland. The first time their supremacy was seriously challenged was by the white men of the Collins Overland Telegraph Company in 1866, who were building a line between New York via Moscow to Europe. At first the Kitselas refused passage to the telegraph men; however, when they saw the well-stocked arms chest and were told that the Company was not a trading company, the Kitselas helped pull the laden canoes through the rocky crags of the canyon.

The last decade of the nineteenth century brought the steamboat to the Skeena River but no change to the strategic position of Kitselas. The canyon is the only major constriction in the Skeena River between Hazelton and the ocean. In high water the canyon is too difficult to navigate; in low water the bars at its upper end are impassable. Consequently, ships sometimes had to wait for days for the water to rise or fall to make passage through the canyon possible. One early traveller described the canyon as follows:

It is the most justly dreaded inland waterway of the Northwest, for, aside from the tremendous force of the contracted river over an uneven rocky bottom, forming great swirls and riffles, the upper entrance is obstructed by two high, narrow rock ridges that divide the waters, forming two narrow channels at all stages and a third at extreme high water. The walls on either hand are precipitous or strewn with immense boulders to a height of from 50 to 100 feet, where narrow benches slope back from them to the mountains 3000 to 4000 feet in altitude.

Although the natives' hold in the canyon had been challenged, it wasn't until the Omineca gold rush that it was finally broken; by the early 1870s miners were streaming up the Skeena to the new Eldorado. Many of the Kitselas made money taking canoes through the canyon; however, they no longer controlled the river.

By the turn of the century, the four Indian villages at Kitselas were deserted: Tsune-ee-yow (the landing place), where the railway is at the bottom of the canyon; Kit-lah-soak (the people of the place where they steal the canoe bottom boards), where the totem poles stand; Kit-Ousht (people of the sand bar), the present site of the archaeological dig; and Kit-lth-sahok (people at the edge of the lake), on the flats at the top end of the canyon. Where once a thousand Kitselas Indians had lived, controlling the canyon, there were now only empty lodges and decaying totem poles. Most of the people had moved to the coast to fish or work in the canneries since the white man had changed the traditional life at the canyon. About sixty of them moved four miles down river and built a new village, An-dee-dom, or Newtown.

As more white settlers moved into the area, some to homestead, like Bruce Johnstone and Frank Whitlow, and others to mine such as James Wells and Tom Thornhill, Kitselas became a focal centre for the white pioneers.

New buildings rose on the site of the ancient Indian village of Kit-Ousht. First the Hudson's Bay warehouse and in 1907, J.W. Patterson built a store which doubled as a post office; then the Big Canyon Hotel where superstition changed room 13 to 31. At this time the townsite was owned by W.D. Clifford, Magistrate and MLA for the Skeena riding. Lots could be bought for the munificent sum of $25 for an inside lot and $50 for one on a corner.

The halcyon days of Kitselas were beginning—steamboats belching around the bend below Kitselas, whistling at the top end of the canyon before their treacherous trip through the white water; unloading foodstuffs and trading goods; loading wood for the voracious boilers; letting off homesteaders and prospectors, taking on Indians and trappers—the usual hustle and bustle of frontier river life.

By 1908, there were signs of civilization at Kitselas—a telegraph office and a provincial police lockup. During that year the steamboats were busy—the *Hazelton* made 26 trips and the *Port Simpson* made 12.

"After an outbreak of smallpox amongst them, the natives decided to move their village across the river to a site a short distance further down. This was known as New Town. The railroad eventually placed their station at that point and called it Van Arsdoll after the chief engineer. The days of Kitselas were numbered, for as soon as the railroad reached Hazelton, the river boats were withdrawn, and the construction crews having moved on, there was no one left to patronise the town's facilities. Today no trace remains of the village of Kitselas. On the railroad side of the river a small band of Indians still occupy 'New Town.' The name Van Arsdoll has been dropped and once more the village is called Kitselas." [6]

The Omineca Herald:
July 11, 1908
*The Indians at Kitselas are
attempting to collect tribute
from anyone setting foot on
their reservation. They want a
dollar for each person pitching a
tent and they propose to mulct
the Hudson's Bay Company
severely for the privilege of
landing their steamers.*

March 27, 1909
*A large warehouse capable of
holding from 150–200 tons is to
be built at the head of Kitselas
Canyon, if the requisite
permission can be secured from
the Indian Agent. The* Port
Simpson *will, on her third trip,
unload at this warehouse if the
river is not too high to get
through; otherwise she will
unload below the canyon. From
then on the* Hazelton *will
remain on the upper river and
the other boat below the canyon
and furnish a continuous service
during the high water period.
Three teams will be used in
transferring freight around the
canyon. There will be no
warehouse charges for storing
freight at the canyon, only
actual transfer cost being
charged up to the consignees.*

Kitselas was an anthill of activity. Foley, Welch & Stewart, the contractors for the Grand Trunk Pacific, built an aerial tram from the bottom end of the canyon to the top and put a boat on the river above the canyon so they could ship goods through even when the canyon was impassable. Surely Kitselas was coming into its own—or was it? The price of a lot jumped from $50 to $200 to $400. Kitselas now boasted its own newspaper, the *Big Canyon Weekly*—E.R.L. Jones, owner and editor; circulation 300.

Across the river the railroad was being built; there were three tunnels to be drilled, hungry men to be fed, thirsts to be quenched, and Kitselas was in the right place to supply the action. A ferry was operated between the railroad and the townsite. The Big Canyon Hotel supplied the liquid refreshment and further back in the bush were a couple of houses that slaked other manly appetites.

By 1910, Kitselas was in full swing. There was the Kitselas Contracting & Building Company, T. Mitchell, manager; the Lee Bakery and OK Mountain Restaurant; the Big Canyon Hotel and *Big Canyon Weekly*; W.B. Bateman's Tobacco & Soft Drinks; the Bornite Mining Company Ltd., J.E. Bennet, agent; Joseph E. McEwen & Merryfield General Store; the Riverside Hotel, Ray Tafel, proprietor; Dr. Traynor, M.D., as well as the warehouses of Foley, Welch & Stewart and the Hudson's Bay Company. For the year 1910, there were 30 voters registered at Kitselas. Although this does not seem like a huge metropolis, barring the railway camps, this was the largest white settlement between Port Essington and Hazelton.

One of the frequent visitors to Kitselas at this time, who did not share the optimism of the local residents was a man with a high-pitched voice who opined that although Kitselas appeared to be a fine site for a town, he felt his pre-emption below the Little Canyon was a better place. His name? George Little. This pre-emption is the present location of downtown Terrace.

The cause of the increase of tempo at Kitselas also held the seeds for its downfall. With the completion of the railway, the riverboat transportation, which was the lifeblood of Kitselas, came to a close. As the Indians had moved away to Port Essington, Port Simpson and Metlakahtla, so the whites moved to other settlements. The newspaper moved to Hazelton, the storekeepers to Pacific and Hazelton and the miners to Usk. The river ate into the banks; floods obliterated the townsite and the forest reclaimed the cleared land. Kitselas had been a town of opportunists and as the opportunities had moved to other centres, so did they.

Today there are only a few reminders of the once busy centre of upriver steamboat trade. The road that leads to the canyon and the past is part of a logging road built in a later era. About three-quarters of a mile from the highway, the road divides. The right-hand branch leads to the top of the canyon. The left-hand branch leads to the townsite; some of this branch is part of the original wagon road between the top and bottom ends of the canyon. The Foley, Welch & Stewart aerial tramline which starts above the townsite is still visible but in many places is overgrown. The road to the garbage dump and the houses of the "fallen women" is partly obliterated by a mudslide. At the top end of the canyon one can find the remains of an Indian gravestone; one of the broken gravestones is dated 1889. In the muddy bank where the upriver steamers tied up is a rusted shovel blade. In the rock at the edge of the water are ringbolts once used to line the boats through the ever-turbulent waters of the canyon.

On the site of the town itself one may find an old miner's boot, broken bottles and in the dense thickets of willow and devil's club can be found old drainage ditches or perhaps the faint outline of a building and a few boards or pieces of tarpaper, maybe the rusty remains of a stove. Above the townsite proper are the burnt and twisted remains of a bathtub, once a part of W.D. Patterson's house. Much of the townsite has disappeared into the river.

The Indians have left more permanent reminders of their past. On the railroad side totem poles thrust up out of the bush. If you search you may find an old tombstone or two. On the site of the white settlement amateur archaeologists dig for the artifacts of the people who lived here 4000 years ago. Today Kitselas is a mixture of overgrown bush and moss-carpeted wooded parkland, more deserted now than it has been for thousands of years.

May 8, 1909
The Hudson's Bay Company warehouse at the upper end of Kitselas Canyon is nearing completion and will be ready to receive freight as soon as the water is too high to allow the boats to pass through the canyon.

May 15, 1909
The proposed tramway around the Kitselas Canyon to avoid the necessity of using teams in transferring freight, seems to be in a fair way of being carried to completion. Engineers have been engaged in surveying the line and work is expected to commence before long.

May 29, 1909
While at Victoria last winter, R.S. Sargent contracted to transfer freight for the Hudson's Bay Company around the canyon at Kitselas. To that end he purchased a fine team on the coast, which, after high water, will be brought to Hazelton. A teamster has been sent to the canyon to meet the horses, due to arrive there June first. In the meantime T. Wilson will look after the transferring.

Main Street---Kitselas in its heyday.
(26-A) / BCARS

Post Offices

A consultation of the Canadian Official Postal Guide *reveals that a post office was established in Kitselas in 1907 when a listing was first made. J.W. Patterson was listed as the postmaster. From 1907 to 1916 he occupied this post; in 1916 C. Durham took over. The last listing in the Guide was for 1917. Kitselas: "A settlement and station on the G.T.P. Railway and the Skeena River at the Big Canyon 95 mi. N.E. of Port Essington and 13 from Kitsum Kalum, which is the nearest post office."*
Wrigley's B.C. Directory, *1918.*

The 1920 edition of Northern B.C. Index and Guide *lists the post office for Kitselas to be Usk, and suggests people requiring further information address a J.E. Wells at Usk.*

Kitselas: *". . . site of old Indian village on Skeena River 4 miles east of Vanarsdol, the post office."*
Wrigley-Henderson, *1925*

Kitselas: *". . . site of old Indian village on Skeena River 4 miles north of Copper River, the nearest Post Office."*
Wrigley-Henderson, *1935*

Hudson's Bay Company warehouse, Kitselas September 1903. Front row: Sim Dobbie (caretaker, Singlehurst Mine), Charles Durham with Nell (Adams) & Mary (Blackhall). Back row: E. Youngdahl (rancher & miner), George & Fred Durham, Margaret Durham & Elsie (Whitlow). Side and rear: Hank Boss (telegraph operator). Telegraph office & stable/storage space for Singlehurst Mining Co.

The Charles Durham Story

◆ Kathleen Varner (1963)

Charles Durham, christened Halvard Carl Joseph, was born in 1861 in Molde, Norway, the sixth child of Palle and Elizabeth Dorum. Palle was a professor of mathematics and philosophy. He also wrote and composed the music of *Molde Sangen*, a tribute to the beautiful town. In appreciation, a Molde street was named in his honour. In 1864 the Dorum family moved to Oslo, at that time named Christiania.

After school hours the young son, Charles, worked as a proof-reader for a newspaper. However, like young people the world over he wanted adventure, so he ran away to sea to be a cabin boy. Sailing on several ships and seeing the world, he became an able-bodied seaman. On one of his visits home he met Margaret, daughter of Captain Caspar Evensen. Charles and Margaret were married in Oslo in 1885, moved to England then, several years later, moved across the sea to Portland, Maine. But Charles became ill with yellow jaundice and was forced to leave the sea. Times were tough. The Durhams stayed with friends in Montreal until Charles got a job with the CPR and was transferred to Sudbury as dining car storekeeper. Later he was paymaster for the Coppercliff Nickel Mine. In Sudbury their first two children were born—Fred in 1889 and Elsie in 1891.

In 1892 the family moved to Vancouver. Charlie made his first trip north on the *Princess Louise* to Port Essington and nearby canneries. Then he sailed on the CPR's *Empress of China* as purser and interpreter, worked in the hotel business, worked for the Rogers Sugar Refinery and fished the Fraser. A son, George, and daughters Helen (Nellie) and Mary were added to the family.

In 1901 Charlie, once again came north, this time on government telegraph work. He took up a pre-emption on the north bank of the Skeena at the foot of Kitselas Canyon. He brought his family to "The Ranch" in August 1903, worked as a telegraph lineman, mail courier and prospector, and ran a ferry service across the river. Daughters Irene and Kathleen were born.

Main Street, Kitselas, 1912
(26-A) / BCARS

Departure of the winter mail service, Kitselas.
(41-A) / BCARS 88166

The tramway from the Foley, Stewart and Welch warehouse to the wagon road is tested with three tons of flour.
(41-A) / BCARS 88161

It was a boom time for the Skeena district. The Grand Trunk Pacific Railroad was being built—in fact, it ran right through the Durham ranch. For seven or eight years Kitselas, at the foot of the canyon, was a busy little village.

In 1914 war broke out. Charlie, not to be left behind by son George and son-in-law Frank Whitlow, enlisted with the 102nd Battalion and went overseas to the Aldershot Training Base. There, owing to an old injury and his age, he was discharged and sent back home.

In 1917 the Durhams moved in with their eldest son in Tacoma, Washington, but after a few months Charlie returned north to Usk. He got a job as bookkeeper for the Kitselas Copper Mining Company, sent for his family and took over the Usk Hotel from Mr. and Mrs. Earl Hays. When the mine closed down, Charlie again worked as government telegraph operator and lineman. Then he built and ran a pool room, was watchman at the Kitselas tunnels and the Prince Rupert railway yards, did government road work, ran the Usk Ferry, and even spent a summer tending the Cape St. James Lighthouse.

When World War II began Charlie, a staunch pro-Britisher, joined the volunteer reserve. He was assigned to guard the Shawatlan Lakes, the water supply for Prince Rupert, and later worked for the US Army. After the war, Charlie and Margaret spent their remaining years in Usk with their daughter and son-in-law, Nellie and Dick Adams, visiting family in Vancouver during the winters.

On February 26, 1948, the family was bereft by the death of Margaret Durham, who had been in poor health for some time. Charlie continued living in a little cabin by the Adamses and going south in the winter. After enjoying remarkably good health most of his life, he passed away suddenly on September 13, 1958, at the age of 97.

After carrying all that flour, a load of men proves to be no problem for the F S & W tramway.
(26-A) / BCARS

Durham Townsite

Being in the N.E. 1/4 Lot 304 R.V. Coast District

Scale 200 ft to 1 inch

Kitselas Indian Reserve

The Ranch at Kitselas

The Canyon Trail, Kitselas—the wagon road built before river boats could make it through the canyon.
(11-C)

♦ Elsie M. Whitlow

The old steamship *Danube* plied its way up the coast of BC from Vancouver in August 1903. On board were Charles and Margaret Durham with their five children, Fred, Elsie, George, Helen and Mary.

It was adventure to the children; to the father a sailor's dream of homestead and farm life. But the mother was filled with anxiety and doubts as to the family's welfare in moving to a strange, unsettled country without schools or doctors. Charles had come up first in 1901 or 1902 to work on the old Dominion Telegraph line along the Skeena River. Lonesome for his family, he pre-empted a 160-acre homestead at the mouth of the Kitselas Canyon across from the old Hudson's Bay post, which was a 10-acre block in the midst of a 3-mile square of Indian reservation.

The three-day journey (first class fare $16) was pleasant and sunny, but Spokeshoot was a cannery town, water-soaked and damp, with a population consisting mostly of Indian men who were, during the summer, busy fishing for salmon and Indian women who were employed in canning salmon. They lived in rows of shacks built out over the water or on the beach next to the cannery. Each of these shacks seemed to accommodate a family of countless adults and children.

After about three days the sternwheeler *Hazelton* finally came into port from its trip to Hazelton, situated as far up the Skeena as the river was navigable for steamers, and after hastily preparing for the next trip, the family embarked on the last lap of their journey.

Up the river the hard-working sternwheeler chugged under the command of Captain Bonser, the most famous and popular of river captains, with a full cargo for the interior residents whose year-round supplies all had to be brought in during the few summer months. The number of trips depended on the stages of the water. If too low or too high, navigation had to cease!

The family were the only first-class passengers aboard. The lower deck was aswarm with Indians, who bag and baggage, were returning to their homes as the fishing season came to a close. These Indians were sorry-looking, unkempt and dirty—not to be wondered at considering the conditions in which they lived. Almost all the children had open sores around the glands under the chin or on the neck. Some of the older people too had scars which must have had the same cause. It is fine today to see how much healthier and nicer they look and it is a credit to any of those who have been responsible or have helped with their welfare. If only they could, or would, leave liquor out of their lives, we would have no finer or more lovable people among our population.

Beyond stopping for cordwood piled on the bank at various places there were no stoppages, and beyond the telegraph station at the Hole-in-the-Wall, no point of interest was passed until Kitsumkalum Indian village appeared, followed by Thornhill's Landing, just below the Little Canyon; Red Bill Bostead's homestead, a little to the west of what is now Copper City; Dave Stewart's ranch, now Dobbie's, across the river from Copper City, where a flock of girls came running down to the beach to see the boat go by. A mile after this, at the Indian village called New Town, near what would later become Kitselas, were a number of nice new houses. Next Kendal's Landing,

A busy day at Eby's Landing, Kitsumkalum, with sternwheelers Port Essington *and* Distributor *taking on firewood and another riverboat coming up fast.*
(1-B)

Above and opposite page: The Hazelton *at Ringbolt Rock.* (25-A) / *BCARS 62235*

about a mile west of Kleanza (Gold) Creek, and then Kitselas at the mouth of Kitselas Canyon, generally called Big Canyon to differentiate from the Little Canyon where the Terrace bridge now spans the river.

Here, at the Hudson's Bay post and the telegraph station, on the south side of the river, was an excellent place for tying up. A fair-sized hemlock tree, which I believe has now been washed into the river, was used for snubbing and holding the boat to the bank.

The arrival of a steamer was the happiest of days for the old pioneers, who looked forward to getting mail and whatever glimpses of the outside world they could get. As a steamer slowly edged up the swift current, whistling here and there to announce that she was coming, the folk would gather at the landing place. Sometimes it was a wait of many hours from the time the whistle was first heard until the boat arrived. This depended on the stage of the water—when too low, the boats in some places literally had to be dragged by cable to get by a sand or gravel bar. If the boat carried many Indian passengers on the return home after the fishing closure for the season, they would all be sent ashore to walk up the bar or river bank to a point where the boat would again have sufficient draftage.

At this particular time of the *Hazelton*'s arrival at Kitselas, on a mid-afternoon about the end of the summer, 1903, there was nothing to indicate it was, or had been, a Hudson's Bay post, except for a freight shed near the aforementioned hemlock tree. Prior to steamers operating above the Canyon, this was the point of portage and transfer of freight etc. to canoes at the head of the Canyon for the remainder of river travel. An excellent graveled wagon road had been constructed over this distance approximately one or one and a half miles long. This road was also used, as long as steamboat days lasted, at times of high water when the canyon was unnavigable by either boat or canoe. A water gauge was maintained at the steamer landing under the charge of the telegrapher, and when the water reached a point called "four feet on the gauge," or over, there was no thought of going through the Canyon. It was told that Captain Bonser once made the trip through at the four-foot level successfully, but his was the one and only try.

The Hudson's Bay boat, the *Caledonia*, was the first of the sternwheelers to operate through to Hazelton. On one of her trips she met with grief on a rock at Hankin's Riffle near Philips Creek, which flows into the Skeena about halfway between the railway station at Kitselas and the Big Canyon on the north side of the river. The rock was henceforth known as Caledonia Rock by rivermen and is all there is to be reminded of this old vessel. She was replaced by the *Mount Royal*, which, part time, was also used for service on the Stikine River.

To return to the Hudson's Bay post—down river from the landing was a much larger building which had been used for a store or warehouse, barn and stable, and had belonged to the Singlehurst Mining Company. This was a New York company which had become interested in prospects in this part of the world and had started mining operations in the 1800s on Singlehurst Mountain, a peak at the end of Bornite Mountain and beside Kleanza Creek. After several years of development and ore production the mine closed, probably because of high transportation costs. Mr. Singlehurst died and his widow paid a brief visit to the district about the year 1906.

A beautiful, rather large, long-haired black and white dog, said to have been a Klondike or Northern dog named Tanner, left behind by someone in the mining company, habitually lay or sat outside this building and generally spent the nights telling the moon his story of loneliness and desertion. As he was the lone dog in the place he managed to survive by the scraps fed to him by the few residents, but he never took to a new master after his old one left.

Between the two buildings, a little further back was the three-room frame house known as the Dominion Government Telegraph Office, occupied by the operator, Hank Boss, and a lineman, Charlie Durham, who in 1903 were the only residents in Kitselas. Mr. Boss used his bedroom for an office and had his telegraph equipment installed in there. Their food, which was supplied by the government in one large consignment during the steamboat season, sufficient to last them through the winter and until the boats were running again the following summer, was mostly stored in the attic. Ham and bacon, those days, with the exception of a bit of mold which would come on the outside sometimes, and could be wiped off, kept marvelously well; canned cornbeef and sausage and powdered or crumbled dried eggs were the main protein foods. In vegetables they had desiccated and dried potatoes and onions to take the place of the fresh, and plenty of other keepable dried vegetables and fruits, some canned fruits and vegetables as were then available and other grain foods etc. to the amount they thought to order. These orders were supplied by Kelly, Douglas & Co. of whom Bob Kelly was Secretary-Treasurer of the Liberal Association in Vancouver during the time of the Laurier regime.

One other small log cabin a short distance away, the home of a

Foley, Stewart & Welch landing, Kitselas Canyon.
(41-A) / BCARS 88160

couple of prospectors, was the total number of buildings at the post. Besides this, about a mile off at Swede Creek, lived a couple of Scandinavians who had taken up a homestead there and also Milo Kendal at Kendal's Landing where he also had a pre-emption.

At the head of the Canyon were the remains of the deserted old Indian village with one quite modern (at that time) house standing in which dwelt "Kitselas" George Ellis, who was chief of the tribe—although the tribe now lived at New Town on another reservation about four miles farther down the river. There were several very large totem poles standing here at this time and several more opposite, on one of the islands along with the remains of Indian lodge houses. An old cemetery, which later caused the railroad some difficulty in negotiating, was on the other side of the river.

So here we are at Kitselas. We can't wait for the boat to tie up and get out that gangplank, but are finally ashore and greeted by the residents. Hank Boss, the telegrapher, Sim Dobbie, who had been filling in as lineman in Charlie's absence in fetching his family, Olalie Johnson, Jim Wells and the two homesteaders, Ed Youngdahl and Louie Anderson.

But I had eyes only for a young Indian woman who had also come off the boat with three small children. I followed her into the large shed. She hung up her papoose in the little wooden crib which she had been carrying on her back, fastened around her head and shoulders by a tumpline, the tape-like rope of red and yellow which used to be made by the Indians from the inner bark of the cedar trees. This line she threw over a rafter, leaving the babe there while she attended to other business; but not before I could ask her the baby's name.

"Annis," she said. It was a long time before I could figure out that "Ernest" was the name. The other children were Martha and George, and the mother, Lizzie, wife of Chief Kitselas George, who of all the tribe were the only ones that remained at the old village when the rest had left after an epidemic of smallpox.

As Charlie had only recently applied to the government and been granted the right to his pre-emption, it was still in primeval condition. With, as yet, no shelter provided for the family, Boss kindly made us at home in the telegraph office where we stayed until quite late in the fall. We gradually got acquainted with the surroundings, the forest immediately behind the office and surrounding everything else save the small clearing and grass patch between the three buildings. A little brook running behind and past the office gave an ample supply of clean, cool water and crossing this brook was a path to the sandbar—a two- or three-minute walk toward the canyon—where there was a fine place for trout fishing, tying up canoes and camping. As children, we spent many hours here playing in the sand, fishing or wading in the slough between the upper end of the bar and the mainland.

At the head of the canyon was a pretty bay and back of it the house of the chief (with no George or family in sight), his totem pole with a cache box fastened a few feet up on the trunk of another pole. I was told this box was for holding the bones of the dead. Probably somebody was spoofing me. There were a few other totem poles about, several of them on an island nearer the other side of the river.

Kitselas Mountain is very close to this place and we could spot goats on it. The mountain was especially interesting to me on account of "The Castle." At that time it was complete with a square fair-sized turret which sometime later broke off, spoiling the look of that seeming old ruin.

One day we were invited to visit Anderson and Youngdahl, and went up a steep sidehill after which another half-mile or so of pleasant walking brought us to their ranch at Swede Creek—so called on account of their settling there. Here, they had about an acre of clearing done and a two-room log cabin—one room as bedroom, the other as general living-room. Mr. Anderson (Norwegian) was probably about 50 years old. Youngdahl (Swedish) was a little younger. They had been working at the Singlehurst Mine until taking up this homestead of 360 acres.

They gave us our first sampling of bachelor cooking—coffee and bannock fresh from the oven. After inspecting the garden in which some rather miserable-looking potatoes and vegetables were growing, and taking a trip down the bank to Swede Creek, their water supply, which at this time of year consisted more of humpback salmon struggling to get upstream, than water, we returned home to the office.

The steamer season was over now, so there was nothing exciting to look forward to except the rare event of a canoe going by, the only one I can recollect particularly this fall having five men on board who were returning to the outside world after a season in the Omineca or Ingenika. Elmendorf was one of these and two doctors from Spokane. I cannot remember the others. They arrived from Hazelton in the evening and Mother cooked a supper for them, giving them hot baking-powder biscuits over which they raved and supplied their own syrup from a large can with a handle on top and a screw-top, which they carried among their groceries. In the morning after they had departed, it was discovered they had left their almost-full can of syrup behind, so we ran down to the riverbank calling to them and waving the can. However, they were floating down the swift current and an hour's work wouldn't have brought them this far upstream again. I think they purposely left the syrup as a treat for us kids.

Elmendorf is a place name in Alaska and I have often wondered if the Elmendorf I speak of is he for whom the place is named.

Weather permitting, and between times when Charlie was not occupied on lineman's duties, great work was going on at the ranch. The bachelors around, including Red Bill from Copper River, chipped in to help fell trees for a clearing and to get suitable logs for the cabin.

They took as much pleasure in getting the Durhams settled as could be had in any kind of "bee." In fact it was fun to have something to do to break the monotony of a dull existence, since so late in the season there was nothing much for them to do but lay-up for the winter.

To reach the ranch it was necessary to cross the river by poling—together with paddling or rowing—a boat or canoe up from the sandbar to the necessary distance in the mouth of the canyon and then angling over, the swift current carrying the craft down to a gravel bar lying in the river where it had widened out considerably after it escaped the canyon. The trick was to catch an eddy at the head of this bar which would carry the craft into the comparatively calm water flowing around in a large, bay-like area back up to the mouth of the canyon again. If one did not catch this eddy just right, escaping the main flow of the river, they were in great danger of being carried to almost certain death in a race which went down the narrow channel between the bar and the north bank of the river, running with tremendous force and speed against a log jam at the head of an Island at the lower end of the bar.

The nearest part of the ranch was behind the border of the Indian reservation, a few moments' walk up from the river bank. Here was a dense growth of both large and small hemlock trees which the men attacked with great gusto. Young Fred and George, getting initiated into this kind of education (instead of school books) were having a wonderful time trying to make themselves as useful as best they could.

Kitselas Canyon, also called Big Canyon, a place of narrow passages, precipitous rock walls and dangerous waters. Said one old sourdough about the trip through the canyon, "If anything gives, there's going to be an unrehearsed somersault into hell."
(41-A) / BCARS 88163

A ringbolt on Ringbolt Rock.
(33-C)

The men all being experts with axe and saw, did not take long to clear enough space to let in a little daylight, and to select a site for the cabin near a small stream of clear pure water.

Being in a hurry to get the family moved in before the winter's snow began, no time was lost more than was needed in barking and peeling logs, and it was not long before walls were being put up—one log on top of another laid in opposite directions, fitted and fastened together by notches made near the ends. A partition of logs across the cabin divided it into two rooms, each approximately twelve feet square—one designed as parlor and bedroom for the parents, the other as kitchen and general living quarters. A flooring of rough boards was put in, windows across the front and an outside door into the kitchen; the windows, door and shingles for the roof had been ordered and brought in while the steamers were still running as were also all other supplies of groceries, clothing etc., sufficient to last until the following spring or summer.

Olalie Johnson turned out to be the chief carpenter in these operations and while he smoothed inner walls and fitted chinking into any open spaces between logs on the inside, Red Bill attended to filling up spaces and plastering on the outside. He had found clay in the bed of the creek and with clumps of this wet stuff thrown enthusiastically against the cracks between the logs, Olalie on the inside received much of the splashings. He and Bill were not the best of friends, due, maybe, to differences in character and nationality, Olalie being of Swedish descent and Bill, Bluenose. Whether there had ever been any trouble between them is not known. They simply did not like each other. So Olalie finally came to the conclusion that Bill was aiming at him purposely. He came to a window opening to really give Bill a calling-down, only to receive a large clump of clay against his face and fine bald head. That really irked him, but with Bill's abject apologies and assistance in cleaning up the mess, Olalie's good nature came to the fore and he finally had to forgive Bill and laugh along with the others who had witnessed the incident.

At last came the time for moving in. The stove, a new-fangled "Star" set on legs with plenty of open space beneath, and with an oblong oven set about one stovepipe length up from the stove, was installed on the side of the dividing wall. It gave good service as long as the family remained on the ranch and the oven proved an excellent baker. A cupboard was put in the corner between the outside door and doorless opening into the bedroom. A bench along the whole length of the far wall and a homemade table with only room enough left at the ends for a person to slide by or sit, a couple of chairs and a small rocking chair completed the kitchen furnishing. A bureau, bed and sewing machine furnished the other room until, later in the winter when the river was frozen, the piano, the one luxury which had been brought from Vancouver, was hauled over on the ice and a place was made for it between the head of the bed and the outside wall. This space became the parlor for evenings of song when everyone crowded in front of it or sat around on the two sides of the bed. Charlie was a natural-born wit and entertainer, gifted with an ear for music and could chord to any tune once he heard it. He loved company, so happy evenings were spent with all joining in on the old-time songs.

A bed-spring with mattress was laid on the floor at each end of the attic which became respectively the boys' and girls' rooms. As there was barely room under the centre roof rafter for even a child to stand upright, bedmaking was rather a problem and crawling into bed was literally what the kids had to do—as well as climbing up the log partition and through a hole in the ceiling to get to their rooms. However, this was all fine with the kids, especially as they were allowed to have lamps and to read as late into the night as they wished.

Winter set in, with gloomy days of rain, slush, snow and darkness. Daylight hours were fully occupied with chores—boys keeping the woodbox and water buckets filled, and Mother cooking, washing, mending etc. with Elsie as general help. Charlie was as often as not out on his "beat," as with bad weather there was always trouble on the line—a break from a fallen tree or heavy snow, power leakages, or one thing or another. The "beat" covered many miles both east and west. A trip in either direction often took several days, according to travelling conditions and the extent of the damage. If I remember correctly, the

The Port Simpson *at Ringbolt Rock.*
(3-B)

beat extended halfway to Graveyard Point where there was another station, or beyond Kitsumkalum River to the West and Lorne Creek to the East. When the river was open, generally a canoe was used for carrying supplies and repair materials, some of which would be left in caches for winter use, and the telegraph operater came along. In winter, Charlie went alone with backpack and snowshoes.

Sometimes he took Fred along for company. Once in the late autumn, they went east on an overnight trip. The temperature dropped and the rain turned to heavy snow, so that trudging through it became most tiring. By the time they reached home it was late evening and the family was waiting anxiously. As soon as they got in the door, Fred collapsed on the floor and sat with huge silent tears flowing down his cheeks.

Came Christmas, marked this time only by the traditional Norwegian Christmas Eve rice pudding, which as far as we were concerned was simply boiled rice made richer by the addition of milk and plenty of seeded raisins, served in a soup-plate with butter, milk, sugar and cinnamon added according to taste. Christmas cake was also experimented with, using dried eggs and whatever could be found to use in place of the usual luscious ingredients. A visit from the neighbors from across the river with an evening of games around the table completed the celebration.

Later Christmases were really gay, with every bachelor in the country there to spend the holiday week. Whatever special delicacy in the way of food was saved for this occasion; Jimmy Wells was "it" when it came to making Christmas cake and other fancy cooking.

A large tree was set up in the centre of the living room, trimmed with coloured tissue paper chains and baskets containing nuts and raisins, wild cranberry strings and the gifts. Festivities always started Norwegian fashion on Christmas Eve, with hands joined and dancing in a ring around the tree.

Such games as chess, checkers and cribbage amused visitors during much of the daylight hours and during the long evenings card games such as Trump and Old Country, or High-Low Whist, Pedro and cribbage were played. When there were "parties" Hearts, Fan-Tan, Old

Dance programme, Kitselas Bachelor Ball, May 24, 1910.
(16-B)

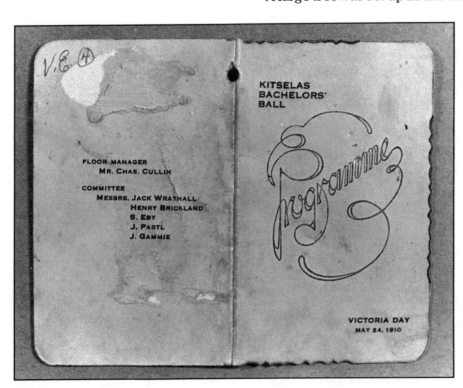

KITSELAS
BACHELORS'
BALL

Programme

FLOOR MANAGER
MR. CHAS. CULLIN

COMMITTEE
MESSRS. JACK WRATHALL
HENRY BRICKLAND
S. EBY
J. PASTL
J. GAMMIE

VICTORIA DAY
MAY 24, 1910

S.S. Distributor, *with* S.S. Skeena *following. Sleeping Beauty Mountain is in the background.*
(1-B)

Maid, Black Peter and Greasy Pig, as well as memory games and tricks with the cards were highly enjoyed.

With these the main diversions in the long winter evenings, often one or other of the bachelors crossed the river on the ice, with his "bug" to visit the family.

During the summers the men were usually out in the hills prospecting or doing assessment work on their claims. The main source of their income was cutting cordwood for the steamers, which they were generally glad to do by contract, but cut anyway on the chance of selling, as this work was a good winter occupation.

In January when the river was frozen solid and the piano brought over, it made diversion for Mother in the afternoons by playing both for her own pleasure and to make sure that Elsie practised both playing and singing. Her favourite melody was *The Lorelei* and poor Elsie, whose voice to say the least was not a soprano, did much sweating and croaking in an effort to reach the high notes.

After the house was built, many gay evenings were spent in dancing and music, Durham vamping on the piano and always someone or other who was an artist on the violin, harmonica or even the comb.

With such a lack of womenfolk it was fun for the small girls to be chosen as partners, and in the quadrille there were at least two of the men with a white cloth tied about one arm to denote "sex."

The Fandango-Sarabandi or other dances with fancy names were generally the events of the evening, with two men strutting about

S.S. Pheasant *wrecked at*
Beaver Dam Rapids,
November 6, 1906.
(25-A)

each other with their finger-tips lifted elegantly on the thighs of their not-so-elegant pants, making pretty faces and fancy steps about each other.

During the summer, should a steamer lie overnight at the canyon, nothing pleased Durham more than to have the passengers and crew all in for an evening of entertainment.

During the winter, when there was no river traffic, once a month one of the Tomlinson boys—generally Richard, with his gang of several Indians from Meanskinisht—camped overnight on his mail-carrying trip to or from Kitimat. We then had an evening crowded in front of the piano, singing hymns, the favourite being *Shall We Gather at the River*, *I Will Sing of my Redeemer* and *Wonderful Words of Love*. The Indians, all lovers of music, were able to carry the tunes beautifully.

As winter progressed into the more settled weather of February, land clearing began to take place. While the snow was still quite deep, felled trees were cleared and burned. The three older children took part in this and enjoyed keeping the fires blazing. Later, digging out stumps required much harder work. No dynamite was used. When it seemed that no more digging down on a stump could be done, a pry was used to try to lift it out. This pry was not a peavey or any such tool, but a stout pole or piece of timber about eight feet long—the thick end placed over a block of wood lying as close to the stump as possible, and the point of the pry under the likeliest part of the stump for a good grip to get it heaved out of its reluctant bed. We were lucky if there wasn't another couple of hours digging before that pry could do its job, and it was a matter of rejoicing when finally the stump was uprooted.

This, however, was not the most arduous task of breaking ground. When it came to digging a vegetable garden, besides other miseries, the soil was found to be full of these tough hemlock roots—layers upon layers of them, crisscrossed in every possible direction so it took hours and hours of backbreaking work to make any progress in clearing sufficient space to plant potatoes and other vegetable seeds expected to arrive on the first boat in the spring. The gardening was pretty well left to the kids who, since there was no other way to amuse themselves, or pass time, worked diligently and had a fair garden considering everything. We did have potatoes for the following winter and they gave a greatly humorous point to the song we used to sing in which "They growed potatoes small, over there, over there."

Since our arrival in Kitselas our food supplies had come partly from Charlie's half of the stores supplied by the Dominion Government Telegraphs for the operator and the lineman. The balance of what we needed from the first winter arrived from Kelly Douglas & Co. in Vancouver at about the same time as the family did. A storage place had to be constructed for these. Fresh foods were out of the question so everything we ate that first winter came out of a can, a box or a bag: cereals, dried beans—white, brown or limas for variety—dried eggs, potatoes, onions and spinach and dried fruits. Spinach, by the way, was the most natural tasting. Hams and bacon, unlike what is to be had nowadays, kept very well through the winter, as did cheese, although by the time it was consumed there was about as much mold as cheese to it.

On the river bank, which had a moderately steep slope and no beach, a small landing place had been made for tying up a rowboat or a canoe. This landing was a fine place for the children to try their hand at fishing and as soon as the ice had gone out of the river they produced many delicious meals of trout.

Charlie had experience as a gillnet fisherman on the Fraser River, so he lost no time in getting hold of a net and putting up a rack on which to hang it. An excellent place for setting it out was at the mouth of the canyon, just where the eddy in the bay met the outflow of water from there. This net provided the family with an abundance of salmon for year-round use, as that which was not eaten fresh was salted down in barrels. At that time we had no other way of preserving the fish. Even if we had, the cans and jars now available would have been too expensive a method for a food which was practically a daily item on our table.

On top of the riverbank, on a small grassy plain to the left of the path leading to the ranch, a number of weather-beaten decorated cedar storage boxes still showed the work of an Indian artist who had adorned them with designs or coloured motifs and mussel shell inlays. But there were no other signs of habitation. These all disappeared during the construction days of the railroad. The Indians, in former times, had undoubtedly found this a good spot for fishing and camping, but too vulnerable to enemy attack to be a good site for a permanent settlement. Their location at the head of the canyon—which, from this place, was reached by a trail uphill and over the bluffy heights of the canyon wall—was the perfect site for a village as far as defence was concerned. Here, with high, rocky banks on each side and water entering the canyon only through narrow channels, an enemy could easily be pelted with missiles from above. On the larger island between the channels there were still remains of a lodge house built of cedar boards or planks, up to about three feet wide and three or four inches thick. The corner posts of the lodge still stood, each wearing a wooden cap that might very well be taken for a Top Hat. Totem poles stood adjacent to the building and across the river on the south side, where the old chief still lived. Nearby, on the north side was a graveyard for which, because it happened to be in the path of the railway right-of-way, a settlement had to be made in which the graves were moved to another location.

Anticipation ran high as the ice on the river slowly broke and drifted away. Every day the gauge showed how much the water had risen. At last came news that the first steamer was on the way and when the first whistle was heard from maybe still a dozen miles away, arguments broke out as to where the sound came from. The old timers had already prepared for this event by washing and mending their clothes so they could appear in their Sunday best, and by giving each other shaves and haircuts.

Where *did* the sound of the whistle come from? With each succeeding toot a fresh thrill was felt and a new argument began until the bow of the boat, watched for from the landing, came into view past the bend of the river. When the boat finally docked at the landing and the gangplank was out, there was a scramble to get aboard to hear outside news and to receive long awaited mail from the purser. Only letters had been delivered during the long winter, the mail carriers having had a limit of 100 pounds of load to distribute through the whole interior from Kitimat eastwards. The going was often very grim with the carriers having to break trails through deep and wet snow.

Badly needed boots and clothing parcels were looked for from orders out of Eaton's catalogue. For the Durham parents, keeping abreast of the needs and fittings for their growing children was quite a problem.

In the winter and spring of 1903 Olalie Johnson and his then-partner in the cabin, Charlie Carlson, had a grim food shortage. Only by eating whatever could be spared from the telegraph station and the little game Carlson managed to trap or snare were they able to survive. Olalie had had an experience of starving once in the Omineca district. He had been lost for several weeks and had subsisted on berries, which gave rise to his moniker, Olalie—the Indian word for "berry." His real name was August Edward. He saved his energy by lying in bed and taking an occasional spoonful of raw flour.

During the summer of 1904, when the river was fairly low, Durham decided it was time the family paid a visit to all those neighbours who were so kind and hospitable to him when he was out on line duty. First, we had to go visit Thornhill at Little Canyon and his native wife Eliza, for whom Charlie had a very high regard. Thornhill himself was rather a quiet and well-bred-appearing type of Englishman. Together they seemed happy and contented in their neat little home.

We set off by canoe for the Thornhills one sunny Sunday morning. Olalie was along both to visit and to help with the canoe, as

S.S. Inlander *entering Kitselas*
Canyon
(25-A) / BCARS 29365

on the return journey it would be impossible for one man to handle alone. The trip down was short, and after a lunch and as much time as could be spared in visiting, inspecting the garden and being presented with flower plants, the return home was started. Charlie sat in the bow of the canoe, Olalie at the stern, Mrs. Durham and the children on seats between, young Fred feeling very important with his own paddle. All went well until a place beyond Copper River, where it was impossible, even after repeated efforts with poles, to force the canoe up against the swift current. Charlie got out with a towline. There was a lot of brush along the riverbank here, and he was out of sight when the canoe suddenly tilted over and water rapidly rushed in. Like a flash Olalie was out of the canoe and up to his neck in water, steadying it while Charlie, hearing the frightened screams of the passengers, quickly snubbed his line and came hurrying back.

Such happenings may have been common occurrence with practised canoemen as neither of the men seemed unduly concerned, and after bailing out the canoe, reassuring the passengers and doing some replanning to get past that point we were soon on the go again—a sobbing Elsie clutching tightly the little sister she had at her side.

Later on we made another visit by canoe, this time to the Stewarts, and returned without mishap, except that we overstayed our visit and by the time we had got past Philips Creek it was too dark to proceed further by water. The canoe was secured on the point of the island where the water between the island and the mainland was fairly shallow and quiet; Charlie and Olalie, waist deep, acting as bearers to Mrs. Durham and the younger children across the 20- or 30-foot channel. Then we trekked a mile or so home through the woods along the riverbank.

Dave Stewart must have been a brave and sturdy Scotsman in his younger days, but was now a heavy elderly man with grizzled hair and beard, helplessly crippled with rheumatism or arthritis. He had been engaged in the fishery business around Spokeshoot but since had settled here, building a comfortable log house and cultivating enough ground so that he already had a small orchard. His wife had died after they settled here and a cared-for little plot towards the riverbank marked the place of her burial.

His daughters Mary and Jemima, still teenage girls, to the admiration of all in the district not only cared for their crippled father but for the house, and did all the outside work such as gardening and cutting firewood. They also cared for their three younger sisters—the eldest of these, a sweet bed-ridden patient, died a couple of years later.

After this there were no more excursions. We got down to regular existence. During that summer and the next we continued clearing land and burning stumps and debris. In the second summer, for a spell of a month or six weeks, fires seemed to break out all over the country. While a fire raged up Bornite Mountain we heard one loud blast after another—due, we were told, to the numerous dynamite caches made by prospectors from the stores belonging to the Single-hurst Mine, to which they had helped themselves after the mine closed down. Although we had stopped all burning when the weather became so dangerously dry, fires continued to break out in unexpected places in our clearing, so we were kept constantly on the alert with water-pail and shovel. These outbreaks were caused from underground rotten logs and other plant material, in which it seemed a spark could smoulder forever, only to flare up and start a new fire at the least sign of a breeze. A strong wind finally came up which kept the whole family on the go all day and the older children watching through the night with Jimmy Wells (now Olalie Johnson's partner in the cabin), who had come to help, staying up to keep things under control. In the early hours of the morning we got hungry and Jimmy spitted a salmon which he cooked for us over the small campfire that we sat around. No stove-cooked fish ever tasted so good.

The wind fortunately brought a change in the weather and relief, both from the fire hazard and from the heavy pall of smoke which had hung over the valley. We could breathe clean, fresh air again.

By this time a few scrawny hens had been acquired from someone in the Indian village at New Town—possibly "Old Kate," who was kind to Charlie whenever he passed through the village. Old Kate was kin to Chief Kitselas George and upon his death she became the head of the tribe—a branch of the Tsimpsian Indians.

The case in which the piano had been shipped was put into use as a chicken house with fish-net fencing to hold in the birds—although it mostly didn't. Since winter was hard and feed scarce there was no production of eggs until the spring and even then these old biddies never produced anything to cackle about. When summer came they all wanted to "sit" and after obliging a couple of them with sittings of eggs, the others lived off and on under boxes or buckets, which was supposed to break them of the mothering notion. Those hens Old Kate sold Dad were mighty old. Still Mother hung on to them and if we ever had one for a meal it was an "occasion"—even if it was mighty tough eating.

A couple of young dogs were also acquired. Charlie, the wit of the family, promptly named them Bonser after the captain and Clifford for the local Member of Parliament at that time. Bonser lacked accomplishments, but Clifford climbed trees. This amusing creature, was sometimes also a source of anxiety as he was better at going up than coming down.

On the northwestern corner of the ranch, reached via the trail from Kitselas to New Town, was a large meadow with a good growth of wild grass. Enough hay could be produced there to feed a cow. Scythe and pitchforks were procured and a good many summer days were spent by the kids in the cutting and stooking of hay, with lessons and occasional help from the neighbourhood bachelors. A crude log barn with a shake roof was built and a fine Holstein cow was procured from somewhere in the Fraser Valley. In the journey up the coast on the SS *Cardena*, Sarah Bernhardt (as she was named upon her arrival) delivered a son, which was as warmly greeted as his mother, and promptly named Moses.

S.S. Operator *heading up Skeena River.*
(25-A) / BCARS 23240

Madam Bernhardt produced great quantities of milk, but it was lucky for her she had the calf to nurse while the boys were getting practice in the art of milking. Moses, though only milk-fed, was soon full of wild oats and getting to be rather a nuisance around the farm, so as soon as he could be weaned he was taken across the river to fend for himself on the grass growing around the Post.

In the spring of 1906 Mrs. Durham gave birth to a daughter, attended by the Chief's wife, Lizzie, who made an excellent midwife. Lizzie was called into attendance again in 1908, when the last of the Durham children was born.

The first child, Irene, was christened by Bishop Du Vernet, on the steamer *Hazelton* as it was making a trip through the canyon. The other child was christened at a later date, after the Reverend Thomas Marsh became missionary at Kitsumkalum.

More people gradually began drifting in, lured probably by rumours of the new transcontinental railway to be constructed in the near future. Quite a number of homesteads were taken up between Kitselas Canyon and New Town. There was Ed Erickson—who after he settled managed to find a very pleasant and cheery wife for himself—his brother Dave, Charlie Hillstrom, Pete Brusk and Gabriel Elbring.

J.W. Patterson came to Kitselas and built a small store and hotel, which were both enlarged in time for the boom when railway construction started.

Among the other outsiders who came about this time were Al Johnson (who later settled in Terrace) and family, with Mrs. Johnson's brother Walter Washburn and her sister Mattie. Al was chief carpenter on the building of the Patterson property.

Frontiersmen like Jim Bates, Dan Olsen, Bobby Burns and T. Hansen came in and stayed for awhile.

Andrew Kelch and Billy Doyle took up pre-emptions near Anderson and Youngdahls.

Hank Boss left Kitselas and in his place came a man named

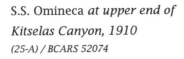

S.S. Omineca *at upper end of Kitselas Canyon, 1910*
(25-A) / BCARS 52074

Grahame, who did not remain long, but while he was there he carried on a romance with Miss Lily Tomlinson, operator at Meanskinisht, over the telegraph keys. They were later married and lived in Victoria.

He was followed by Enoch R.L. Jones, accompanied by his little Spanish wife from the Philippine Islands and their small son.

The Water Gauge

◆ Elsie M. Whitlow.

The water gauge at Kitselas was simply a tall white-painted post anchored near the riverbank where the steamers tied up in front of the telegraph office. It was marked in numbers up to about 10 feet, and one of the telegrapher's duties was to keep his eye on it and report the water level, which was very important during the summer while the sternwheelers were running. Around the two-foot mark on the gauge the water was considered good for steamer traffic. Four feet was fine as far as the Big Canyon, but no captain would navigate through it at that level except Captain Bonser, who only tried it once. At about six feet or over the river was considered to be very high.

"At the lower portal of the canyon is a gauge. When it registers a rise of 12 inches in the water at that point, it means that an additional four and a half feet have been piled up at the higher entrance. And the variation may take place in a few hours, for the Skeena, fed by melting snows from the mountains far to the north, is a fickle river. Its behaviour is entirely governed by the strength of the sun during the day and by the depth of the snowfall at night!"

F.A. Talbot, *The New Garden of Canada*

Boom Days in Kitselas • Elsie M. Whitlow

Sternwheelers moored at Kitselas.
(26-A) / BCARS

Surveying for the Grand Trunk Pacific—now the CNR—started about 1906, and as the surveyors made progress along the line they were followed by the usual flock of speculators, businessmen and so on. Among the first people to come at this time were Frank Whitlow, the four Kenney brothers—the eldest with his wife and three small children—Charles Giggey with his wife and son, Clair, and Lee Bethurem, who all remained to become good citizens in this northern country.

Among those who came in and opened up businesses, but left when the boom was over, were McEwen & Merryfield, (general store); W.M. Bateman (tobacconist & soft drinks); D.C. Savary (contractor and builder); Brickland Billiard & Pool Rooms; J. Shannon (general contractor); *The Big Canyon Newspaper,* owned and edited by E.R.L. Jones; Mr. and Mrs. Taft, (Riverside Rooms); Lee Bethurem (cafe & bakery).

As the railway was being built across the river from Kitselas, including three tunnels through the canyon and one a short distance west, there were camps for each piece of work, or contract, so this was where most of the population was during the boom days. The railroad went through the Durham property—the house had to be moved a couple of hundred feet back to make room for the right-of-way.

At the head of the canyon, on the Kitselas side, was situated the railroad hospital, a rough board and tarpaper building, as were all the other camp buildings, with Dr. Seymour Traynor in charge. He lived there with his wife and three children. Dr. Traynor later settled in Terrace until he went overseas in the First World War. A large Foley, Welch & Stewart warehouse was also situated here on the bank of the river. It was used principally for storing freight which had been portaged from the lower end of the canyon, where FW&S also had a warehouse at a different spot from the Hudson's Bay Company landing. From this warehouse, an aerial tramway to the top of the hill behind Kitselas connected with the old wagon road, over which they transferred their freight.

During these days everybody was busy. There was not much going on in the way of social activities. An approximately 24-foot square tent with flooring and partially wooden walls was set up in which church services were held by the Reverend Mr. Marsh, who made the special trip up from his mission at Kitsumkalum by any means he could find, sometimes on foot. A large building erected towards the end of the boom—for what purpose it cannot be remembered—was used to hold a couple of dances, probably put on by the engineers. These were elaborate affairs that even featured program cards.

Much of the social activity went on at Swede Ranch, so called from being the home of Anderson and Youngdahl, who now were both dead, Youngdahl by drowning in the river, and Anderson in a fall from a bluff. This place, with new buildings, became the red light district, and along with the licensed saloon at Patterson's Hotel and a few other questionable establishments, the constable, Frank Jones (who had come with his wife and family from Victoria) was kept fairly busy. A jail was built, but it cannot be remembered if there were any important cases of confinement.

C.W.D. Clifford now resided in Kitselas with his wife and daughter, having built a home for himself. He carried on a real estate business and acted as magistrate. Frank Whitlow, who was Postmaster in Patterson's store, was appointed Justice of the Peace, but after a few samples of justice, between magistrate and constable, resigned the honour.

As the only really permanent residents with children of school age at Kitselas were the Durhams, there was never any agitation for a school, and outside of the Christmas celebrations and parties held at their home, there were no other entertainments, nor events for other special holidays.

By 1913 the tunnels were completed and trains ran through to Smithers, so a large proportion of the population moved on too. The town slowly disintegrated. The First World War came, and the few remaining young men joined up or went on to greener fields. Finally, even though the railway ran by the ranch, it became a more isolated place than ever, and even the Durhams left.

Looking for Kitselas now, it is very hard to find any trace of it at all.

BC Voters List ◆ Kitselas

1900
Schwarz, Samuel — miner
Anderson, Lewis — miner

1903
Ross, Henry Newton — mining engineer
Johnson, August Edward — miner
Kendall, Milo Cecil — miner
Thornhill, Thomas — miner
Wells, James D. — miner

1907
Durham, Charles — lineman
Graham, J.W. — tel. operator
Johnstone, John Bruce — rancher
Johnson, August E. — miner
Kendall, Milo Cecil — miner
Paterson, John Walker — merchant
Wells, James D. — farmer

1908
Durham, Charles — lineman
Johnstone, John Bruce — rancher
Johnson, August E. — miner
Kendall, Milo Cecil — miner
St. Aubin, Joseph — farmer
Thornhill, Thomas — miner
Wells, James D. — miner

1909
Anderson, George — logger

Brickland, Henry Esmond — clerk
Brilliant, Frank — labourer
Clement, Anthony — rancher
Clifford, Charles Wm. Digby — miner
Durham, Charles — lineman
Erickson, David — farmer
Falconer, William R. — labourer
Falk, Andrew R. — farmer
Graham, Peter — miner
Harris, Bernard W. — miner
Johnson, August E. — miner
Johnstone, John Bruce — bencher
Kibbey, Edwin C. — farmer
Long, Bert
McDonald, Alexander Rod
McEachern, Ronald — labourer
McEwan, Joseph E. — merchant
McGregor, John — miner
Milne, Clifford — rancher
Mirabelle, Antonio — section foreman
Patterson, Joseph Edmont — miner
Paterson, John Walker — merchant
Rowe, Arthur F. — rancher
St. Aubin, Joseph — farmer
Shannon, John — contractor
Watson, Richard — cook
Wells, James D. — miner
Whitlow, Francis M. — farmer
Whitlow, Frank M. — rancher
Winter, Albert Oldham — farmer
Winter, Albert O. — lineman

Henderson's *British Columbia Gazetteer and Directory*, 1910

Postmaster—J.W. Paterson
Provincial Constable—Charles L. Cullen
Justices of the Peace—C.W.D. Clifford, Frank M. Whitlow
Government Telegraphs—E.R.L. Jones

Anderson, George	logger
Bateman, W.M.	tobacconist and soft drinks
Bennett, J.E.	agent, Bornite Co. Ltd.
Big Canyon Hotel	John W. Paterson, Prop.
Big Canyon Weekly	Enoch R.L. Jones, pub.
Bornite Co. Ltd. (mining)	J.E. Bennett, agent
Clement, Anthony	rancher
Clifford, C.W.D. (J.P.)	townsite owner
Cullen, Charles L.	provincial constable
Cullertson, Edward	cook
Durham, Charles	lineman
Erickson, David	farmer
Falconer, Wm. R.	farmer
Falk, Andrew R.	farmer
Foley, Welch & Stewart	railway contractors, branch warehouse
Graham, Peter	miner
Johnson, August E.	miner
Johnstone, John Bruce	miner
Jones, E.R.L.	agent, Gov't telegraphs
Kendall, Milo Cecil	miner
Kitselas Contracting and Building Co. Lee	T. Mitchell, Mgr., bakery and OK Mountain restaurant rancher
Long, Bert	miner
McBridge, James	

McDonald, Alex Rod	
McEachern, Ronald	labourer
McEwan, Joseph E.	labourer
Merryfield Joseph D.	General Store (also Prince Rupert)
McGregor, John	miner
McPhee, James	labourer
Mirabelle, Antonio	section foreman
Paterson, John W.	General Store and Prop. Big Canyon Hotel
Patterson, Joseph E.	miner
Riverside Hotel (lodging)	Ray Tafel, Prop.
St. Aubin, Joseph	farmer
Savary, D.C.	contractor and builder
Shannon, John	carpenter
Tafel, Ray	Prop. Riverside Hotel
Thornhill, Thomas	miner
Watson, Richard	cook
Wells, James D.	miner
Whitlow, Frank M.	Justice of the Peace
Whitlow, Frank M.	farmer
Winter, Albert O.	farmer
Winter, Albert O.	lineman

Boom Town Editor

◆ Enoch R.L. Jones Sr.

Sternwheelers putting into port at Kitselas.
(32-A) / BCARS 80803

I came to the town of Kitselas on the Skeena in 1908 as a telegraph operator on the Dominion Yukon Telegraph Line. Previously I had been a telegrapher on the Pennsylvania Railroad, an officer in the US Signal Corps during the Boxer Rebellion in China, and a miner in Wyoming. When Kitselas began to boom I decided to provide the new metropolis with a newspaper.

I telegraphed an order to Vancouver for a complete printing plant, together with a printer. At the same time I drew plans for a two-story house, and bought a supply of lumber from the William Ellis sawmill, recently installed at Hardscrabble, a few miles upriver from Kitselas Canyon. When the printing plant and printer reached Kitselas, I had a building ready. On Thursday of the following week, the first issue of the *Big Canyon Weekly* made its appearance in Kitselas, and a bundle of papers was on its way to Little's News Stand in Prince Rupert.

I received splendid support in the way of advertisements and subscriptions. Prince Rupert businessmen filled a page with one or two-inch advertisements, and land locators began bringing their location notices to me instead of taking them 90 miles upriver to the Hazelton paper.

News items were never lacking. There were passengers on every steamer that tied up at Kitselas who had news of some kind. In winter, when river navigation was closed, "Barney" Mulvaney and Dutch Cline, packing mail between Telegraph Point and Hazelton by toboggan and dog-teams, were good sources of news. And Omineca placer mine operator Beach, "French" Bodine, land surveyor Brownlee, and others who passed through Kitselas every spring and fall could be depended upon for stories of life and doings in the interior.

There were other "space fillers." The first winter, 1909–10, in collaboration with Mrs. Lily Graham, telegrapher at Meanskinisht, daughter of the Rev. Robert Tomlinson, I published a serial on the missions of northern British Columbia. The next winter, in collaboration with George Kerr, clerk at Patterson's store, I published Kerr's story of the 1884–1885 Louis Riel Rebellion in northern Saskatchewan.

The other little townsites were also sources of news. Downriver from Kitselas, W.J. Saunders was promoting Copper City; telegrapher Sim Dobbie, son-in-law of pioneer rancher Dave Stuart, had a pre-emption that might be made a railway stop and become the junction point for Copper City and Kitimat. Some thought that Kitsumkalum had advantages over the other prospective townsites in the area.

George Little came to Kitselas occasionally to make purchases at Patterson's store. At such times we heard much about the advantages of his pre-emption at Little Canyon for a townsite. Like the people of Kitsumkalum we paid little heed to his talk. One evening, though, George met more than his match in the person of "Tony" McHugh, one of the railway sub-contractors.

In a spirit of jest, Tony took George on to divert him from me. For every advantage George claimed for a townsite at Little Canyon, McHugh advanced a dozen disadvantages that seemed to carry sense. Finally George was silenced but not convinced. Only a few months after that, Little had an interview with Grand Trunk Pacific officials, convinced them of the advantages of a townsite at Little Canyon, made the railway a present of acreage, and Littleton (future Terrace) was born—and the handwriting appeared on the wall at each of the nearby hopeful townsites.

I found that publishing a politically independent paper, and being in charge of a Dominion government telegraph office wouldn't mix. The party in power was Liberal and my paper should have been Liberal. I took the hint and resigned. I was succeeded by Jack Wrathall as telegrapher. Frank Dowling, manager of the Prince Rupert office, succeeded me as circuit manager.

The Kitselas townsite was owned by W.D. Clifford, ex-member of BC Parliament. When the township of about 200 lots was first surveyed, he sold lots fronting on "main" street to friends and acquaintances at bargain prices. When the little boom came, those lots fetched high prices, but I do not remember Clifford having sold a lot of his own, nor realizing a dollar on the 185 lots he had left during the boom.

By the fall of 1910, we knew that when the railway was finished, Kitselas would become a ghost town. Some of the businessmen began preparing to quit the town before doomsday hit. On the invitation of "Peavine" Harvey and other businessmen I moved to Hazelton, but that is another story.

Indeed, when construction ended Kitselas not only became a ghost town, but a few years later a flooded Skeena washed the townsite away.

Compiler's Note: There is some confusion over the name "Little Canyon." In this instance "Little" has its usual meaning—small—to differentiate it from the "Big Canyon" which was at Kitselas. It was not named for George Little.

The *Big Canyon Weekly*

◆ Wiggs O'Neill

The *Big Canyon Weekly* was printed at Kitselas Canyon on the Skeena by Mr. Enoch R.L. Jones, owner, publisher, and the local telegraph operator. He had worked on newspapers in his younger days, and still had printer's ink in his veins.

It was the first paper to be published anywhere near Kitimat, just across the divide on the Skeena. Jones was a very interesting person. He had been taking part in a mining venture in the southern part of the province and ran into hard luck. He called at the office of the Yukon Telegraphs in Vancouver and met John T. Phelan, the superintendent. In conversation, Mr. Phelan discovered that Mr. Jones was an old telegraph operator and persuaded him to forget mining for awhile and go up to the Skeena division and help him out, as he was short of operators.

Enoch Jones, being a real soldier of fortune and hard up, was always open for adventure, so he moved to Kitselas with his wife and small family, as operator and boss of the Skeena Division. He was very efficient at his work, but the printer's ink began to boil up in his veins and he saw an opportunity for a weekly paper in his town. Kitselas had started to boom in 1910, with the advent of railway construction, and with many river steamers going into service and the town bustling with activity, the *Big Canyon Weekly* was born.

Jones was owner, manager and reporter. Mr. Loran Kenney, a brother of E.T. Kenney of Terrace, was his printer's devil. The paper did a big business in 1910 and Jones proved himself a top dog newsman and an able writer. So successful was he that in 1911 a delegation from Hazelton high-pressured him to move his paper up there and get in on the big money from land and coal claim advertising. The railway building activities would soon be leaving Kitselas behind, so he shipped his plant to Hazelton, resigned his operator's job, and went into publishing full-time, in competition with two papers already established there.

There was a Dominion election that year. One of the other papers was openly supporting the Laurier government and the other one was sitting on the fence. Jones, who was an American and did not savvy much about Canadian politics, took Hobson's choice and supported Clements, the Conservative candidate. Jones was such an able writer that his paper did a lot towards electing Mr. Clements.

However the government was in charge of land advertising and the government agent, to play safe, placed it with the paper that had sat on the fence. This tough break, after his good job on the election, discouraged Jones so he sold out and left the country.

In his early life he had gone through the Boxer Rebellion in China and the Spanish-American War in the Philippines. While in the Philippines he had seen quite a lot of fellows get rich with coconut plantations, so Jones headed back to the Philippines, bought himself a little island and started to grow coconuts. He expected to grow rich and retire in a few years. But by a strange quirk of nature—it was the first year it ever happened—no coconuts grew! In a letter I received from Enoch Jones, he said, "I went broke faster than I got into business."

He applied for a job from the American government as a wireless operator on an island, although he knew nothing about wireless, but he figured he could master it somehow. It didn't take long for the retiring operator to find out that Jones was hopeless at wireless, but he was so anxious to be replaced that he conveniently missed the boat and stayed on for two more weeks. By constant drilling he turned an old Morse man into a pretty good operator. Jones stayed on the new job for some time until he built up his depleted finances, then resigned and went back to San Francisco where he joined the Western Union and went back to his old love, the Morse Code.

Enoch Jones stayed with the Western Union the rest of his working days, handling some big jobs for the company until his retirement. He was the type to whom retirement spelt boredom, so he took on the job of secretary for the Veterans of the Spanish American War and is still doing a bang-up job at the age of 85.

While on holidays in 1955, my wife and I paid a visit to Mr. and Mrs. Jones in San Francisco. We had a wonderful visit talking about old days on the Skeena River. I found him still full of pep and going strong—although I missed the big black cigar, as he quit smoking many years ago. When I looked at my friend, I thought of how true it is that old soldiers never die. I remember him best when the *Inlander* pulled in to the river bank at Kitselas. He would be the first one up the gangplank with the inevitable black cigar, a big black moustache, and a pad and pencil in his hand, news hunting for the pages of the *Big Canyon Weekly*.

S.S. Inlander, *its foredeck stacked with cordwood.*
(25-A) / BCARS 40234

Christmas in Kitselas -- 1909 • Enoch R.L. Jones Sr.

"Indian Freighter" between Hazelton and the Omineca River, a distance of 200 miles. Each load weighed about 400 pounds. Winter 1911.
(26-A)

During the winter of 1908–1909, the Enoch R.L. Jones family lived in a house in Kitselas which the Dominion government leased from the Hudson's Bay Company for use as a telegraph office. The house had four rooms: the telegraph office, bedroom, living room and kitchen. The telegraph line ran from Port Simpson and Prince Rupert to Hazelton, where it connected with the line from Dawson to Ashcroft. I was the circuit manager. The only other buildings in town that winter were J.W. "Jack" Paterson's store, his hotel and a house at the edge of town occupied by Kitselas Indian chief Richard Cecil. The Charles Durham family lived on their farm across the river.

Early in the forenoon of January 3, 1909, Constable Charles Cullen came over from the hotel and asked, "Is it true that you have had an increase in your family last night?"

"Yes," I replied, "a girl baby born at two o'clock this morning."

"What are you going to feed her?" was his next question.

I told him, "My wife is taking over that responsibility."

Then he asked, "What are you going to feed your wife? I hope you have enough grub to see you through the winter."

Without interruption from me, he explained, "When I heard that you had an increase in your family I wondered how you were fixed in the way of food. I guess you haven't heard that Foley, Welch & Stewart's commissary department bought up all of Paterson's food this morning. The construction camps are facing a food shortage and the Company is buying the entire stock of every store up and down the river. Paterson wanted to keep some supplies for his regular customers but he was told point blank that he had to sell everything or nothing."

It seemed unbelievable. I hurried over to the store to ask Paterson about it. He was out, but his clerk, George Kerr, confirmed all that Cullen had told me.

"They've bought everything in sight except a couple of kegs of nails, several cans of paint, a bolt of table oilcloth and the rat poison," Kerr shouted.

As an afterthought he added, "Let's see. Seems to me Jack (Paterson) didn't take them to the little storehouse over there," pointing to a little 8 by 8-foot shed nearby. "Let's take a look."

Unlocking and opening the door we found inside, four 25-pound sacks of flour and 10 pounds each of lima and navy beans. That was all, and I bought the lot on sight. These he helped me to carry home.

Going into the telegraph office at once, I contacted Eddie Cox, manager of the Hazelton telegraph office. I told him about our serious food shortage and arranged with him to send me a case of evaporated milk and two slabs of bacon by first mail team coming downriver. "Barney" Mulvaney and "Dutch" Cline were running the mails that winter, using eight or ten "huskies" to the toboggan.

Cox purchased the milk and bacon for me at "Dick" Sargent's store and the next morning it was en route to Kitselas, loaded on a toboggan with the outgoing mail. I believe the case of the milk cost $3.50 and the bacon was 37 cents per pound. The total weight was around 65 pounds. Cox didn't know just what Barney would charge me for transporting it, but he was sure the charge would not be less than one cent per pound, per mile—a staggering cost which would have amounted to $65 for the 95-mile haul. When Barney delivered the load, in true Christian spirit, he charged me only $16.50.

Sim Dobbie, in his telegraph office at Copper River, heard the tale of woe I had related to Cox, and when I had finished, Sim broke in and remarked, "I guess that barrel of salmon bellies is going to come in very handy."

"What barrel of bellies?" I asked him.

He reminded me that when the steamer *Hazelton* tied up at Kitselas on its last trip downriver that fall, before the close of river transportation, he had arranged with me to have Captain Joe Bucey bring him two barrels from the warehouse. He had left those two barrels there when he transferred to Copper River. I had done as Sim requested, without noticing that there were three barrels in the warehouse, and I didn't know whether they were empty or not.

So it was thrilling news when he told me that morning that all three barrels contained salmon bellies he had packed himself that spring, and that he had left the third barrel in the warehouse for me.

What a change in hardly one hour! At 10 o'clock that morning I had been threatened with starvation and now within the hour I had flour, beans, a barrel of salmon bellies, and soon to be en route from Hazelton, a case of milk and two slabs of bacon.

There was more good news. The previous spring, Sim Dobbie had not known that a telegraph office was to be opened at Copper River, and that he would be transferred there. So, already having a pre-emption adjoining Dave Stewart's land, he had planted potatoes around the house I was now living in. Before I came to Kitselas, Dobbie had purchased two steers from the Hudson's Bay Company, and these animals had trampled around completely obliterating the stalks, so that there was no sign of any potatoes when I took over.

One afternoon I was digging a posthole and near the fence I uncovered a whopping big spud. On taking it out of the ground I noticed another, and then another. I showed one to Paterson, asking him if he knew anything about the mystery of potatoes in the ground—and there being no signs of a potato patch.

He understood at once, and explained to me. I went to the wire, called Copper River, and told Sim about my find. He answered, "If there's a crop of potatoes there—they're yours."

I took more than 500 pounds of potatoes out of that patch. I stored them in the root-house Sim had made. With this new addition to the larder, along with the provisions already listed, the Jones family's winter needs were fairly well provided for.

That same January 3, Elsie Durham (Mrs. F.M. Whitlow) came over to stay with us for a few weeks. In addition to being a help to Mrs. Jones, she was also the family cook, and I was the baker. Mrs. Whitlow, who has recently been writing her reminiscences for the *Daily News*, will remember that I specialized in Vienna Twists.

One bread-baking day, I held out some of the dough, and made "bloody" duff, as the British Marines called it (I served temporarily with them in China during 1900). But instead of cooking my duff in a muslin bag, as the Marines cook it, I made it into dumplings. They were perfect—big, and as light as a feather. Duff was a new dinner course to Elsie.

"How do you eat these? she asked. "Like dessert," I replied, "with milk and sugar."

After eating one, and part of another, Elsie suddenly stopped, took a deep breath, and then began to laugh, until she fairly shook with laughter.

"What's so funny?" I asked.

Checking her laughter, she said, "I have eaten two of these things and now I am so full I can't eat another bite, and I am just as hungry as before I came to the table." So no more "bloody" duff for Elsie.

Shortly before Christmas 1909, Sim Dobbie sent word that he wanted to meet me at Newtown (now, I believe, New Kitselas), midway between Durham's and Copper River. That was months after I had started publishing the *Big Canyon Weekly*, and was no longer connected with the telegraph office.

I met Sim at Newtown at the time he requested, and he handed me a gunnysack which contained a turkey.

"Here's your Christmas turkey," he said cheerily, adding, "Pat Burns and Company sent a load of turkeys up from Vancouver to be distributed to the construction camps for Christmas. I have been able to do a few favours for their commissary manager, Bobby Grant, and in return for these he gave me three turkeys. Two will be plenty for my family, so I've brought this one for you."

Glory be! A Christmas turkey in that far north where I never expected to see such a thing. I lost no time in hurrying home with that 12-pound bird.

I noticed a group of newcomers at the hotel and went over to try and pick up a few news items. Bobby Grant was with the group and upon seeing me asked, "Did you get the turkey I sent you?"

"Yes," I replied, "and it's a beauty—thank you."

"It certainly ought to be. I picked that one for you myself. P. Burns and Company never overlook a good man, particularly at Christmas time."

Now I thought this was strange. Sim Dobbie was 100 per cent, a square-shooter, and not one to tell anybody he had given a present when really it was a gift from somebody else. He wouldn't take credit himself if it were due to others.

"Well," I said to myself, "I must have misunderstood Sim."

When I returned home my wife greeted me with, "Now what in the world are you going to do with two turkeys for Christmas?"

She told me that a few minutes after I had left for the hotel, a strange man came to the door and handed her a turkey, saying, "Merry Christmas, Mrs. Jones, and compliments of the season, from P. Burns & Company."

That second turkey was no problem at all. We had Sim's turkey for Christmas dinner and for several dinners after Christmas. The second turkey was held over until January 3, our daughter's first birthday, when we combined New Year's dinner with her birthday dinner.

That was the "spirit" that reigned in the North during my time up there.

Bakery and lunch room, Kitselas.
(26-A)

Foley, Stewart & Welch riverboats at Prince Rupert. (4-B)

The Battle of Hardscrabble Rapids

◆ Wiggs O'Neill

In the year 1900 business conditions began to pick up on the Skeena River. The building of the Yukon Telegraph Line was getting under way from Quesnel north. It was to follow pretty much the route projected and built as far as the Kispiox River, just north of Hazelton, by the Collins Overland Telegraph Company, and abandoned with the successful completion of the Atlantic cable in 1867.

Advance parties were surveying the route to be followed north of Hazelton and south from Telegraph Creek, with parties working from both ends on the Skeena and Stikine rivers. Robert Cunningham, the mastermind of R. Cunningham & Son, had a big trading post and cannery operation at Port Essington—or "Spokeshoot" as it was generally called—at the mouth of the Skeena. He also operated a branch trading post at Hazelton, at the forks of the Skeena and Bulkley rivers. Robert—generally spoken of as "Old Diamond C," from the brand on his "Diamond C" salmon tins—saw business opportunities in the advance of the telegraph line construction and in the general atmosphere of the country. He decided to buy his own river steamer to save on the freight charges which he now paid to the Hudson's Bay Company who owned the *Caledonia*, the only steamboat on the river.

He was a wily customer, and he made overtures to Captain J.M. Bonser of the *Caledonia*, painting him a rosy picture of the advantages of aligning himself with his firm and leaving the Hudson's Bay Company. "Diamond C" sent him south to find and buy a river steamer. Captain Bonser had a hard time locating something suitable for the Skeena River, but he arrived back with a small steamer named the *Monte Cristo*. She only made one trip to Hazelton, then the government contractor for the telegraph line, who was having difficulties with transportation on the Stikine River, chartered the *Monte Cristo* to do all their work on the Stikine until the line was completed. The Stikine was a millpond compared to the Skeena, so this arrangement suited everyone and was very profitable to the Cunningham firm. "Old Diamond C" was always credited with having the luck of the devil.

Cunningham immediately sent his skipper to Victoria to build a new riverboat for him according to his own ideas of the size and power that were needed for the Skeena. The new steamer—*Hazelton*, built by the Alex Watson Shipyards—arrived in the spring of 1901, and soon the Hudson's Bay Company were scratching their heads. The *Caledonia* was hopelessly outclassed and something had to be done.

That winter the Bay built a brand new steamer. In the spring of 1902 the *Mount Royal* arrived on the river. She also proved a splendid boat for the Skeena.

These two new boats, the *Hazelton* and the *Mount Royal*, with their skippers, both first-class swift-water men, became bitter rivals on the river. To add a little zest to the situation these two skippers had no use for each other, mainly, I gathered, because of the old demon, jealousy.

Rivalry went on for some time, each boat trying to collar the trade and beat his rival out. Consequently it came to pass that these two skippers were running up and down the Skeena with loads of freight too light to make it pay, in an effort to satisfy their passengers with their speed to Hazelton. This went on all summer until there came a time on one trip when both boats were pretty close together. The *Mount Royal* caught up with the *Hazelton* steaming the Hardscrabble Rapids, near where the town of Usk was to spring up in later years.

It would appear that the skipper of the *Mount Royal* tried to crowd the *Hazelton* and pass her on the crest of the rapids to prove his boat's superiority. He crowded his rival so close that he forced him into shallow water and he had to ring a stop bell and drop back about half a length. Then he rang full speed ahead, caught the *Mount Royal* about midships and pushed her across the river to the opposite crest of Hardscrabble Rapids up on the bar. To add insult to injury he went on over the rapids and tooted his whistle at his adversary.

This battle between the rival skippers was the subject of conversation up and down the river for a long time. It was hashed and rehashed, some favouring one skipper and some the other.

In the late fall when the season closed down for the year and the famous battle was more or less forgotten, an item appeared in the *Victoria Colonist*—"Investigation is demanded in the Battle of Hardscrabble Rapids by the Merchants' Service Guild. Complaint made to the Minister of Marine." It would appear that the skipper of the *Mount Royal* was trying to have his rival's Master's Licence taken away for bad conduct.

Lawyers for both the swiftwater skippers got into the fray. They collected evidence that the complaining skipper, during the battle, had abandoned his steering wheel, left his pilot house and called for a gun, thus endangering the lives of his passengers, with no one in command. Also, he crowded his rival while negotiating dangerous rapids. The more the law boys got digging into the affair the more they became convinced that both of the hot-tempered captains were at fault, which could result in both of them losing their Master's Tickets.

The lawyers must have got together and put some of the fire out before it came to trial as nothing much came of it, but it was generally understood that both captains got a good warning.

That winter something happened that changed the course of any future hostility, which might have resulted in a tragic ending. A courier from the head office of the Hudson's Bay Company in Victoria arrived at Spokeshoot and went into conference with Cunningham.

He pointed out the folly of running their boats up and down the river with part cargoes and both losing money, which he termed the height of folly and poor management. The result of the conference was that the Hudson's Bay Company agreed to pay Cunningham $2,500 a year to keep the *Hazelton* on the ways and not operate her. They also wound up with an option to purchase the *Hazelton* at a set price in a given period of time and during that period they would haul Cunningham's freight to his Hazelton store free of charge.

Later on, the Hudson's Bay exercised their option and purchased the *Hazelton*. She had a long and honourable career, and flew HBC at her masthead to the end of her days.

This arrangement did one of the skippers out of a job. Bonser left the Skeena and went to the Upper Fraser River to make steamboat history. This was probably a good thing as it kept the two hotheads apart and avoided any further battles between them. However he returned to the Skeena in 1911 as master of the *Inlander* and wound up his career on her in 1912, the last boat and the last skipper to ply the waters of the old Skeena.

The Battle of Hardscrabble Rapids, fought under the shadows of the town of Usk, before the days of Ma Cameron and her hotel, is still remembered by a few old timers on the river. Both of these impetuous swift-water men have long since gone over the Great Divide. Knowing them both so well, I would not be surprised if in the Great Beyond they are looking around to see if they can find a new river to

Captain Bonser briefly captained the Monte Cristo *(left) before taking command of the* Hazelton.
(25-A) / BCARS 38221

match the old Skeena, where it took prowess and expert riverboating to do the job.

INVESTIGATION IS DEMANDED
The Serious Charges Preferred against Capt. Bonser referred to Minister of Marine

The Merchants Service Guild of Canada, which includes the foremost shipmasters of British Columbia ports, is destined to make itself an important factor in pressing claims of its members and marine men generally upon the attention of the authorities. It has recently systematized and forwarded to the Minister of Marine for investigation a complaint which on its face appears almost too sensational to be within the pale of the believable. And yet members and officers of the Guild assert that evidence of direct character has been transmitted with the request for inquiry, which permits of no other course than thorough and searching investigation, and adequate punishment in the event of the charge being sustained.

In the current issue of the Guild *Gazette*, published in this city, which is the official organ of the shipmasters association, the matter of complaint is referred to in very specific terms. The investigation is sought with respect to the action of one Capt. Bonser, late master of the steamer *Hazelton*, operated on the Skeena River, whom Capt. Johnson, of the rival steamer *Mount Royal* charges with having deliberately, and with malice, run his vessel into the *Mount Royal*, with the purpose of injuring the latter craft. Capt. Johnson claims that he is able to establish by reputable witnesses:

1. That Bonser threatened hostilities before the act complained of;
2. That Bonser boasted of his achievements after the act;
3. That Bonser purposely ran out of his course to ram the *Mount Royal*;
4. That Bonser rammed the steamer *Ramona* on the Fraser River in the same wanton manner;
5. That he suggested to a member of the crew the tampering with an aid to navigation so as to bring to grief a rival boat.

The Guild has asked that a commission be appointed to examine into the entire matter; and if these charges be sustained, or any of them, that Bonser's certificate be canceled.

Victoria Daily Colonist
May 10, 1905.

SERIOUS CHARGES AGAINST MARINER
Dominion Government Instructs Capt. Gaudin to Hold Investigation of Accusations
Capt. Bonser Accused of Trying to Ram Steamer

As an example of governmental promptitude, it is doubtful if any official action has yet been recorded which takes precedence of that following the protest to Ottawa of the Merchants Service Guild ... (see charges as laid down in May 10 account).

As may well be imagined, the proof of such charges as these would properly result in criminal prosecutions—indeed the wonder is that the police, with the facts so prominently before them, have not long since taken action—but in the first place the Guild, in its communication to Ottawa, asked that a commission be appointed to examine into the entire matter, and if the charges, or any one of them were sustained, that Bonser's certificate as a shipmaster be cancelled.

The petition to the Minister of Marine went forward early in this present month—about the 8th or 9th. Action thereupon must have been practically immediate, for on the Friday, the Secretary of the Merchant Service Guild, Mr. J.J. Martin, received a reply from the Minister, Hon. Raymond Prefontaine, to the effect that an immediate and thorough enquiry had been ordered as suggested, instructions in this regard having been forwarded to Captain James Gaudin, the resident agent, who is now engaged in making the necessary arrangements.

Captain Gaudin has not yet determined when the investigation will be held, though he is endeavouring to bring on the enquiry as soon as possible. It is quite probable that the investigation will be held at this port, although this has not yet been determined. Captain Gaudin is now in communication with the parties connected with the matter, those making the charges and the accused captain, and will arrange the meeting to suit the convenience of those interested.

Victoria Daily Colonist
May 28, 1905.

*The Union
steamship* Camosun
and the S.S. Port
Simpson *at Prince
Rupert.*
(25-A) / BCARS 1052

My Wild-Indian Summer

✦ M. Duncan

The *Camosun* would sail on May 8th. If I waited longer, the Skeena would be at high water, with no further navigation for a month or six weeks. It was a dilemma, for the earthquake had put all my plans at sixes and sevens. But a desperate "now or never" feeling came over me, and I replied to the ticket agent, "I'll go! You can make out my coupon."

A few hours later I was speeding toward the Canadian line.

Vancouver belied its rainy reputation; I found it warm and dusty, a fire in North Vancouver blurring the landscape with a smoky haze. I reached my destination with little ado, counting upon a night's rest before the departure of my steamer. Alas! no. My hostess phoned; then—"Miss Duncan, that boat sails tonight at midnight."

My ticket secured, we repaired to the CPR station to await my belated trunk. An imposing structure, this station, a great credit to plucky Vancouver! Victoria placidly folds her hands, well-content with present population. Peace to her smiling shores! She holds a warm spot in my memory. But in Vancouver breathes the Spirit of the West, brave, bright and free!

It was after ten when I walked aboard the *Camosun*. Various miners and "prospectors" were stretched on the benches, too provident, or improvident, to secure staterooms. No female-kind were visible, but in the ladies' cabin I found indications thereof, and learned that I was to have at least one companion. With four berths, this was no hardship; I promptly appropriated a lower one, ascertained that it was a case of "feet forward," and proceeded to make myself comfortable. When you are almost the only lady aboard, comfort is easily attained, for the men treat you like a queen. Such a scampering for extra overcoats when you appear on deck! Such coaxing to partake of extra little suppers! Such solicitude—bless them!—in behalf of your devoted trunk!

The first to appear was the steward, pleading with me to accept tea and sandwiches. At first I declined, but he was equal to David Copperfield's waiter, so I succumbed.

My trunk was late again. Repeatedly came the purser and steward, to ask "what it looked like." Finally the latter appeared, to beamingly inform me it was safe aboard. So I could lie down, with mind at rest. Half an hour more; the "throb throb" had begun, and I could see Vancouver lights receding.

Those next three days! The thought of them makes me homesick for the *Camosun* and the rainbow-land—the land of magic and of fairy gold. The earth-gold of the miners may turn to dross; but the glowing splendour of those enchanted fjords in that Norway of the West! Fadeless, ever-brightening, as the vision of the seven circles of Paradise!

The *Camosun* was ideally in keeping with the spirit of that region. So deliciously "boat-ey," all free-and-easy aboard. The passengers were of various types—surveyors, prospectors, and so on. My room-mate was a little Newfoundlander, shy as a rabbit, going to join her husband at some cannery or lumber camp. Thirteen years of the West had not "rubbed off" her terror of mere "people"; on that first morning, she so shrank from facing the breakfast crowd, that I actually had to take her hand and lead her downstairs like a child. We ladies were grouped at the same table—four of us—a bright little mother, with baby and nurse, going to join Papa, up the coast—and the two of us already introduced. The others at our table were pleasant courteous gentlemen. These men of the great Northwest have their own way of appreciating a woman; to them she is, not an ornamental target for flattery and compliments, but a rational being, to be taken seriously, conversed with naturally, her opinions weighed and respected, agreed with or not as may be. Yet this give-and-take matter-of-factness is combined with a kindness equal to "old world chivalry." Wherefore, commend me to the gentlemen of the Canadian West!

I was talking with one from Ketchikan, Alaska, describing my room-mate's horror of appearing at meals. "Rather hard on us men!" he remarked dryly. "The fact is," he continued, "so many women think of men as being about ten times worse than they really are. Now take this boat. If there were a young girl on board, alone, and sick or in any trouble, there isn't a man of them but would do anything he possibly could, to help her."

This may not always be true, but I do believe it was true of most of our *Camosun* passengers. As to the one now speaking, I soon discovered two things. First, he was an American. Second, he was a married American. For all who were neither American nor yet married, he seemed to feel sincerest pity; for the former deficiency, indeed, the pity was mingled with contempt—which failed to endear him to some of the Britishers on board.

Midnight had seemed a strange hour for departure; the reason, it appeared, was to make Seymour Narrows at low tide. I had ensconced myself nicely in a steamer-chair on the stern deck, with maps and circulars—"enough to go to Europe with," declared the married American. This gentleman was talking with a missionary from Alert Bay. From their calling my attention to some point of interest, we drifted into general chat—the rough voyage of the *Amur*, to the stricken California city—my destination on the Skeena, and other matters. Referring to the Indians on board, I complained that they were too civilized to be interesting.

"Ah, you'll have to blame this gentleman," said the American. "That's his work."

"What! don't you believe in civilizing them?" inquired he of Alert Bay.

"Well, it does make them seem neither fish nor fowl."

I fear my heresy shocked him. The question is a large one, but the harm done to the Indian by "civilization" is not usually to be laid at the door of the missionary.

Sunrise had greeted us in a wide stretch of water, with a long line of snowy Alps to our left. Has no poet yet found the Gulf of Georgia? Or does poetry belong with "historic associations"—thus doubly a thing of the past?

"You'll want to come forward to the upper deck very soon now," said the American. "We shall be in the only really dangerous part of this trip—Seymour Narrows."

A recent writer describes his adventures in a canoe, at this place. For my part, I have no desire for such an experience. The water has the appearance of suction, and of being swollen rather than rough. The *Camosun* put on her utmost steam-power, yet progress was slow; the wind rushing down the Pass, nearly tore my soul from body, as it shot a south-bound boat down the current with the speed of an arrow.

Now the mountains draw closer around us; by noon we hover at Eden's Gate. A mirror, is that, below us? The word conveys but the faintest idea. "Afloat in translucent space, rather than water," says the above-mentioned writer (Roger Pocok, author of *Following the Frontier*). Look down into opalescent, dark green depths—the very surface is invisible; you see but the flashing diamonds flung from the vessel's prow. The *Camosun* might indeed seem a bird soaring home to her mountain.

Surrounding, enfolding us, huge crags, mantled with forest and crowned with snow.

In the afternoon, we reached Alert Bay, famed for its totem poles. Here we deposited our missionary, in exchange for a young lady bound for Namu.

My little Newfoundlander succumbed to a wave of timidity and feebly declared her preference for dinnerless solitude rather than appearing below. Inwardly marveling, I flew to the friendly steward, announcing that the lady did not "feel like coming down; couldn't he send her some dinner?"—so at all events the poor little thing did not sup on starvation. The next evening brought us to Bella Coola, where her husband met her. ("Beaming all over! See what it is to be married!" enthused the American).

Queen Charlotte Sound is the only uncomfortable part of the journey, and as we passed it after bedtime anyway, it mattered the less. I had stayed on deck rather late, unwilling to admit seasickness.

Next morning I lay in my berth too late to see Bella Bella, which really was a loss, if the place be so doubly beautiful as the name would imply. It is said to be the most modern and progressive Indian village on the British Columbia coast.

Mentioning to the American my recent occupation as teacher in a boarding-school, I was met with a sly twinkle, and the quizzical reply: "How you all must have loved each other, after a little while!"

This was too much for my gravity! After all though, we teachers weren't such bad friends, "considering." Perhaps it was a case of companions in misery.

Agreeing or disagreeing, the time whiled away—sometimes on authors; Ralph Connor, Owen Wister, Jack London, Fra Elbertus, and others who write of the life of today.

Sunset on the last evening, as we lay anchored at Claxton, awaiting the tide. A landscape clear-cut, steely-blue, sharply outlined as you see only in the far North. We were only a few hours distant from Ketchikan.

"But I've got to go to Portland Canal first," mourned the American, whose homesickness seemed to increase as the distance waned. "Oh! I'll get out and walk home. Can't wait to get hold of those kids. Going up the Skeena, you said? to Hazelton Hospital. You'll be needing a hospital," he chuckled, "by the time you get there."

It was at Claxton I drew my first whiff of the pungent fragrance of an Indian village; here also that I had my first view of the husky-dog, or Mahlmoot, the packhorse of the snow-trail. Half dog, half wolf, he eyes you in grim silence. Never a bark from those horrid jaws; but the gleaming fangs are there, and you venture no compliments of word or touch.

Midnight brought us to Port Essington, formerly known as "Spokeshute."

Possibly the earthquake had put me in an optimistic mood toward all else, for not even Essington seemed as black as it had been painted. What matter if all the streets were wharves or the extensions of them? Needs must, for solid ground is not to be had. The mountains rise well-nigh perpendicular, leaving a border of—well, bog! there is no polite name. But for the board roads, the inhabitants would be in the Slough of Despond, with no Hopeful to pull them out. Needless to remark, horses and vehicles are conspicuous for their absence. Wheelbarrows are muchly in demand, and they shake the wooden boulevards until I shuddered with renewed "quake" sensations.

But the place boasts two hotels, a church, several stores, and—what place does not?—its share of pleasant, kindly folk. Everybody is friendly and wants to "shake." You count for something in this new world; you are part of The One Event, the arrival of the steamer!

The *Camosun* already seemed as an old friend and I really felt homesick at leaving her, but the *Mount Royal* lay alongside, and I hopped over the rail, feeling that at last the final stage of my journey was reached. But alas! I had yet to learn the Skeena River. "High water" was coming on apace, though for the present all seemed placid.

And now the *Camosun* bade us farewell, and steamed away for Aberdeen. The men stood out on deck, waving their caps, while "Auld Lang Syne" echoed over the gray waters.

The *Mount Royal* began her upward pull late in the afternoon; or late it looked, for we had what Scottie called a "wicked sky." Gazing aloft into the snowy chasms; "I'd like to be up there," he declared, "hunting a bear!" I could not appreciate the wish. Steaming between those dark and gloomy mountains, veiled in mist, cleft with glaciers, seemed like passing into the sternest of Dore's Dantean visions. "Ye who enter here, leave hope behind!" Was I indeed going to the ends of the earth? Black as the Stygian stream, this wild, wide, rushing torrent! Heaped into apparent ridges and valleys, it seemed like several rivers in one. Falling eight hundred feet in one hundred and eighty miles from the Forks to the coast, just midway cutting through a dangerous canyon, the Skeena merits all that is told of its terrors. Until recent years, indeed, this river was not considered navigable by steam; those who in former days braved its perils, went the entire distance by canoe.

And this was the beginning of the spring flood. How the boat "jiggled"! I nearly bit pieces out of my teacup, whenever I tried to drink the contents thereof.

The second evening, we tied up at Lorne Creek. The others walked up to the mine, but, being tired, I remained behind. As I sat alone, the purser approached, accompanied by a pathetic figure—"One of our good old placer miners" was the introduction. Learning that a lady from near San Francisco was on board, he had come —like grasping at a straw, I suppose—to ask me how possibly to learn aught of his daughter and brother, from whom he had heard nothing since the disaster. The street he mentioned was, I knew, in a locality completely wiped out, with much loss of life. I gave what encouragement I could, saying how difficult it was to manage the mails, for the present, or even get telegrams through.

"But it's been three weeks now," he urged piteously. "It's just awful! All this distance and I can't hear a word! And my wife—she ain't right in 'Frisco, so I ought to hear from her."

Later in the summer, I was glad to learn from another miner that "Mr. J. heard from his folks and they were all right—yes, of course they lost everything, but none of 'em hurt."

Life, and to be unhurt—that was all that counted in those first days.

Threading Kitselas Canyon is the crucial point of a voyage on the Skeena. Lying just halfway between Hazelton and the coast, it falls, I was told, seventeen feet in its three-quarters of a mile. There are three narrow channels, between islands of jagged rock, while on one side rises sheer from the water a mountain-side three thousand feet high. As at Seymour Narrows, the waters are deep and treacherous, with many a whirlpool. I hardly realized, at the time, the perilous nature of the passage. Since then, the canyon has claimed its awful toll, and brave souls have gone down in its sullen flood; the staunch *Mount Royal* has fought her last fight with the dark Skeena, her river of death.

Proceeding upstream, the mountains recede somewhat from the banks, giving a rather milder aspect to the scenery. There is more sunshine, too, as you go further inland.

We passed Kitmun-gah, a village "presided over" by a Church of England missionary. Kitzegucla, under the auspices of the Methodists, makes up the "Amen corner" in totem poles.

These Indian names have their etymology. "Kit," the first syllable, signifies "The people"; the rest of the word is supposed to describe the particular people in question. For instance: "Kitselas"—the people who live where the water is rapid and a whirlpool; "Kitmun-gah"—the people who live where many rabbits are; "Kitanmauksh" (Hazelton)—the people who live at the place where they fish with nets.

As for orthography, that is purely according to "the taste and fancy of the speller, my lord." I have given a spelling to follow the sound as nearly as possible. These tribes have no written language, the nearest to it being a set of symbols, invented for convenience sake by one of the Catholic missions.

Thus, learning to write is an accomplishment that fills the Indian with pride. Whereof a notable example is to be found in the person of "I Paul of Hazelton." This worthy, being a convert to the Church of England, baptized "Paul," and a most devoted reader of the New Testament, enjoys especially the style of the Pauline epistles; so much so indeed, that the temptation to imitate has become irresistible. He loses no occasion to pen a message, even when a verbal one would suit the purpose better. If he calls to see you on business, he will smilingly hand you his part of the conversation, on paper —with the invariable preface. At the time of King Edward's coronation, it was the heart's wish of this loyal subject to telegraph his congratulations. The message, of course, began: "I Paul, of Hazelton," etc., and all went sweetly as a summer's day, until he was gently informed of the extreme unlikelihood that His Majesty would personally foot the bill of a "wire" from Hazelton to London. Poor "I Paul"! The will had to go for the deed.

On another occasion, desirous of making some purchases on credit, he was vouched for in writing, by the minister. Not long after, his wife wished to go shopping; I Paul reasoned that if a few written lines would secure the goods, why, what could be simpler? Therefore, the good dame departed, armed with a modern "Pauline"—but alas! returned empty-handed. To this day, I Paul never has been able to make out why his chirography would not work the same charm as the minister's.

Unacquainted as yet with "I Paul," and other characters of the wilderness, I lay in my berth for a Sunday siesta. "Only two hours longer," I reflected, and was sinking into a comfortable half-dream, when:

"Bump! Crash!! Bang!!!"

Then stillness. Silence. The boat had stopped. I looked out the window. Had we struck a rock, or was it a new kind of earthquake? a riverquake, maybe? The steamer did not seem to be settling, nor taking in water, and the bow remained in position. Just ahead of us lay McIntosh Bar. Yet it was evident that we were slowly but surely drifting downstream. But as no one seemed to be excited, I decided not to be the first, and dressed myself quietly. Had just closed my suitcase, when the captain's wife came to the door and explained the trouble. The engine was broken; one of the cylinders had exploded, and we were helpless unless we could tie up to the bank. Otherwise we must take to canoes and let the poor *Mount Royal* go to her fate.

We stood watching the efforts of the crew; several Indians, also, were out in a canoe, struggling with the line. All worked almost without directions, swift and skillful, as if it were a thing of every day. Once we were fastened—no! the weight of the steamer, swept by that terrible current, came against the cable and snapped it like a thread. Things began to look ugly. Once again the attempt was made, this time with success. We were drawn out of midstream and moored in safety. Meantime, we had drifted five miles down; but for the heaviest anchors, retarding our progress, and holding the boat in position, we might have gone farther and fared worse.

Time now to hunt up damages, so we went below on a tour of inspection. We found the cylinder a minus quantity, the stove smashed to flinders, the wall behind it burst out, and last but far from least, the two cooks in a state of complete disrepair—scalded with steam, bruised, their clothing in shreds. Indeed, they had barely missed being blown to atoms, for the cylinder had flown directly between them as it crashed into the stove.

For a touch of the ludicrous, a tin pail had been fired out the window, and floated off merrily down the Skeena. How far did it go, I wonder?

The captain sent up Indians in a canoe, to bring the doctor from Hazelton. The magic "written word" accompanied them, else they would have had us all in various stages of dismemberment. Meantime, the crew set to work, and improvised a stove of rocks on the bank. We expected to be thankful for bread and butter and coffee, but accident is the mother of enterprise, and the next two meals compared more than favourably with any we had enjoyed on the way.

Arriving at half-past nine, the doctor found the patients in a much better condition than expected—not even candidates for the hospital. Frightened out of their wits, however, they lost no time after reaching the coast, but bade their last farewells to the *Mount Royal.*

The following morning, I resumed my journey in a canoe with the doctor and two or three Indians. Somehow my umbrella got smashed. We blamed the explosion—and actually secured damages!

The other passengers prepared to "foot it" for the remaining ten miles to Hazelton. Either out of benevolence to me, or by way of getting their things "toted" for them, they piled my canoe with their overcoats for my throne, until I declared that Cleopatra in her barge could not hold a candle to me. I was assured that there was no danger, so long as I sat quite still, which advice I obeyed so rigidly, that on reaching Hazelton I was almost past the power of purely personal navigation. The Indian canoe had made me unfit to paddle my own.

All the luggage and freight were dumped on the bank, in charge of an Indian boy, to await a larger canoe. The *Mount Royal* began gingerly to test her powers, with half an engine, for during the night the river had risen nine inches, and no time was to be lost in reaching the coast. How they accomplished the canyon is a mystery, but they did so, and safely reached Port Simpson, where all damages were repaired.

We set forth, quite theatrically. Out in midstream, front, the *Mount Royal* wheezingly trying her paces—paddling up the bank, right, a canoe containing two or three men, and one small woman muffled to the teeth—below us, left, another canoe, piled with Indians—above us, behind the wings (i.e. birch trees), a party of walkers, one in a brimstone-coloured mackintosh that ever and anon flashed vividly through the green curtain like Mephisto, about to appear.

Our bark was a hollow log, scooped to the thickness of perhaps less than two inches. Cedar or cottonwood, I was told, furnished material for these canoes, birch being fatally frail for the Skeena. They tried it once, and seven men went down.

Cheering, as a starter!

It was towing, poling, paddling, baling. On the steamer I had felt no discomfort, but now I often covered my face to shut out the sight of the dizzying current on a level with my eyes. It seemed to be the banks moving instead of the water, and the illusion made one's head swim.

Repeatedly we were driven across stream in search of gentler waters, thus losing considerable time, so that our journey consumed five hours in all. Once we stuck on a bar in mid-stream, often we headed against rapids that well-nigh defied the united strength of four men, the canoe straining as if ready to burst asunder.

One stop we made, at the home of a young woman, who since her father's death, lives alone on the shores of the rushing Skeena. Sometimes actual residence is necessary to make good one's title; so Bessie keeps her "lone vigil"—respected by all—molested by none, save the wolves she has trapped at her very door in the long winter nights. (N.B. It's only chickens they are after, but you needn't mention it, lest you spoil the effect.)

Clouds and mist floated above us and around, veiling the sight of great Hazelton Mountain. Now and again the veil half melted, showing faint glimpses of snow-crags colossal, peering down from mid-heaven.

"Prepare for the ordeal," remarked the doctor; "you are the first woman who has ever had this adventure, and I expect the whole of Hazelton to be lined up to witness your landing."

But the doctor was mistaken—owing, perhaps, to the uncertain hour of our arrival. At the Forks, our tow-man skipped 'cross country, his services no longer needed.

Here the raging Bulkley tears down to unite with the waves of the Skeena. For some distance below, the two streams still maintain separate existences, as shown by the colouring.

Hazelton village, chief "town" on the river, lies just above the Forks. Twenty years ago, the Hudson's Bay Company was the only sign of white life. In those days the Indian was not the subdued creature of today, and tribe preyed on tribe. The white man venturing in, bore his life in his hand.

"Missions" have tamed the child of the wilderness. Nowadays he takes to them more or less kindly. Departed forever, the day of his power; his own life fades in the mist of the past. Missions mitigate the sorrows forced upon him by the pressure of civilization. And of all mission-work, not the least in importance—perhaps greatest of all—is the hospital work.

After lunching sociably with the ladies of the Hudson's Bay Company, a wagon ride of a mile up the hill, brought me to my long-sought goal.

The Pheasant *on the Skeena
River, 1906.*
(25-A) / BCARS 3586

Last Trip of the *S.S. Pheasant*, 1906

◆ Walter Warner

We started from Port Essington about the middle of April and if we had returned to Essington we would have set the record for the longest season on the river but we did not. This was the year of the San Francisco earthquake.

Now this boat was small potatoes compared to the Hudson's Bay Company riverboat which was its competition. The Indians asked some white man what HBC stood for and he told them "hunger before credit," but I found them a good outfit to work for. I was with them on the Stikine and Skeena Rivers, dolled up in blue suit with gold braid. Some class—I was only Chief Steward!

S.S. Pheasant cost about $10,000 to build compared to the $50,000 to $75,000 cost of the *Mount Royal*. She had everything including Japanese waiters, who were smart, clean, neat and knew their work.

We landed at Tom Thornhill's, just below the present Skeena River Bridge. George Little came over in a canoe, wanting to know what we would charge him to take a bunch of lumber across the river and up the slough. I told him to go up and see Captain Bonser, so he did. The captain asked him who brought the lumber up; George told him the Hudson's Bay Company. Then why did they not take it across and land it where he wanted it? Captain liked to get something on George, who told him they would not do it. I did not blame them because if they got stuck and had trouble they would have a time with the insurance. Anyhow, Captain told him he would take it. We got the deckhands to load it on the bow, so that if she did stick she could back out of it. We charged him ten dollars, and George was tickled to death to get it done. Ours was a much smaller boat than the Hudson's Bay Company's.

We finished the season, and had a busy time. Being small, we could pack only 35 to 40 tons. We had to make two trips to keep up with the others. The river being just right, low and no ice, we were chartered to the government to work on the river blowing up the rocks in the channel. The government engineer, C.G. Wosfold, picked up a crew in Port Essington. We made one trip to Hazelton to mark the rocks to be removed.

I had some freight bills to collect along the way, which had been left with the missionaries to collect from the Indians. I left the boat at Hazelton and walked up to Kispiox, where an Indian came over to fetch me across the river. I returned to Hazelton, bought a dugout with lots of beam that looked like a good sea boat, and paddled down to where the *Pheasant* lay just above Kitseguecla.

Here there were three big boulders—just enough room to get through, no more. They decided to leave them because at the steamboat stage of water they did not present a problem, so they started to go downriver and go between these rocks. Something went wrong and the *Pheasant* hung up on one rock and jackknifed over another. Then the force of the river—and it was swift at Red Rock Rapids—caused it to jackknife the other way. The ship started to fill and drift downriver. Windows were broken and everything turned upside down—what a mess!

We had put a heater in the Ladies' Salon for the crew to dry their clothes. It upset and in a few minutes we would have had the choice of being drowned or being burned. If you had ever seen one of these boats being built you would know how fast it would burn. The hull is strongly built with natural crooks and well timbered. But the house work is just gingerbread and built of the lightest dry cedar. Lots of canvas and paint—it would go up like a balloon.

I grabbed a bucket and put the fire out. The Captain swore at me: Didn't I know the boat was insured against fire but not against wreck!

Deckhands jumped ashore, made fast some lines and that was that. We were not far from the village, just above where the railroad crosses.

We were busy for awhile piling everything out on the rocks. We were invited to the village in the evening. There was a table set for us in one of those big Indian houses with a dirt floor and a hole in the roof for the smoke to go out. The rest all sat around the big log fire.

After supper the entertainment started—old-fashioned Indian dances. One old lady had a frame filled with feathers and danced. Every time she stomped a bunch of feathers flew out. The cleverest turn I saw was done by an Indian named Haldene—a sleight-of-hand act—a real good turn. We all enjoyed the evening very much.

I bought a canoe that could carry about a ton, paid $120 for it, for the crew to go downriver to Port Essington. Next day I got them loaded, with Walter Wright as pilot. Dave Blainey, the second engineer, stayed with me and we went down in the dugout canoe. Our load included a lot of scotch, rye and brandy. As the Indian reserve was handy, we had to take the liquor with us, but we could not make room for a case of ale splits so I left it in care of the missionary at the village and I have not seen or heard of it since.

Dave and I were ready to go. I steered and he rowed. Just a minute or so after we got out into the swift water I felt her suck down until there was only about an inch of freeboard. I knew that would not do. We had too much of a load. I steered the canoe into the eddy and threw all that good booze up against a boulder and smashed it (but the worst of it was, along came Prohibition!). All I kept was a bottle of Hennessey's brandy in case we got wet.

Now we were lighter and could travel. Just ahead a few miles was Sheep's Head Rapids. That was bad enough on a steamboat, but if you really want a thrill just try it in a small dugout. We could not pick out a channel so we had to take a chance. We grazed one large rock, but luckily it was round and smooth. Anyhow, we shot the Kitselas Canyon and got down to Port Essington without further mishap. I never did find out what became of the wreck until last Sunday. I was up to the hospital and Carl Pohle was in. He told me he bought the boiler from the Indians, fixed it up and ran a sawmill with it, about 3 miles north. It has done good service.

I went down to New Westminster and as I was purser of the boat, the government paid me and I paid off the help. I took their receipts—captain, engineer and second engineer—and a barrel of beer I borrowed from Mrs. Kirby at Port Essington. It's lucky I did, because there were some lawyers in the Company and if the government had paid them, the crew would have had to whistle for their money. So all is well that ends well.

The Wreck of the *Mount Royal*

♦ Ed Kenney

Although much has been written about the wreck of the *Mount Royal*, little has been written about the ship herself. The *Mount Royal* was named after a Governor-General whose full title was "Lord Strathcona and Mount Royal."

She was built in Victoria at the shipyard of Alexander Watson, a Scot who had the reputation of always putting a little-something-more into the ships he built. The *Mount Royal* was built for the Hudson's Bay Company. The Company desired a ship especially designed for the turbulent Skeena River, to skim the cream of the passenger trade away from Cunningham's *S.S. Hazelton*, yet still carry everyday cargoes of furs, gold, livestock and mining equipment.

The Victoria *Daily Colonist* described the *Mount Royal* as "the best of her type on the Coast." She was to be the Queen of the Skeena, built of Douglas-fir and Eastern oak, to carry her passengers in comfort and safety.

Being designed for the Skeena, she had a moulded depth (from her main deck to her keelson) of only five feet, and unloaded drew only 18 inches of water. She was 138 feet long with a beam of 28 feet—narrow enough to navigate the treacherous channnels of the Skeena and large enough to house powerful engines which, with 200 pounds pressure coursing through her 16x72-inch cylinders, turned the paddle shaft 37 times a minute, producing a speed of 12 knots with which to buck the muddy Skeena.

The *Mount Royal* was supposed to be launched April 8, but due to a low tide the launching was postponed to the next day when, at 3:45 p.m., Miss Thelma Thompson christened the ship. The *Mount Royal* began to slide slowly down the ways—then stopped. Two hours later

Many versions of the wreck of the Mount Royal *are to be found. Several are included here, to present this tragic happening from different viewpoints.*

the workmen got her moving again and into the water—but she was moving too slowly to steer and ran up on the bank where she remained for two days. Superstitious sailors would say this launching was an ill omen foreshadowing the fate of the *Mount Royal*.

Although her end was tragic, the *Mount Royal*'s life was filled with distinction. In 1904 she carried President Hayes of the Grand Trunk Pacific and his party for eight days of sight-seeing along the coast and inlets. She raced with the SS *Hazelton*—sometimes winning, sometimes losing—in the contest to be first up or down the river. One such race ended up in the marine court at Victoria. For five years, the *Mount Royal* carried passengers and supplies from the sea to the hinterland; grizzled prospectors, hopeful settlers, silent Indians, Englishmen, Irishmen, Scots, Swedes, Japanese, Chinese—all walked her decks. Furs, flour, gold, whiskey, horses and mining equipment filled her hold. Her whistle was heard at places such as Bateman's Landing, Eby's Landing, the Big Canyon, Meanskinisht—dropping supplies and news, denuding riverbanks of trees to feed her voracious boilers.

At night, tied to shore to avoid sandbars and driftwood, the poker games got underway and money passed across the tables in the *Mount Royal*'s plush saloon. On one such occasion, the evening's entertainment was interrupted by a blood-curdling scream from the Chinese bull-cook, who later discovered the apparition he had seen was not one of his ancestors but a bear cub which had crawled into the flour barrel.

Such was life aboard the *Mount Royal* before her rendezvous with Fate at Kitselas at 3:04 p.m., July 6th, 1907.

"Lining" a riverboat through the Devil's Elbow.
(18-A)

The End of a Fine Riverboat

◆ Mrs. E.M. Whitlow

The really big thrill of the year was the coming of the first steamer in the spring. Although the arrival of every steamer was an event for which everyone dressed up in their best clothes and went down to the landing stage, the first boat was the really big occasion. It was nice to see new faces, hear new voices giving the latest news, to get long-awaited parcels of new and badly needed clothing and shoes. Also there were letters, papers, magazines and fresh food. It was a long and impatient wait sometimes, because though one might hear the steamer whistle in the morning, it might be late afternoon before the boat appeared in view from the landing. In low stages of water they often had great difficulty in getting over bars and shallow places.

The *Hazelton*, belonging to Robert Cunningham of Port Essington, and under the command of Captain Bonser, and the *Mount Royal*, belonging to the Hudson's Bay Company with Captain S.B. Johnson commanding, were the two boats operating in those days. The *Mount Royal* was the larger and finer of the two.

In the early afternoon of July 6, 1907, while coming down through the Kitselas Canyon, at about a two-foot level of water on the gauge—this was fairly high but not considered dangerous—the *Mount Royal* was caught by a gust of wind which swept it across the channel, between the south bank and Ringbolt Island. The boat started to turn over and Captain Johnson hurriedly got his passengers, including his wife and two other women, off the bow of the boat and onto the Island. The purser and steward, in trying to save valuables from the boat, were drowned, along with four other members of the crew when the boat broke in two parts, as it completed its capsize. Five members of the crew managed to save their lives by climbing up on the outside of the boat as it went over.

Meanwhile the Durham children were at the mouth of the Canyon, waiting for the arrival of the boat. They heard it whistle as usual, then again, but this time a long, long, eerie, mournful whistling that caused them to look at each other with wonder and premonition. The whistling was soon followed by a great shouting, and everybody including the men who were about the hotel and the store, came running to the river bank, from which could be seen bottom-up the hull of the boat, drifting from the mouth of the canyon. It stranded on the Kitselas side of a gravel bar, in the middle of the river, which widens out to quite a width, after the rushing waters escape from the narrow passage of the canyon. Durham, at once, with one of the other fellows about, took his skiff that was tied up at a sandbar two or three hundred feet further up the bank from the steamboat landing place, rowed over to the wreck and brought these men over to Kitselas.

While on the rescue trip, a man who had somehow jumped onto the mainland from the stern of the *Mount Royal* as it lay across the channel came running into Kitselas with the story of what had happened, and of the people stranded on the island. Durham, taking two whom he knew to be first-class canoe men familiar with the canyon, Olalie Johnson and Walter Washburn (now of Kitwanga) with him, got his canoe from his own landing place on the other side of the river, and with these men he worked his way up the canyon to the island where the refugees were stranded.

They took them off the island to the north shore in several trips. The people had to climb the steep canyon bank and follow the telegraph line trail to Durham's Ranch, where Mrs. Durham consoled them with tea and coffee whilst they waited to be taken over to the Kitselas side of the river. These people were stranded there about three days before rescue came from outside. One old fellow, Andrew Falk, who was very deaf, was so scared by his experience that he would not, for a long time, go on the water. He stayed on at the Durham place, then eventually took up a pre-emption nearby.

During the three days that Captain Johnson was in Kitselas, holes were cut in the hull of the wreck in the hope of finding the bodies of the drowned men, the safe, and valuable bales of fur which were being shipped south. None of the bodies were ever recovered. The safe had dropped somewhere in the canyon and the furs that were recovered were in a mess when spread out to dry. The bow part of the vessel also drifted through the Canyon and went down the channel on the far side of the gravel bar, on which the hull stranded on a logjam at the head of what now shows on the map as Whitlow Island.

The old and the new: the S.S.
Craigflower *passes by a dugout on the Skeena.*
(25-A) / BCARS 55000

Swiftwater Pilots

◆ T.W. Paterson

Captain Johnson was one of the best-known swiftwater pilots on the Skeena. The test of his skill and courage came without warning on the bright summer afternoon of July 6, 1907.

Bound for Port Essington at the mouth of the Skeena, *Mount Royal* cleared Hazelton on her last voyage at 9 a.m. "In a few minutes," recalled passenger Edward Potts, "we were in the forks of the Skeena and Bulkley Rivers on a first-class and powerful steamer, commanded by an excellent, cool and calculating captain.

"There was very little freight on board, but that, unfortunately, was of considerable value. About 11 o'clock we stopped for fuel and this took considerable time. Lunch was now served and the majority of us did justice to the same, and I fancy now I see purser O'Keefe by my side, smiling, and mate Lewis, with his quiet ways, aloft.

"A powerful blast of the whistle told us we were close to Meanskinisht, known to most travellers as the Holy City, and in charge of Rev. R. Tomlinson. Here we let off two prospectors and took on Miss A.L. Tomlinson, who was making her first trip outside in 19 years."

The voyage proceeded uneventfully until 3 o'clock, when: "An extra long blast of the whistle announced we were going through Kitselas Canyon. O'Keefe remarked to me that the ship had not touched a rock this year. At 3 p.m. by my watch, we entered the head and O'Keefe said, 'Hold on tight, boys!' for a gust of wind had caught her bow and no one on earth could prevent the crash on the flat rock, throwing her bow up at least three feet."

Mount Royal had confidently barrelled into the mile-long gorge as she had so many times before in her busy five years on the river. Captain Johnson caressed the large wheel as he deftly guided his surging craft through the hell of raging water known as Kitselas Canyon. Ringbolt Island, a long low reef jutting up in mid-channel, began to flash by.

Swiftwater navigation was a delicate art, pitting skill and nerves of steel against a vindictive foe. But even experience and courage could not cope with the unknown. Kitselas Canyon allowed not the slightest margin for error or the unexpected. When a squall knifed through the pass, it slammed the lightly-laden steamer's bluffhouse-work like a sail.

High above, in the wheelhouse, Captain Johnson felt his ship shudder as she nudged the island. Even before he could think *Mount Royal* groaned to a halt, her spoon-like bow impaled on the rocks. Almost by reflex, Johnson ordered the 27 passengers ashore and began bawling instructions to his crew to save the ship.

With Johnson directing operations from the wheelhouse roof,

mate W.L. Lewis threw the gangplank overside and bundled the passengers, including Mrs. Johnson, onto the rocky island. There was no panic; indeed, hardly any haste, the passengers seemingly reluctant to abandon their comfortable ship for the inhospitable beach. All had been deceived by the light crash. They did not realize, as did the experienced crew, that time was their only ally. If *Mount Royal* could be secured to the island, she might be saved. If the frothing Skeena regained control, the valiant steamer was doomed.

Calmly the deckhands attempted to moor their stranded ship fore and aft to a tree. Lewis hoped to winch her snugly to the island but found the capstan had been damaged and was useless. *Mount Royal*'s precious minutes had run out.

Pivoting on her trapped bow, the ship began to spin towards the opposite shore. Slowly, then gaining speed as the current grabbed her, she whipped around. As the horrified passengers watched dazedly, the pride of the Skeena splintered her mighty paddlewheel against the other bank. The steamer now was wedged cross-river like a dam!

The end came suddenly, violently. With her engineers and firemen at their posts below, Captain Johnson on the pilothouse, the gallant *Mount Royal* heeled before the overpowering fury of current and wind. The merciless river writhed over the starboard rail, flooding posh cabins, then, with the strength of a tidal wave, shouldered her over.

To the gasps of those on shore, and the wail of straining, breaking wood and iron, *Mount Royal* turned turtle and started downstream, bottom up, at a murderous 10 knots.

Miraculously chief engineer Madigan and his assistant made their escape from below, reaching deck just as the steamer capsized. The frightened pair were instantly sucked away by the boiling current, remaining afloat by clutching pieces of wreckage.

Their passage through the swirling waters must have been of the most thrilling character, and how they kept afloat is regarded as marvelous by those who know the awful speed of the waters of Kitselas Canyon. For nearly a mile they raced against death. Only when they had passed out of the canyon were they able to make the shore, to spend a shivering four hours until they were rescued by Indians.

One of the Japanese deckhands had scrambled over the ship's rolling hull "like a squirrel in a revolving cage," to join three others on a wild voyage through the rapids on *Mount Royal's* bottom.

Bert Frayne, a fireman, had been off watch at the time of the crash. He had helped the passengers ashore and secured a hawser to the tree trunk, then hurried aboard to join his shipmates. He disappeared when the ship rolled.

The heroic purser, James O'Keefe, had been the first to help passengers disembark, then hastened back to the ship. He was last seen by deckhand Joseph Offett, bravely swimming for shore. He vanished

The S.S. Strathcona.
(25-A) / BCARS 50053

in a giant whirlpool. It would have been his twentieth birthday the following Sunday.

Thirty-two-year-old steward Archie Willis and mate Lewis were last seen handling the lines on deck. When *Mount Royal's* shattered hulk drove aground on a sandbar downstream, Willis' mangled body was chopped from the wreckage.

After the passengers had been evacuated, "orders were given to throw out a cable and make fast to the Island," recalled Offett. "This couldn't be done, as the capstan had been damaged and put out of action. The mate ordered a cable on the after cleat to keep the boat from swinging. This was impossible, for the boat was tilting with each succeeding drop of water coming over her guard, and started to turn and tear herself away from the portion anchored on the ledge. Offett went over with the boat as she started down the waters of the rough canyon, and landed below. Entangled in the lifeboat when the ship overturned, the deckhand was dragged onto the hull by fireman William Jones. Steward Willis, he said, "was working with me on the cable and I did not see him alive after the vessel tipped."

A passenger, Mrs. F.M. Phillips, of Oregon, told how purser O'Keefe had stormed into her stateroom, saying, "Quick, the boat is going to crack in 10 minutes!" and carried her ashore. He then returned to the ship and she "never saw him again."

Captain Johnson, she said, had "stepped down the companion-way to the deck below and to the shore just as the *Royal* was turning." Johnson did not even wet his feet; a split second after he landed *Mount Royal* capsized.

"Throughout the disaster, Johnson had been cool and collected," reported K.H. Rolley, a passenger from Matsqui. But when he saw "the best and most loyal crew that ever stepped on the deck of any boat" being whisked downstream, he "broke down and cried piteously . . . and the efforts of passengers Edward Bissett and E.E. Potts were necessary to keep him from jumping in the river."

Word of the tragedy reached Victoria almost instantly. Government operator J.W. Graham manned a tidal gauge at the foot of Kitselas

Canyon, telegraphing daily reports to Hazelton. He immediately wired Victoria.

"*Mount Royal* total wreck in canyon 3 p.m. today; Don't expect loss of life will be large as I can see a large crowd on Ringbolt Island, including the Captain. First and Second Engineers came through canyon on debris. Indians in canoes are now working to get passengers off island. Expect to know full particulars at 7 p.m.—Graham."

The news "cast a shadow of gloom over the city," home of *Mount Royal*'s six lost crewmen. As Skeena Indians courageously conducted the ticklish rescue of survivors stranded on Ringbolt Island, newspaper and telegraph offices were swamped by inquiries from anxious Victorians.

Lost Japanese deckand, Frank Amata, had been an "interesting personality," a veteran of the famous torpedo boat raids of the China–Japan war. He knew every part of the *Mount Royal* and for general handiness was unsurpassed among the crew. One of the most devoted servants of the company, he could turn his hand to carpentry and painting and was useful in many other respects.

Sixth victim had been another Japanese carpenter, J. Morishima. During winter lay-up he and Amata had worked as waiters in the Pacific Club.

When all survivors had been attended to, Captain Johnson spent five days at the grim task of searching for bodies. Only Stewart Willis' was found. Johnson dynamited river pools in hopes of driving bodies to the surface, but without success. Disheartened, he returned to Victoria.

A year before, the steamer *Pheasant* had wrecked in Kitselas Canyon, without loss of life. Earlier, eight men had drowned in the deadly gorge when their barge was overturned.

As we said, it took guts—and lots of them—to go riverboating way back when!

Charles Durham Remembers . . .

◆ Rita Mary Rogerson (c. 1954)

Charlie Durham, a lively old timer of ninety-three, waved the Omineca *Herald* at me. "Did you see this?" he demanded.

"No," I answered, wondering just what was in the paper.

"Well, that chap that wrote the *Big Canyon Weekly* at Kitselas in the early days has a letter in the paper and he says, 'Is Charlie Durham still around? He must be close to a hundred. I remember forty years ago, he had one foot in the grave.'

"Well," said Charlie indignantly and winking, "I wonder where the other foot was!"

Conversation drifted to the early days along the river.

"Charlie," I said, "do you think there is gold in the canyon, from the wreck of the *Mount Royal*?"

"No," said Charlie. "If there was, the Hudson's Bay Company would have been after it years ago."

"Did you see the wreck?" I asked.

"I was there," said Charlie. "I used to ferry people back and forth across the canyon. I was the ferryman."

"Well," I said, "tell me about the *Mount Royal*."

He meditated for awhile, then said, "The whole population of Kitselas was waiting for her at the head of the canyon. We heard her whistle. I wondered why she was taking so long to come through, when a Frenchman beside me said, 'Oh, see! The men on the raft coming through the canyon!'

"I looked and before I could get my mind used to the strange phenomenon, another fellow came running and shouting up behind us, 'The *Mount Royal!* The *Mount Royal!* She's turned over!'

"My vision cleared. 'That's the *Mount Royal*, bottom up!' I cried, as a feeling of horror rushed over me at the calamity that had befallen. I jumped into my big canoe and hurried to the scene of the disaster. We took the six men off the bottom of the *Mount Royal* and turned them over to competent hands who rushed them up to the hotel.

"Somehow, as the *Mount Royal* was coming through the canyon, she struck her nose into Ringbolt Island. Her stern swung over to the mainland. They put fifty terror-stricken passengers off on the rocky terrain of Ringbolt Island. There they weren't any too comfortable, but they had solid rock under their feet.

"The mate and part of the crew, about twelve men, tried to get a wire cable from the stern to right her. The current instead rolled her over and six men were drowned. One fellow got over on the sternwheel and made it to shore. He was the one who ran down to tell us. I took six or seven passengers off the island at a time. I transported them over to my place, on the other side of the canyon. There was a good trail there; besides it was the most convenient place at the time. The passengers were in varying degrees of shock and fright.

"The last off the Island was a man by the name of Falk, who was stone deaf. He absolutely refused to move; he was terrified. When a seal came up near him he looked at it with horror, 'A ghost! a ghost!' he cried and jumped into the canoe and I took him to my landing. He gladly got out of the canoe, then met my daughter, Elsie, coming down the trail. He was certain he was in the other world. 'An angel, an angel!' he murmured.

"Then I transported all the passengers back to Kitselas, all except Falk, who refused to leave. In fact he took a pre-emption beside me and lived there for years. We became real friends.

"A wire was sent to the Hudson's Bay Company informing them of the disaster. Captain Johnson hired me the next day to go look for bodies.

"Two Indians and I had an unsuccessful search down the river.

"The *Mount Royal* was loaded with furs; bales were lashed to her outside railing. The Indians picked up quite a bit and had it drying at New Town. The safe fell out when the boat turned over and rumor had it that there was $100,000 in gold in the safe.

"The *Mount Royal* lay for several years on the sandbar at the mouth of the canyon. As she was a menace to navigation the Hudson's Bay Company finally had her blown up."

Skeena River Sternwheelers

◆ Walter Wicks

The many sternwheel riverboats on the Skeena River were very fascinating to us as we often watched them plow the water over the stern on their way up or down the river. At times they would call at the cannery to pick up some passengers on their way from Port Simpson to upriver points and eventually to the head of navigation at Hazelton, a distance of about 180 miles from the river mouth.

The first sternwheeler, the *Caledonia*, was put into operation on the river by the Hudson's Bay Company in 1891, making many successful trips to Hazelton for a number of years. She was later replaced by a new and larger *Caledonia* which operated on the river when I first came to the Skeena in 1900. Before the riverboats, all freight was transported by dugout canoes.

Robert Cunningham, the founder of Port Essington, then came into the picture, discarding his canoe transportation system and putting a sternwheeler named *Monte Cristo* on the river in competition with the trading company. Within a few years, five boats between these two groups, were operating in upriver transportation.

Keen rivalry sprang up, and many old river characters shook their heads at a private trader like Cunningham trying to compete with the Hudson's Bay Company, but I well remember my Dad saying, "If any man on the river can buck the Hudson's Bay, it's Old Bob." His words were proven correct, at least for a number of years.

One day a riverboat called at our cannery to load on several hundred cases of empty salmon cans to be delivered to the B.A. Cannery at Port Essington.

My brother Paul and I had been prowling around on board, prying into everything—and there was plenty. Suddenly the boat's whistle let out a blast, indicating she was about to cast off, and I jumped on to the dock—but I missed Paul. It now dawned on me that he was still on board heading upriver. I ran for the house to inform my parents of the predicament.

At that time there were no Sunnyside, Cassiar or Haysport canneries on the steamer route—these three canneries were built at a later date—and therefore the boat had no place to put Paul off until it arrived at Port Essington some 17 miles upriver on the opposite shore.

A very sheepish and frightened boy arrived home the next day on a cannery tugboat. He missed punishment for that escapade as Mother was glad to have him home all in one piece.

The river was a rough and treacherous piece of water for those boats to navigate, sometimes resulting in bad wrecks.

I was about 14 years old when one day we brothers, while hunting on Cassiar Flats, spied a box on the mud flat which proved to be a 40-pound case of butter. Then we noticed a white, painted board, shaped like a transom of a small boat and an oar, floating nearby. On the white board was stencilled the name *Mount Royal*. Having remembered a riverboat by this name, we surmised she had been wrecked.

Several days later, word came that the *Mount Royal* had broken in half in Kitselas Canyon, with the loss of six men.

Our family was well supplied with butter for it turned out to be perfect since the river water was unable to penetrate it.

One day we noticed a sternwheeler floating downriver sideways with no sign of power. Some commotion seemed to be going on out there, and being curious, as youngsters are, we pulled out in a skiff to see what the excitement was about.

The boat had run over some Japanese fishermen's net, winding several fathoms of it around the big wheel. Everybody was feverishly working to untangle the mess, and the fishermen were very angry, as they looked at the damaged net. But the captain and mate—oh my, what language they used! The Japanese answered abusively in their language, a little of which I understood but would not dare to repeat to the captain as I did not wish to witness a murder.

A large, pleasant-speaking man was on board, who seemed to have some authority as he spoke to the captain. Then he leaned over the rail and said, "Byes, ye better go home—and say 'hello' to your Old Man for me." We later learned he was the illustrious old Irish trader, Robert Cunningham.

Whatever he thought of the foul words being used in our presence we could only guess, but two young boys that day acquired additional knowledge of the English language that would certainly not be tolerated in a living room or accepted at a box social.

The glorious days of the sternwheeler have long since gone but the fast disappearing Old Timers still speak of them in a wistful manner as though they were sweet women of a colourful past.

Majestically they churned the water white
With blades that glistened in sunlight,
and stacks which belched the rolling smoke,
We watched them go to lands remote.
Then came the horse of iron rails
That spurts hot steam, the whistle wails,
While Watermen, once bold, now lying cold,
Your riverboats are but the ghosts of old.

An Early Trip Up the Skeena

◆ Eric R. Thomson

My father, the late James Thomson, then of Victoria, was in charge of building the *Mount Royal* and the *Port Simpson*.

In about 1900, the Hudson's Bay Company had two old stern-wheelers on the Skeena and the Stikine—the *Caledonia* and the *Strathcona*, and decided to replace them with one good new steamer. My father was then in charge of the company's affairs in Victoria, and received instructions to have this new steamer built there.

He was an Orkneyman, and although he entered the company's service as a fur trade clerk (and retired as chief factor), he had that knowledge of ships and shipping which is inborn in those islanders and he saw to it that everything that went into the *Mount Royal* was just a bit better than the specifications called for. I was on her trial trip in Royal Roads, off Esquimalt, and later, about 1902, I was on her from Essington to Hazelton in the capacity of a very minor assistant to the purser. My father was taking me with him on his fur-trade inspection trip. I don't remember who the purser was, but I do remember going ashore with him, and carrying his papers, which he called "manifests."

At that time, some distance up the river, there was the village of Meanskinisht (now Cedarvale) and this village was the brain-child of a missionary. The villagers were Indians, except that the missionary had several pleasantly-spoken daughters. Observance of the laws, human and divine, was so strict in that village, which had its skookum-house (jail) on the ground floor of the village bandstand, that even the nearly-omnipotent Hudson's Bay Company found it necessary to make sure that the *Mount Royal* called there on a week day, for Sunday business was taboo.

We called there on a week day, and I sallied ashore with the purser, who I noticed had on his best uniform, and was groomed for the occasion. We went the length of the village, stopped at a large house, and were shown by an Indian maid into a sitting room and were left there while devotions, which we could overhear, were completed in another part of the house. The next thing that happened was that the purser stepped to the fireplace, and removed from in front of the grate a very large pair of wings, either those of an eagle or a fallen angel, then lit a cigarette and blew the smoke up the chimney. I had seen some curious customs in the northland, but this led me to ask why he was behaving like this, and his reply was that the missionary was against smoking, and that he, the purser, wasn't looking forward to meeting the gentleman, had got nervous, hence the cigarette. Mr. Purser had his money on the wrong horse, for when the door opened, it was one of the daughters who entered, and—time being of the essence all round—the welcome was a warm one.

My duties on those trips included the task of stirring up the Chinese bull-cook just before dawn, to make the early morning coffee, for the *Mount Royal* tied up at night, and was off next day at first light. One day, on my way along the freight deck to start the Chinaboy on that job, he came past me on the dead run, screaming that "the devil was in the kitchen." When I got to the galley, sure enough, in the half light, there was something rocking backwards and forwards and screaming. It gave us a fright, too, but was in fact a bear cub which had come down over the riverbank in the night, crawled through the galley window, and got upended in the sugar barrel. It was his wails and waving hind legs that had terrified the Chinaboy. The purser and I, taking one leg apiece, extracted the cub from the barrel, shook the sugar back to normal, and gave the bear a free ride to a likely-looking place where we stopped to take on wood, and put him ashore, but by that time he was loath to leave us.

The *Mount Royal* was wrecked while I was away in Scotland at college, and by that time the CPR had taken over the old Canadian Pacific Navigation Company in which the interests of the late Captain John Irving and the Hudson's Bay Company were in some way blended, and the U.S. tourist trade was beginning to boom.

Then my father got instructions for the *Port Simpson* and he decided she would be the largest, most powerful, and best appointed river steamer that had ever graced the northern rivers. She was just that. My mother had the choosing of the chintzes, linen, cutlery, china and so forth, the general idea being that everything had to be just so, and a bit better than on the CPR. My mother had a flair for these things. She and father got the best Chinese cook on the Coast, and when the *Port Simpson* entered service she was a beautiful and a happy ship.

I got back to Victoria in 1911 and my father took me on another inspection trip, this time into Dease Lake and Liard.

Note: It was on a trip up the Stikine aboard the *Port Simpson* that I first sampled a to-me gastronomic delight. I mentioned that we had a number of American tourists, and it was evident that their ways were not our ways. I remember the horror with which we watched them pave the top of their helping of apple pie with cheese.

One night, after the passengers had retired, the rest of us were having a mug-up, and the matter of this curious combination came up for discussion. It was decided to use me as the guinea pig on an experimental slice. I was newly back from seven years in Scotland, and was no doubt green to the ways of my country, but not so green as all that, for when I bit into that apple pie and cheese combination set before me, I was emphatic in my praise of it, so much so that the rest of those present fell for it and that is how this habit started in northern British Columbia.

Down the Skeena by Canoe in 1907

♦ James D. Cumming

In the summer of 1907 I was the very junior assistant to Walter W. Leach of the Geological Survey of Canada, whose job was to map and geologize the headwaters of the Telkwa River in northern British Columbia. He was also to report on the coal claims of Frank Dockerell and the copper showings of Harry Houston at Mooseskin Johnny's Lake.

There were five of us—the Chief, myself, his brother Ainslie, Fred Walters—cook, friend and helper to everyone—and the packer who looked after the pack train of five horses. For a callow youth, the mountains and pack horses, the diamond hitch and the Carrier Indians—still occasionally hostile—made for a most romantic summer.

In May we embarked at Vancouver on the coastal steamer *Princess Sophia* for the 400-mile trip up the Inland Passage, steering by echo when foggy. We reached Port Essington at the mouth of the Skeena River after three days of smooth sailing. They were still arguing over the alternate routes for the projected railroad from Prince George to the seaport of Prince Rupert, so at Port Essington we took the Hudson's Bay Company steamer, *Mount Royal*, for the trip up the wild Skeena River, 180 miles to Hazelton. These river steamers were shallow draft with big stern paddle wheels and enormous wood-fibre boilers. On the front deck were steam winches to haul the boat by steel cables fastened to "deadmen" on shore, up the boiling rapids.

On the way up through the Kitselas Canyon a cable parted and only skillful work by the steersman landed us in an eddy so that another cable could be put out. Among the passengers was the famous Captain Hector MacLean, the hero of Jack London's *The Sea Wolf*. On the return trip from Hazelton, the *Mount Royal*, with the whole winter's catch of furs from the interior Hudson's Bay posts, was wrecked with some loss of life at this same point in the dreaded canyon.

After a wonderful summer spent mountain climbing, mapping and geologizing in the Bulkley Valley and the headwaters of the Telkwa River, we walked back out to Hazelton in the fall. Our sternwheeler for the trip downriver to the coast was the *Assiniboine*.* This time we did not get as far as the Kitselas Canyon.

A few miles upstream is the "Beaver Dam." At this point a wide dike of diabase crosses the river, making a shallow crossing, a sharp bend in the river, and a big sandbar in the eddy below.

The trick was to cross the hard dike, running like a submerged dam, without scraping bottom, then speed up to make the sharp curve in the river before the stern could be swept around crossways of the vicious current. Well, we did not make it and the *Assiniboine* piled up on the sandbar, breaking her hog rods and the steam pipes. No one knows why we were not blown sky-high, but after an hour or two we went back on board and re-occupied our staterooms.

A couple of deckhands took the ship's boat and the current quickly whisked them down to the telegraph station at Kitselas Canyon. They wired back to Hazelton, and next morning two enormous dugout cedar canoes from the Indian village of Kitwanga, each manned by two Indians, arrived to take us and a ton or two of baggage the remaining 100 miles to Port Essington.

At the head of the canyon the women and non-yachtsmen walked the mile or two across the neck, while the rest of us, four men to a canoe, volunteered to paddle to give steerageway through the violent gorge. The current in the canyon was so fast that the water rose in a central comb and the canoes had to ride this crest. When the steersman, standing in the stern and handling an enormous sweep, yelled, we had to paddle like mad. Once on the comb, the Indians at each end kept the canoe rushing along at terrifying speed with their sweeps.

We made the run through the canyon and felt quite heroic about it all. On reloading, our canoe held 16 people and two tons of baggage, and in the other were 24 men and their packsacks, some craft and some steersmen. By nightfall we had made about 60 miles and camped on the warm sand.

We had about 30 miles to go next morning and had to time our arrival to cross the dangerous "bore" in the Skeena estuary at slack tide. It was a relief to put up at the "Blackjack Macdonald" saloon and gambling den, but we would not have missed the trip for anything. The Vancouver boat had gone, but in three or four days the *Princess Sophia* came back and we returned to Vancouver.

This ill-fated boat, a few years later, hung up on a reef in the foggy Inland Passage. Seemingly hard aground (until help could arrive) the passengers and crew went back on board for the night. Without the slightest warning, she suddenly plunged to the bottom, carrying more than 400 people to their deaths. The sad list included some well-known Cobalt mining men.

* Aside from this story, there is no record of a Skeena riverboat named Assiniboine.

The Wreck of the *Northwest*

• Charles Durham

"WRECK . . . Navigation on the Skeena River is at a standstill following the wreck of the steamer *Northwest*, belonging to the Northern BC Transportation Co. The wreck, which occurred 40 miles above Port Essington, involved no casualties."

I was aboard this boat at the time of the wreck and here is my personal experience in connection with it.

Captain Bonser, who for a long time had been in command of Robert Cunningham's sternwheeler *Hazelton*, had just lost a smaller and probably more dilapidated sternwheeler, the *Pheasant*, on the Beaver Dam just above Skeena Crossing.

A newly-formed company then bought the *Northwest*, which was a very large, rotten old boat and engaged Captain Bonser to take command of it.

On the first trip up the Skeena River the Chief Steward went on a spree, so at Kitselas I was hired to take his place. I also got a position for Jimmy Wells for a trip. This is how it happened that Jim and I were returning to Kitselas as passengers on this second trip of the boat upriver.

There were very few white passengers on board, but several hundred Indians, returning home from the canneries as the fishing season was over. Among the passengers were either Mr. Welch or Mr. Stewart (I can't remember which) of Foley, Welch & Stewart, who had his wife and, I think, his little daughter along.

The first night out of Port Essington we tied up on the south side of the river on what used to be called the Hudson's Bay Flats—apparently on top of an old log lying on the river bottom, as during the night the silt had washed away from around the log and in the morning we found the boat's back broken across the middle, so that both the bow and the stern were hanging down.

It seemed that there was only one lifeboat belonging to the steamer. Captain Bonser took this with the Welch or Stewart family and also a message from me to Telegraph Point asking the Dominion government telegraph operator there to get word to Kitselas to my son, George, to come down with a canoe to get me home.

Where the boat was tied up one could hardly put a foot ashore before one had cleared away the willow and all kinds of scrub bushes. The only kind of trees to be seen were cottonwoods so there was not a stick of dry wood for building fires.

After Captain Bonser had gone, the purser whose name, I think, was Whitney, sent all the crew ashore to clear land so as to get the cargo unloaded. Meanwhile Big Bateman, who homesteaded at Remo, and his wife, who had brought a skiff on board with them, asked Jimmy Wells and me to help them launch it—which we did, but to our indignation they went away without offering to take us, which would only have been fair appreciation of our help.

It was a miserable place to make camp, with only mud and this willow stuff and scrub around—no dry wood, millions of mosquitoes and flies to torture us, and swarming with Indians so one could not move without bumping into one or the other of them.

I was happy a couple of days later when my son, George, aged only 13, arrived in my canoe which he brought down alone from Kitselas. This was quite a feat for such a young lad, and only one of his experiences to bring pride to a father's heart.

I then gathered up Jimmy Wells, who also belonged to Kitselas, a big fellow who came from Switzerland whom I only remember by the name of Louie, and Eric Forsman, who took up a pre-emption near Copper City. The canoe was small, but with the exception of Big Louie who weighed 250 pounds, we were all small men and made a heavy enough load for that craft.

Now, to the best of my knowledge, nothing whatever was done to take the Indians away from there, neither by the steamboat company nor by the government. So how they managed I don't know, excepting I do know that some of them were still around there the following spring when the river was again navigable.

Reminiscences

◆ Frank D. Rice

We arrived at Port Essington from Stewart on the old *Capilano* on our way to Hazelton on September 25, 1907. When we got to Port Essington we found that all three steamers had been wrecked on the Skeena River but that the *Hazelton* was being patched up and would be coming down the river soon for repairs. She arrived at Port Essington for repairs. They worked day and night and finally got off for Hazelton on October 15, much later than the trip had ever been made before. The trip, which normally took two days, took us six, mostly on account of low water and shorter days. To add to the excitement there was an outbreak of measles among the boat's 30 passengers, which included a two-year-old. The daughter of Constable and Mrs. Kirby of Hazelton, she took quite a shine to me and I had her in my arms for the best part of the last two days of the trip.

We finished our work about January 15 and started out at once for Kitimat, along with our large dog, weighing about 150 pounds, that was half St. Bernard and half wolf. There was only about three inches of snow in Hazelton, not enough to let them get their firewood in for the winter. We got to Kitseguecla that night to find that the ice had gone out in the river, so we turned the dog loose and bought an old dugout canoe for $15 and started out next morning. We made about 35 miles that day to Meanskinisht where the river was again frozen over but the snow was about three feet deep. We bought four pairs of snowshoes from the Indians and started out with packs on our backs. We made Kitselas Canyon in about four days. We stayed at the hotel overnight and left next morning, making Thornhill's place on the Little Canyon.

We crossed the river there and went downstream to where they had the terminus for the new sleigh road they were building from both ends to Kitimat. We found out that a sleigh had left that morning and that if we caught up with it we could get a ride to the end of the road. So we started out and finally caught up with the sleigh about 10 p.m. In the meantime, in passing Lakelse Lake we had to cross the Hot Springs which were running in several channels and had melted the snow for about 200 feet, so we all got our feet wet. However we had a good night's rest and started out next morning and got a ride to the end of the road.

So we put our packs on our backs and started out in heavy snow on snowshoes. We reached the summit about 3 p.m. and saw two valleys, both running in an easterly direction. I told the boys to cut some wood for a fire and some brush to sleep on, while I went down the valley to the right to make sure it was the right one, as the snow had got so deep the blazes on the trees were covered. After walking about three miles, I came to a thicket of spruce and found the blazes I had been looking for. I got back to where I left the boys at dark and found them huddled up on some logs they had cut. They were almost in tears as they couldn't get a fire started. As it was down to zero and I was wet with sweat, I started out making a circle around the camp and kept going in a larger circle until after watching the sky, I found what I was looking for—a small dead pole leaning against a hemlock. I cut it down and packed it to the camp. After cutting off several short lengths and splitting it up fine, I made some shavings, and in a short time we had a good fire started. We piled on some of the green hemlock that the boys had cut and had no more trouble with the fire. We laid the brush on the snow and spread our blankets and had a good night's sleep. In the morning we went to cook breakfast and found that the fire had burned right to the ground and that the snow was 10 feet deep so we had to cut steps in the snow to get down to the fire.

We started out in the morning and by that night we had come to the end of the road they were building from Kitimat. It was the roughest camp I had ever seen. The ground where they had cleared the snow was mud. The cook tent had several long tables made of jackpine poles and were about four feet off the ground. There were no seats. They had old-fashioned pea soup in bowls. Then we had some beans and salt pork and stewed prunes for dessert. We started out after breakfast and got to the head of Kitimat Arm.

We stopped overnight there with Mr. and Mrs. Taft, who had a cabin on the flats. She was a lady barber and gave us all a much-needed haircut. Next morning we went across to the Indian village where we had to wait three days for the steamer *Venture,* which was an old wooden boat operated by Boscovitch Steamship Co. The boat was northbound and we were quite surprised that the first class fare to Vancouver was only $16 each.

We went to Hartley Bay and then north to the Skeena where we called at four or five canneries, then to Prince Rupert, which was just started. Then we went north to Port Simpson and the Naas River. Turning back we called at Port Simpson, Prince Rupert, Port Essington and afterwards went to Rivers Inlet, where there were several canneries and where there were 1800 cases of canned salmon to load. There were no men at the canneries but the watchman, so we all grabbed a truck and started wheeling the cases down to the boat. It took us two whole days to load the boat and we got some much-needed exercise.

We finally got to Vancouver, and much to our surprise, we were called to the purser's office and each paid $18 for longshoring. So when a most wonderful trip ended, we had enjoyed the most wonderful meals for ten days at no cost to us.

The Hoo Doo Ranch at Swede Creek

◆ E.M. Whitlow (1958)

Highway 16 goes past this place now but from all appearances one would never know that here a pretty stream once flowed by into the nearby Skeena River, about two miles west of what is now the village of Usk.

There was once a plank bridge, and before that just a couple of logs laid over the stream for a crossing, on the trail from the old Hudson's Bay post at Kitselas Canyon down to Kleanza Creek. It was probably a section of the old pioneer trail between Kitimat, Hazelton and the interior of BC.

Before the white man came to Kitselas, legend has it that at the site of this crossing was the house of an Indian. He and his wife made a little clearing beside the stream, and this they found to be an excellent spot for the spearing of humpback salmon, which came here in such abundance that the water was practically hidden by them. The woods around were full of small game and berry patches were plentiful.

This Indian belonged to a tribe whose village was at the upper end of Kitselas Canyon, about two miles distant, but for some forgotten reason to white men, he had been made an outcast. For some time the couple got along quite well, but finally his wife threatened to leave him, so he killed her and himself committed suicide. Nobody ever learned the details of the story, only that the bodies had been found beside the creek, and since that time the Indians shunned the place—it became taboo.

In the closing years of the nineteenth century, a couple of Swedes by the names of Louis Anderson and Ed Youngdahl, came to Kitselas. Both these men were approaching middle age, and Youngdahl had a mutilated hand—two fingers were missing as a result of an accident. It is not known how they came to Kitselas—whether over the old trail from Quesnel, via Kitimat, or up the Skeena from Port Simpson. They were among the first prospectors and had probably worked at the old Singlehurst Mine. They were stakers of the Golden Crown group of mineral claims, on the west side of Kleanza Creek, on the hill which Highway 16 now skirts. They either came as partners, or formed a partnership afterwards, regarding their mining venture. They were partners in a 320-acre pre-emption of land which they took up at the location of the old Indian homestead.

In the year 1900 they had built a comfortable two-room cabin and had cleared enough land to cultivate a good acre, which they unfortunately got the idea of fertilizing with the humpback salmon from the nearby creek. The fish soon became so odoriferous that the very air was polluted, so the partners were obliged to move away until the winter had set in. They eventually returned but the air was still bad. After a while they had a disagreement about something and were no longer on speaking terms. They lived together in this uncomfortable fashion for a whole year, until Youngdahl went to Kitimat, and here he stayed awhile on construction work.

Youngdahl returned to Kitselas and he and Anderson patched up their quarrel. They lived peacefully together again and went on with their ranching, prospecting, working on mineral claims, trapping and whatever else there was to work at, so as to enable them to keep a supply of provisions, tools and powder, this latter being necessary for prospecting and mining operations.

The two men had rather secretive dispositions, as was the custom of old-time prospectors. In those days one had to be careful lest his find or claim be jumped by another person. Everyone was looking for a fortune and wanted to be in on it. Some old prospectors had quite a game, the owners changing from one year to another. A great deal of arguing went on as to whether the required year's assessment work had been done.

Anderson and Youngdahl had a dog, and in the summer of 1905, the two men and the dog mysteriously disappeared. Weeks went by and there was no sign or word from them. Late in the autumn some Indians, who had gone on a fishing expedition up Copper River, found them wandering. They were in a pitiable and starving condition. The kind-hearted Indians immediately abandoned their fishing trip and brought them down to New Town, where the old Kitselas Tribe had set up a new Village, after vacating the Canyon because of a smallpox epidemic. New Town is now called Kitselas, and is a station on the Canadian National Railway.

Soon after this there was talk about the Bulkley Valley opening up, with the coming of the railroad. Anderson and Youngdahl made up their minds to get in on the ground floor, as the saying goes, so they made up their packs and hit the trail. They went down the south side of the Skeena and up the east side of the Copper until the trail became absolutely impassable. At this point they constructed a raft, and made an attempt to cross the river. However, they were unable to manage the raft in the swiftly-flowing water, and before they reached the other side they were upset, losing their packs, gun, axe and barely escaping with their lives. After this fiasco they laid up, recuperating, for some time.

Youngdahl had been visiting a few miles down the Skeena, and was returning to Kitselas by canoe, along with Hank Boss, the Dominion government telegraph operator, and the lineman Charlie Durham, who had been out on line repairs. The Skeena was at a low stage of water and they did not anticipate much difficulty in navigating up the river, but when they reached the mouth of the Copper the water was extremely high and dangerous. They managed to get across it, but in the effort struck a floating tree, and the force of the water upset the swinging canoe. Boss was in the stern of the craft and he managed to clamber onto the trunk of the tree. Durham was bowman and he grabbed a branch as he went under. Youngdahl had a hold on this same branch, but in his weakened condition and owing to his crippled hand, he could not maintain his hold and was forced to let go. The branch Durham clung to sprang into the air for an instant, giving him the breath he needed and the chance for a better hold over the limb. He managed to make his way to safety. Youngdahl was drowned; his body was never recovered.

The following winter, Durham had occasion to go south to Vancouver on business, and in his absence Anderson took on his job as lineman. He made a trip over the line between Kitselas and Hardscrabble Creek, to the east of Kitselas Canyon. When he did not return searchers went to look for him. They found him dead at the foot of a cliff over which he had fallen and broken his neck. His body was taken by sled over the ice on the Skeena River, to Hazelton, some eighty miles away, for burial.

The next individual to settle on the now deserted "unlucky" ranch was known only by the name of "French Joe." He was a stranger in the community. There were no other people of French extraction around the village, and perhaps owing to the fact that he kept himself to himself, he did not make any friends.

He was living there at the time of the construction of the Grand Trunk Pacific Railroad and Kitselas came into its own as a metropolis for the large construction camps, steamer traffic, building, and portaging of supplies over the Canyon, etc.

French Joe may or may not have had the title to the property, but it was one spot that was already cleared out of the forest, with a brook handy, a small cabin, and only a ten or fifteen minutes walk to the little ten-acre township. His became a little respectable dwelling amidst a community of well patronized bawdy-houses.

After his secluded and solitary life in the spot he had chosen to make his home, the rowdyism of "the fancy houses," as they were politely called, must have affected Joe. One cold winter morning early in January, he was found lying over a chair dead—shot through the head with his own rifle, which lay beside him. Kitselas was now equipped with magistrate and a Provincial jail, and the police gave the verdict of suicide.

Eventually the construction days were over for Kitselas, the four tunnels across the river at the Canyon were completed, the trains were now carrying passengers and supplies to points further east. The sternwheeler days were also over. As Kitselas was on the opposite side of the river from the railroad, it quickly became a place of empty buildings. The "Red Light" inhabitants followed the construction camps up the line.

Swede Creek, so called from the time Anderson and Youngdahl first settled there, was now ruined. The wrecks of old buildings made it an eyesore and a sad memory to the few remaining residents who on occasion still used the trail. Finally they too left, and Kitselas was deserted.

If one knows where to look among the trees and new growth they can still find traces of this old "Hoo Doo Ranch," as it became known, because of the ill fate of those who had made their homes there. A culvert and fill takes the waters of Swede Creek beneath Highway 16, and there is now nothing to mark the spot or to tell the story of the old Hoo Doo Ranch.

Hazelton

The pioneer history of Hazelton, though fascinating, is best left to its own local historians. However, as this site became the eastern terminus of the riverboat run, we should know something about it.

Dr. Large, in his *Skeena, River of Destiny*, gives a concise account of its early beginnings, which may be summarized for our purposes as follows —

Before the advent of the white man, there were two native villages near what was later called "The Forks"—Hagwilget, the home of Carrier Indians, situated on the Bulkley River, and Gitenmaks, inhabited by the Gitekshans, on the Skeena.

In 1866 the Hudson's Bay Company sent two of its men, Thomas Hankin and William Manson, on a scouting expedition to locate new trading post sites. The result was the erection at Hagwilget of a small structure that remained in operation for less than two years.

Thomas Hankin then decided to go on his own. He left the Company and settled on the hazel flats close to Gitenmaks.

The Collins Overland Telegraph Company in 1866 had men working in the area, and when that project fell through, several stayed on to try their luck at mining. Many wintered at the little settlement, and in 1868 it was named Hazelton because of the abundance of hazelnut bushes in the vicinity.

There was an old Indian trail running from Gitenmaks to Babine Lake which the miners used to get to the Omineca country. Hankin and Robert Cunningham, in 1871, were given the task of clearing and upgrading this trail to provide a better route to the gold fields. It was a good thing they did because the rush of 1871–72 was on.

Pack trains of mules and later of horses were a common sight on the village streets. The stores in Hazelton—of which "Cunningham & Hankin" was one—did a thriving business. Gradually the town expanded and became a supply centre not only for the Omineca mines but for the Lorne Creek and other nearby holdings as well.

During the time of the Yukon gold rush, miners from the interior headed up the old Telegraph Trail in an attempt to reach the Yukon sooner. This was an extremely difficult route for the pack trains but it did provide the way for the government telegraph line from Quesnel to Atlin, which was completed in 1901.

The year 1880 found the Hudson's Bay Company back in the area again.

S.S. Omineca *and S.S. Operator*
at Nailhead, just below Kitselas
Canyon.
(25-A) / BCARS 70973

The movement of sternwheelers
up and down the Skeena
provided newsworthy items for
the Omineca Herald *and other*
newspapers in those early days,
which today provide a
background to the lives of the
pioneer families along the river
highway:

July 18, 1908
Prince Rupert has now become
the terminal point for the
Hudson's Bay Company's
steamers, the change taking
effect this week. Port Essington
will remain a port of call on the
route.
News has been received that the
new steamer Skeena, *destined*
for use on the Skeena River, is
nearing completion. She will
have an overall length of about
125 feet and is especially built
for service on the upper river at
comparatively low stages of
water.

The new G.T.P. boat, the
Distributor, *left Telegraph Creek*
on the Stikine, July 10th, for
Prince Rupert and Hazelton. The
rates for passengers and freight
have been published and are
about the same as is charged by
the Hudson's Bay Company.

Hazelton Post

In order to facilitate the transport of goods between the mouth of the Skeena River and the Babine Post, the Hudson's Bay Company wanted a post at the Forks of the Skeena, so in the fall of 1879 chief factor William Charles arranged to take over the premises of W.J. Walsh, an independent trader. In 1880, Mr. Walsh turned his premises over and Alfred Sampare, who was at that time in charge at Babine, was put in charge of the new company post which was known as Hazelton.

Once this post was established, goods for Babine were regularly forwarded by the Skeena River route. Some goods for the other New Caledonia posts also came by this route, but an attempt in the summer of 1882 to bring in the greater portion of the New Caledonia outfit by way of Hazelton failed when arrangements fell through for a pack-train to transport goods across the Babine Portage. During the summers of 1883 to 1885 therefore, only Babine goods were forwarded by way of Skeena River. New Caledonia goods were brought in by this route in the summers of 1886 to 1888, but the lack of satisfactory transport up the river made it a difficult task. It was felt that without a steamer the Skeena route could not be largely utilized for New Caledonia. The re-appearance of opposition at Hazelton in the fall of 1888 provided another reason for the introduction of a steamer on the Skeena River.

The construction of the steamer, which was named the *Caledonia*, was completed in the spring of 1891. It was not until the spring of 1892 however, that she made her first through trip to Hazelton. From

July 18, 1908

We are informed that an independent company in which Captain Bonser is interested, will place a new boat on the Skeena River route about the 15th of August. The hull is now completed and the machinery is being installed. She is designed to carry 100 tons of freight with a draught of 24 inches.

September 12, 1908

The steamer Distributor *of the G.T.P. river service arrived last evening, making the trip from Kitselas in one day. This is the first time the* Distributor *has appeared on the upper river. Her passenger accommodations are not so large as those of the* Port Simpson *but she seems to be more efficient as a freight carrier. There are no monogrammed windows at several dollars a pane or fancy woodwork features which make the cost of the* Simpson *so high.*

this time onward the Skeena River steamer was used as a regular means of transport for the New Caledonia goods.

When the post at Hazelton was inspected by chief factor McDougall in October 1890, it was described as situated on the south bank of the Skeena River about one and a half miles from the confluence of the Agwilget (i.e. the Bulkley River) and Skeena and about 125 miles above tidal waters.

The post, at that time, was surrounded by Indian dwellings of the Kitamas tribe. Another Indian village was situated on the Agwilget River three miles distant and Hazelton was the centre of trade for the adjacent tribes hunting on the upper Skeena. It was the depot of the mining trade of Omineca, comprising the camps of Germansen, Manson, Vital, and Tom's creeks and many of the miners wintered at Hazelton.

At the time of McDougall's visit the Company's buildings at Hazelton consisted of a general store and office—which were constructed in 1886 when it was found that the original buildings were no longer in good condition—a warehouse, and a dwelling-house intended for the officer-in-charge, which was still in the course of construction. These buildings were surrounded by a double board stockade with two log bastions at diagonal corners which had been erected in 1888 when there had been trouble with the Indians. Outside the stockade the Company owned a dwelling-house which had been occupied by the trader from whom the Company bought the business and since then by the clerk in charge. There were also four dwelling-houses which were usually occupied by the miners who were regular customers. Aside from the land occupied by the buildings, seven acres were under cultivation.

Visitors to an Indian cemetery, Hazelton
(16-B)

No. 4 ◆ Hazelton Post

◆ C.H. French and Wm. Ware

Established in 1872 by those rushing into the country on account of placer gold discoveries in the Omineca. The Hudson's Bay Company acquired its location by purchasing the buildings and rights of one of these adventurers.

It was soon evident that the Skeena route was cheaper to haul freight over than the Fraser River route; therefore it was adopted, and until the completion of the Grand Trunk railroad, McLeod's Lake, Fort Grahame, Babine, Fort St. James and Fraser's Lake posts all got their annual freight by that route.

From 1872 up to 1893, canoes were the only carriers used, and one has only to know the swiftness of the water and the dangers of the canyons to realize what a difficult undertaking this was.

In 1893 the first steamer was built and, from this on to the advent of the railroad, Hazelton became the most-talked-of town in the interior of British Columbia. It was the head of navigation on the Skeena, the distributing point for Manson, Vital and Tom's Creek mines, and the Bulkley Valley as well as Kispiox and north. It also became an important point in the Yukon Telegraph line. All supplies to north and south were distributed with pack-trains from there.

It has a population of about 216 natives and 100 whites, Dominion Government telegraph, general hospital, Anglican, Methodist and Salvation Army churches, public school, provincial district mining engineer, Indian agent, forestry men, and until recently had other government offices such as mining recording, police, etc.

It is a centre for agriculture, mining, timber, big game hunting, and a fur centre for all natives north and south.

It is on the Canadian National railroad, 177 miles east of Prince Rupert at the foot of the famous Rocher de Boule mountain.

Note: Dates in the above article are always not consistent with those of the previous one.

High Old Time at Skeenaforks
Victoria *Daily Colonist*—Aug. 15, 1873

Editor *Colonist:* What kind of a government have you got down there anyhow? Here every man is his own governor? A short time ago we had what you would call an ejectment without even the colour of law to excuse it. The aggrieved party started for the mines, but finding no magistrate there came back after six weeks' absence and has gone for salt water, determined, if he can't get justice, to take the law in his own hands. Every house sells whisky and trades without a licence for we

September 26, 1908
The steamer Hazelton, *after being nearly a week on the river, was finally tied up near Kitseguecla, Wednesday, the passengers completing the journey afoot.*

Friday morning a large canoe started down river with 12 passengers.

October 10, 1908
It is reported that the steamer Port Simpson *had an accident while passing through the canyon at Kitselas on the down trip this week. In some way the paddle wheel became disabled and the boat, helpless and with no steerage way, drifted about 5 or 6 miles down the river before the crew were able to secure her to the bank. No injury to the hull is reported and it is thought to be one of those minor accidents attendant upon navigation on the river.*

October 24, 1908
Wed. morning a large canoe started down the river bound for Port Essington with a crew of five Indians and seven passengers.

October 31, 1908
The steamer Hazelton *made her last trip up the river this week. She will go direct to Port Simpson, there to be hauled out for the winter.*

November 7, 1908
The steamer Craigflower, *which left Port Essington about two weeks ago for Hazelton, is stalled about 8 miles below Lorne Creek on account of a breakdown to her machinery.*

November 14, 1908
The steamer Craigflower, *which has been making a valiant effort to reach Hazelton for the past 2 weeks finally gave up the attempt when at Andimaul, about 20 miles down the river, and after unloading her freight there, returned to Port Essington.*

November 1908: Victoria
Colonist
It is probable that another sternwheel steamer will be built during the coming winter for the GTP for service in connection with the Distributor *(Capt. Johnson) which has returned to port to be tied up for the winter after a successful season on the Skeena River.*

have not seen a policeman this summer. The Indians think the government is a farce (are they far wrong?) and steal before your face and laugh when you remonstrate with them. There is no chance for a man to do a legitimate business here, for a trader will come in, pitch his tent, sell off his goods and "flit" without paying any tax whatever.

Yours,
HAZELNUT
Skeenaforks, July 26, 1873.

November, 1873
The steamer *Otter*, Captain Lewis, arrived from Skeena River yesterday, bringing $40,000 in Omineca gold-dust and more than 70 passengers.

When Mr. Ferron left Skeenaforks, no ice was making and there was no snow on the flats. He had a rough trip down the river owing to high winds. One hundred miners will winter on the Skeena and either go back to Omineca or proceed to Cassiar in the spring.

March 25, 1948: *Vancouver Daily Province*
There have been so many stories and articles written about Hazelton and the neighboring district that, if they were all put together the result would be merely a collection of contradictory facts.
(*Compiler's Note:* The above statement is certainly correct and tends, very often, to confuse the reader.)

◆

Hazelton has experienced many great booms and sudden depressions since the first white man arrived in 1850. In 1867, Hankin, a former Hudson's Bay employee, started a store and liquor dispensary, the building for which is now the Church of England. Before the railroad was put through in 1909 the district was supplied by dog team in winter and river steamer in season.
In 1900 the Dominion government telegraph was brought through. In 1936 the wire between Hazelton and Atlin was abandoned and wireless sets were put in to replace it.

◆

Constance Cox

◆ Donovan Pedelty

For pioneer tales of old BC it would be hard to beat Constance Cox. She is the first white girl born and baptized in Hazelton, 120 miles north-east of Prince Rupert, and for more than 50 years she was a social and spiritual force in that old Skeena River town.

It is doubtful if anywhere else in the world there is another spry and merry-minded middle-aged lady who can tell from first hand how her mother painted spots on her chest in an attempt to avert an Indian rising, how a dose of quicksilver administered to one Indian saved the lives of 90 besieged white miners, and (at second hand) how a missionary fought a giant battle of fisticuffs with a bishop before an audience of 500 Indians, who promptly followed him to Alaska when he won.

These are among the historical treasures stored in the memory of Constance Cox, nee Hankin, born to Tom and Margaret Hankin in the days when schooling for Hazelton kids involved a 7-day trip down the Skeena in a paddle steamer, followed by an 18-day voyage from Inverness or Port Essington to Victoria.

Constance recalls the *Mount Royal* tragedy, when the old river steamer swung broadside to the swift current in Kitselas Canyon and jammed between the banks.

Says she with the vivid authenticity of one who had the tale when it was new-minted out of local fact: "Purser O'Keefe got the passengers all walked ashore, and then went back with the crew to stand by in case the ship righted. She didn't; she made a dam across the river, built up a wall of water, and turned over. Five were drowned. Captain S.B. Johnson and the engineer, were among those saved. The latter clung to a steamer trunk belonging to Mrs. Johnson and was swept ashore at the foot of the canyon."

For fear of this kind of accident, on her annual summer way to and from a convent school in Victoria, Constance was ordered by her mother to step ashore at the end of the canyon and walk the two miles round to the other end, where the steamer (swept through in a few minutes by the boiling waters) patiently waited for its more cautious passengers.

Her pioneer father, Tom Hankin, went to the post at Mission Point, at the junction of the Skeena and Bulkley Rivers, for the Hudson's Bay Company in 1858. Then a godmother's legacy from England enabled Tom to leave the company, stake a new town of Hazelton, build a store, and partner a cannery at Inverness.

Four boys were born to the Hankins before Constance arrived.

November 1908: Port Essington **Loyalist**
The recent heavy gales have completed the wreck of the old steamer Caledonia, *which was bought by Foley, Welch & Stewart from H. Munro and others, who purchased her from the Hudson's Bay Company. The boat is stripped of all her upper works, and lies on her beam ends on the bar on which she was stranded.*

February 6, 1909
The Skeena River is now in prime condition for ice travel and the number of people going up and down the river increases each day.

February 20, 1909
A conservative estimate of the value of furs shipped from Hazelton during the last year is placed at $60,000.

February 27, 1909
Capt. S.B. Johnson, superintendent of the Company's steamboat service on the Skeena, returned from Montreal where he has been conferring with the executive of the GTP regarding the proposed two sternwheelers to be built for the GTP. Captain Johnson says the two new steamers which they are going to build are to be exact duplicates of the Distributor, *the Company's steamboat which went into commission last spring. They will cost about $35,000 each. Tenders require their completion before the first of June. They will have a length of 135 feet, a 29-foot beam and a capacity of 140 tons. High power engines will be installed—they will be subject to separate tenders.*

March 27, 1909
The Skeena River Commercial Company will build a new $14,000 hotel, modern in every respect, at Port Essington this spring. The building will be located across the street from the site of the old Caledonia Hotel, which was destroyed by fire January last.

The excitement of her advent—the father seems to have been sure that this time it would be a girl—was such that father Tom sent home to England for his own christening robe (it took six months to come out) and made the long trip to Victoria, partly by Haida canoe, to register the birth and arrange for Bishop Ridley, bishop of the diocese of Caledonia, to travel to Hazelton for the christening.

Apparently conscious that this was the christening of the first white female child born in Hazelton, Tom determined the occasion should be marked by a christening cake, the like of which had not been seen in BC before. The only possible makers were the Smiths of Victoria, whose highest flights hitherto had been a soda biscuit. They flatly refused to make a christening cake. Tom flatly insisted they should.

Eighteen years later the Smiths begged Constance to let them make her wedding cake, in honor of the enormous cake business they had founded on that fabulous three-tiered affair of Tom Hankin and which had been the sensation of Victoria before he proudly carried it away up north.

At second-hand, Constance relates how the black-bearded burly Bishop Ridley fell foul of missionary William Duncan when he first came out. Duncan had been working among the Indians ten years before him, had the confidence of the old Chief Paul Legaic who was reputed to have owned 3000 slaves, taken in raids on inland tribes.

Arriving, the bishop ordered Duncan to teach the Indians to call him "my lord." The missionary refused, declining to throw away ten years of work teaching the Indians to think of Jesus Christ as their Lord.

When the bishop insisted, the missionary took off his coat, invited him outside to settle who was the better man. They fought it out, says Constance, at Metlakatla, and when the bishop had been downed for the last time Duncan went off, in 1887, to a new mission in Alaska, with 500 Indians who had watched the battle electing to go with him.

Indians were no problem to the Hankins. Tom encouraged them to settle all round the growing town of Hazelton (they are there yet), and gave a $3000 potlatch to introduce baby Constance to the tribe. Mother Margaret learned seven Indian dialects, and passed some of them on to her daughter.

But there was a situation coming which not even the Hankins could handle.

The gold boom at Manson Creek, up in the Omineca, 180 miles to the north-east of Hazelton, was beginning to result in miners being the winter guests of the town; the pick and shovel boys rested up there between October and May, spending their nuggets on the fare offered by "Red Alec" in the saloon, which included a floor show by Indian dancing girls, to the tunes of a grinding organ which Alec gave any willing miner $5 a night to turn.

At one time, says Mrs. Cox, there were as many as 4000 miners living in Hazelton, and the bishop's wife did wonderful work among them, providing a recreation hall and a library of books, but at the time of the Indian trouble of 1886, "the world's last Indian uprising," there were only 90 miners left, and it was fortunate for the town that there were so many.

"Seven of those old-timers are buried in the old Indian cemetery at Hazelton. I had a railing put around their plot. It cost me $150. But I'm afraid the cemetery is falling into neglect. They should make a historical memorial of it. There was old Jim May buried there, a forty-niner from California and Barkerville, and Ezra Evans, the Welshman, who came up into BC with camels. For years he packed an oak box with him wherever he went, and when I was a child he would never let me look in it, though I used to be always in his cabin getting nuggets for candy. When he died I looked in that box. It contained a pair of lady's white gloves, so small and slender, a lace handkerchief, and a faded, withered bunch of forget-me-nots."

Constance was about four, a child of flying feet and blonde hair streaming in the wind behind her, always playing with the Indians, who, her father had told her, would never harm her since her potlatch, when the trouble broke out.

It began with a departure from custom.

At that time every scrap of BC groceries came by ship from England and there was a rule that none of it except flour, salt and tobacco, might be traded with the Indians. But one ship by mistake discharged an extra cargo at Hazelton, and temporarily it was decided to offer the Indians sugar.

"Many of them refused to buy it," says Mrs. Cox. "They couldn't see why they were being given the chance of it, and it was their nature to be suspicious. But many of the young ones bought it. The next thing was a severe outbreak of measles among the Indian children.

"They didn't know how to treat it. They used to rub the children's chests with snow to make the spots go away. Of course a great many of them died. And their parents blamed us. They said we'd sold them the measles with the sugar."

When Indian deputations called on Mrs. Hankin, whom they had many reasons to like and trust, she tried to get them to understand how measles spreads.

"It's in the air," she said, "it's not in the sugar."

"Then why haven't your children got it?" asked the Indians.

Next time they came they found Constance and the younger of her brothers in bed, with angry red spots painted on their chests out of the school paint box.

"By a coincidence," says Constance, "Mother had just given us a dose of jollop, just in case we did have measles. Listen, if you ever have to have jollop or measles, take the measles. I was just vomiting

April 17, 1909
The Hudson Bay Company is clearing the rocks out of the eddy at the landing place, which will be of considerable advantage to the steamboat captains in times of low water.

May 8, 1909
The steamer Hazelton *arrived at Kitsumkalum Wednesday evening and unloaded, returning to Port Essington for a cargo for Hazelton.*

May 8, 1909
The passenger and freight tariff of the Hudson Bay Company's river service have been received at the local office and show few changes from published rates of last year. The passenger rate down the river has been increased by $7.50, making it the same as that up river, $17.50. The freight rates continue the same with the exception of the 20% rebate allowed to shippers of 15 tons or over, which has been discontinued. Another freight class has been added, which includes gunpowder and high explosives, taking a rate of $75.00 per ton.

May 8, 1909

Tuesday next the Hazelton and Bulkley Valley Stage will begin its weekly run between Hazelton and Aldermere. The stage has accommodation for eight passengers.

May 15, 1909

The steamer Hazelton *with the reliable Capt. Joe Bucey in charge, arrived yesterday morning at 9:30, the first boat up the river for the season of 1909.*

May 22, 1909

The Strs. Port Simpson *and* Hazelton *departed for Prince Rupert Thursday, after waiting almost a week for a proper stage of water.*

May 29, 1909

The Hazelton *left for Kitselas Thursday A.M. and will bring up the load left there early in the week by the* Port Simpson.

up that vile medicine when the Indians came again, and one woman said, "Yes, that's the way mine started. She'll be dead by tonight."

But Mrs. Hankin's ruse came too late. By now 4000 Indians were gathering around Hazelton, lighting fires, dancing war dances. The 90 white miners then wintering in the town had already begun to build a fort, first of sandbags and later of handsawn planks.

The climax came when the two young daughters of the local chief died. "Chief Gitamgldaw," says Mrs. Cox, in the nearest English spelling she can achieve to the Indian sounds, "but everybody called him Kitty Muldore." The Indian braves moved into the town and the whites moved into the fort. The war dances went on under its walls.

Spectacularly, one loyal Indian sought entry into the fort. For him to have gone up to the door would have been to invite death from both sides. He burrowed his way in from the river bank, said his uncle had ordered him to offer his services. His uncle's life had once been saved during a dysentery epidemic by some bold dosing with quicksilver (a kill or cure remedy) administered by Tom Hankin. Now in the person of his nephew, Spokth, he sought to repay Tom's widow.

"Spokth offered to go to Port Simpson for help, said he could make the several-hundred-mile trip in six days. He made it, we never learned how. They sent 80 soldiers and 30 special police from Esquimalt, in command of the police Captain R.E. Loring, later to become my stepfather and Indian Agent in Hazelton."

Shortly before this relief arrived, the miners in the fort stood off attack for several nights by flooding the surrounding countryside with light from hundreds of improvised coal oil torches. The Indians had ceased to dance, which meant they were ready to attack, but none dared cross the bare ground to the fort in that revealing light.

By the time the soldiers arrived, the tribes were gone. There was nothing for the police to do but take three Indians involved in local murders, two of whom were then tried before Judge Pemberton in Hazelton. It was while acting as interpreter in these trials that the widowed Mrs. Hankin met and fell in love with the police chief, R.E. Loring.

Daughter Constance's own romance was with E.R. Cox, the telegraphist. Nine years ago, when radio was installed in Hazelton, Mr. Cox accepted transfer to North Vancouver, but Mrs. Cox still pines for northwest BC. Mr. Cox retired on the last day of the old year.

The walls of her North Vancouver home are lined with photographs and paintings of the glamorous Skeena River country. Her trunks are full of the records of some of BC's most romantic past.

Her greatest ambition is to have a hand in the foundation of an historical museum at Hazelton.

"We mustn't let historical things slip away from us," she says. "You never get them back."

Last Steamer Has Gone Below

Inlander departed Tuesday Noon for Port Essington
Likely operate in the South next Season
September 13, 1912

The last steamer from the port of Old Hazelton has gone. On Tuesday the *Inlander* whistled for the last time in these northern waters and pulled away from her old berth and started down for Port Essington at a good clip. For the last three weeks the *Inlander* has been tied up here for low water. On Monday night the rains in the north caused the river to rise several inches and Captain Bonser ordered steam up and the crew on board to take the last trip while the water was promising, as there is grave danger of it dropping any time, never to come up again this year. It was just noon hour when the steamer whistled and in a couple of minutes the lines were cast and the boat started down while a number of citizens stood on the shore and waved a last farewell to the captain and his crew. With the departure of the *Inlander* ends the transportation on the Skeena River as far north as Hazelton.

The *Inlander* had been on the river for the last three years and she was owned mostly by local people. From the first trip she was a popular boat and was always given a big share of the local business. That the *Inlander* was a good investment is known to everyone. Her days of usefulness are not yet past. There is a strong possibility that after the winter's rest and repairs are made the boat will be commissioned by the contractors on the PGE Railway, Foley, Welch & Stewart, and that next season she will be operating around the southern part of the province.

The crew of the *Inlander* was popular with the people. From Captain Bonser, who has navigated the Skeena River on the different boats for the last 20 years, down to the stoker, they all received the respect of the people and they showed proper respect also. Manager Harry B. Rochester is well known and he is a rustler. Through him and his business ability the boat made a great succes. He will also be missed in this neighbourhood . . .

From now on the Hazelton people and the people of the entire interior are dependent on the GTP for freight and transportation facilities. It is to be hoped that the railway company will display the same consideration for the rights of the people that the steamboats did.

[Note: The Inlander *never took to a river again. It slowly rotted away at Port Essington, and thus was lost a valuable historical artifact.*]

January 10, 1910
Work is now under way at Victoria on the new steamer which is to run on the Skeena next season. The contract for building the steamer has been let to the Spratt shipyards. The boat will cost $25,000 and will, it is expected, prove to be one of the best boats on the river. Her lines and dimensions will be the same as those of the old favorite, Mount Royal, *and she will have a freight capacity of 60 to 70 tons. The local members of the syndicate which will operate the boat are R.S. Sargent, J.C.K. Sealy, and W.J. Larkworthy. Captain Bucey will leave the service of the Hudson's Bay Company to take command of the new boat, which is expected to be in commission at the opening of navigation. Her name has not yet been decided upon.*

March 5, 1910
Charles A. Gardner, formerly mate on the Caledonia *and later master on the* Skeena, *will be in charge of the Hudson Bay Company's steamer* Hazelton *this year.*
Captain Jackman will be again master on the Port Simpson *and nearly all of the other officers are remaining in the service. The* Hazelton *has been undergoing extensive repairs, meaning practically a new hull.*

March 5, 1910

Captain Joe Bucey, who will be in charge of the new boat [the Inlander] being built by the Prince Rupert & Skeena River Navigation Company, writes from Victoria that construction is being rushed in order to have it completed by April 20; at which time he expects to leave Victoria for the Skeena.

The steamer will be 135 feet long, 28 foot beam, 5 foot hold and will draw 17 inches light and 30 inches with 80 tons aboard. Cylinders will be 14 x 72 inches and the boiler will carry 200 pounds of steam. She will be fitted with steam steering gear and all the late improvements, including bathrooms for the passengers. The staterooms will accommodate 40 people. The Captain also says, "There will be no Chinese laundry on the hurricane deck."

Of the other officers Robert Ryder will be chief engineer; Jerry Cunningham, mate; Wiggs O'Neill, purser; Frank Waller, freight clerk; and Joe Doyen, steward.

In securing such a large carrying capacity with such a light draft, Captain Bucey has carried the lines of the hull very full fore and aft. This will make her not so pretty nor so easy to handle as the other boats but should have little effect on her speed.

No "First" Boat This Year

April 25, 1913

There will be no "first boat" this season to hit the shores of Old Hazelton. There'll be no steamer whistle to stir the natives from their winter's sleep into the activity of spring.

For over 30 years the natives and old timers have speculated upon the date of the first boat arriving. Each year about this time (the breaking up of the ice and the rise of the river) the man with the hoe and the rake was out scraping together the debris of the winter; garbage piles were burned; the entire town was given a scrubbing. It was all because the "first boat" might come in earlier than last year. Large sums of money have been wagered upon the arrival of the "first boat." It was the chief topic of conversation for weeks; in fact it was the first excitement of many months—the daybreak of another season.

No tenderfoot, no outsider, no old timer (except those on navigable streams) knows the meaning of the "first boat." But to those who do know, it is like a resurrection, a prisoner liberated, a sick man given a new lease on life. The "first boat" was always wrapped in romance, and no matter what hour of the day or night the whistle sounded, as the steamer paddled up the last stretch, every man, woman and child was out of bed and down to greet the passengers, and greet them they did with cheers and joyous cries.

This year there will be no "first boat." The Hazelton district has been discovered and captured by modern civilization. The old stern-wheelers are a part of history and the modern locomotive takes its place. Railway trains bring passengers and freight to within a couple of miles of town and the boats cannot compete. But the boats will be missed. To the old timer the past winter will be like time wasted. The new supplants the old. New Hazelton today is what Old Hazelton was this time last year—the business centre for the great northern interior.

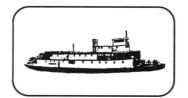

The Last Word

With all the historic material we have on hand, we could easily publish several more books such as this one. This volume has briefly traced the development of trade along the coast of what is now British Columbia, the Hudson's Bay presence at Port Simpson and the growth and importance of Port Essington. We have followed the early navigation of the Skeena River from Canoe Days to the Era of the Sternwheelers. With the advent of this later mode of travel we have seen more people coming in—prospectors, miners, fur traders and settlers.

The frontier was gradually being pushed back, telegraph lines were being built and small settlements were appearing. We have watched the growth of the community of Kitselas and noted its strategic location in regard to river transport.

Finally we have witnessed the riverboats giving way to the railroad and we realize that the entire country will now grow apace.

I mentioned in my Foreword how surprised I was at the amount of material available on the Skeena country if one had the imagination and the patience to search for it. No doubt there is more to be found. I tried to select what might be of local interest and to arrange it in a somewhat chronological order so that it would not seem so much a disjointed collection as a continuous record of development.

Ideally, we would like to follow this volume with one that will deal with the small communities that put down roots along the lower Skeena—Remo, Kitsumkalum, Kalum Lake, Lakelse Lake, Usk and Cedarvale. We have a wealth of personal stories about these places, tales of the triumphs and hardships of pioneer life, many of them told in the words of the pioneers themselves. With them, we can discover how the building of the Collins Overland Telegraph line directly affected Skeena River transport. We can share the hardships involved in the delivery of His Majesty's mails, and we can witness the completion of that monumental task, the building of the railroad, that ended our area's isolation from her neighbours to the east.

Another volume could be done on Terrace itself, a community that has in a short time risen from the wilderness to the stature of a city. Yet another volume could be written telling the stories of Terrace pioneers. Most of them have passed on, and unless their stories are told now they will linger only in the memories of their immediate descendants.

Not to share this knowledge would be to deprive ourselves of valuable heritage. It is not only our duty but our privilege to do so.

◆ Norma V. Bennett

Sources

In the Beginning
(1) McKelvie, B.A., "Pageant of BC" – Vancouver *Daily Province*.

Stepping Stones in History
(2) Dalzell, Kathleen E. – *The Queen Charlotte Islands 1774 – 1966*.
(3) *Encyclopedia Brittanica*.
(4) Wade K.C., F.C., "Early Navigators of the Pacific" – *Art, Historical and Scientific Association – Session 1907-08*.
(5) BC Heritage Series – Queen Charlotte Islands – "Our Pioneers" – *Series 11 Vol. 1*.
(6) Walbran, John T., *British Columbia Coast Names*, Douglas & McIntyre, Vancouver/Toronto.
(7) Marshall, James Stirritt & Carrie Marshall, *Vancouver's Voyage*.
(8) Hudson's Bay Company Archives.
(9) Large, R.G., *Skeena, River of Destiny*.
(10) Anstey, Arthur & Neil Sutherland, *British Columbia – A Short History*.
(11) Howay, F.W., *Trading Vessels in Maritime Fur Trade 1785 – 1794*.
(12) Wagner, Henry, *The Cartography of the Northwest Coast of America to the year 1800 – Ibid* Vol. 1, p.206.

Skeena River Log
(1) Walbran, John T., *BC Coast Names*: Dixon's "Further Remarks on Meares 1791," Douglas & McIntyre, Vancouver/Toronto.
(2) Wagner, H.S., *Cartography of the Northwest Coast* – Vol. 11, p 429 – BC Provincial Archives.
(3) Akrigg, C.P.V. and Helen, *1001 BC Place Names, 2nd Edition (Revised)*, UBC Press, Vancouver.
(4) McNeill, W.H., *Fort Simpson Letter Book, Aug. 26, 1892*, BC Provincial Archives.
(5) Walbran, *BC Coast Names*.
(6) Collison, Archdeacon W.H., *In the Wake of the War Canoe*, pp 288 – 289.
(7) Dorsey, George A., PhD, "Up the Skeena River to the Home of the Tsimshians," Field Columbia Museum, Chicago.
(8) BC Provincial Archives.
(9) Hudson's Bay Company Archives.

The Skeena Was a River!
Downs, Art, "The Skeena" – *Paddlewheels on the Frontier, Vol. 1*.
Large, R.G., "The Skeena" – *River of Destiny*.
Quinn, Vernon, "BC's Beautiful River" -- "Beautiful Canada" -- Vancouver *Daily Province*, Jan. 4, 1932.
Lambly, Mildred, "Skeena Valley Beauty" – Vancouver *Daily Province* – Oct. 1943.
Hallock, Ruth, "Tribute to a Brave Man" -- Terrace *Omineca Herald* – Oct. 1965.

Canoes on the Skeena
Niblack, A.P., "Canoe Building" – *Coast Indians of Southern Alaska & Northern BC*. From personal observations made during surveys 1885, 1886 and 1887. Collection in US Museum.
O'Neill, Wiggs, "Canoe Building" – *Interior News*, Smithers, Nov. 20, 1929.

Port Simpson
Collison, W.H., "Port Simpson" – *In the Wake of the War Canoe*.
Barbeau, Marius, "Old Port Simpson" – *The Beaver*, Hudson's Bay Company Archives, Sept. 1940.
Baxter, Vietta Worsley, "Tsimshian Indians" – *BC Digest*, June 1966.
Downie, William, "Downie's Map and Letter" – Vancouver Public Library, Northwest History.
Morrison, Charles, "Collins Overland Telegraph Co., 1866" – Hudson's Bay Company Archives.

Canoe Travel
Cowrie, G.V., "Canoes on the Skeena" – Vancouver *Daily Province*, Feb. 14, 1948.
Large, R.G., "Canoes on the Skeena" – *Skeena, River of Destiny*.
O'Neill, Wiggs, "Canoe Days" – *Steamboat Days on the Skeena*.
Robertson, Sylvia, "Notes on Paddles" from "BC Dugout Canoes" – *Canadian Geographical Journal*, July 1951.
Crosby, Reverend Thomas, "Travelling with Canoe Brigades" from *Up and Down the North Pacific Coast*.

Port Essington
Morison, John W., "The Story of Robert Cunningham" – Prince Rupert *Daily News*, July 16, 1964.

Port Essington *Star*, June 28, 1902 – Vancouver Public Library, N.W. History.
Bowman, Phylis, "Cunningham Built Port Essington as Base for Skeena River Travel – Victoria *Daily Colonist*, Sept. 10, 1967.
Blyth, Gladys, "The Ghost that Guards the Skeena" – *BC Outdoors*, Oct. 1969.
Wicks, Walter, "Port Essington" – Terrace *Omineca Herald* / Hancock House.
—"Living without Frills" – Ibid.
Prince, Edward E., "The King of the Skeena's Last Voyage" – *Dalhousie Review*, 1926.

Fishing & Canneries
Government of Canada, "Salmon Fishing 1902" – Fisheries Commissioners' Report.
Carmichael, Alfred, "Windsor Cannery, Aberdeen, Skeena" – BC Prov. Archives.
Government of Canada, "Minority Report of Fisheries Commission 1908."

Sternwheelers
McGregor, J. Herrick, "The Country of the Skeena" – *The Mining Record*, 1902 or 1903.
Boss, Mrs. M. W., "Pioneer Pilots of the Skeena."
Stevens, Mrs. C.G., "Riverboats on the Skeena" – *The Beaver*, Dec. 1936, Hudson's Bay Company Archives.
Dorsey, George A., "Up the Skeena to the Home of the Tsimpsians" -- Field Columbian Museum, Chicago. From a lecture delivered at the museum, Nov. 13, 1897.
O'Neill, Wiggs, "Up the Skeena in 1899."
Bennett, Norma & Ric, Wiggs O'Neill, Art Downs, other sources, "Chart of Riverboats on the Skeena."
Rempel, J.G., "Map of Skeena River."

Highlights And Handicaps
Editorial: "In Defence of the River" – *Omineca Herald*, July 25, 1908.

Quotable Quotes
(1) Boss, Mrs. M.W.
(2) Talbot, "The New Garden of Canada."
(3) Rossiter, Lance.
(4) Downs, Art, *Paddlewheels on the Frontier*.

(5) O'Neill, Wiggs, "Steamboat Days on the Skeena."

Kitselas

Duff, Wilson, "Book Review of *Men of Medeek* by Will Robinson.

Kenney, Ed, "Kitselas – Gateway to the Past."

Varner, Kathleen, "The Charles Durham Story."

Whitlow, Elsie M., "Proposed Plan of Durham Townsite."
—"The Ranch at Kitselas."
—"The Water Gauge."

(1) Whitlow, Elsie M.

(2) Talbot, "The New Garden of Canada."

Whitlow, Elsie M., "Boom Days in Kitselas."

BC Voters' Lists – Kitselas, 1900 – 1903 – 1907 – 1908 – 1909.

Henderson's BC Gazetteer & Directory, 1910.

"Investigation is Demanded" – Victoria *Daily Colonist*, May 10, 1905.

"Serious Charges against Mariner" – Victoria *Daily Colonist*, May 28, 1905.

Duncan, M., "My Wild Indian Summer" – *The Westminster*.

Paterson, T.W., "Swiftwater Pilots" – "The Islander," *Daily Colonist Magazine*, Dec. 17, 1967.

Rogerson, Rita Mary, "The Wreck of the *Mount Royal*" – *Northwest Digest*, Jan. – Feb. 1955.

Wicks, Walter, "Skeena River Sternwheelers" – Terrace *Omineca Herald*

Cummings, James D., "Down the Skeena by Canoe in 1907" – *The Northern Miner*.

Hazelton

"Hazelton Post – A Brief History" – Hudson Bay Co. Archives

French, C.H. & Wm. Ware, BC District, "BC Posts: No. 4, Hazelton Post" – *The Beaver*, May 1924.

"Last Steamer Has Gone Below" – Terrace *Omineca Herald*.

"No 'First Boat' this Year" – Terrace *Omineca Herald*.

Photo sources

Our pictures were obtained from many sources, all of which deserve recognition. The same applies to the way in which these pictures were reproduced. Therefore, we employed a simple code whereby full details may be obtained.

At the bottom left-hand corner of each picture there appears, in brackets, a number followed by a letter, thus: (14-A). The number refers to the donor of the photograph, the letter to whoever reproduced the picture.

In some cases, right next to this credit there is a further and longer number. Thus a full credit may read, for example, *(3-A) / BCARS 24567*. This is the identification number of the BC provincial archives (the British Columbia Archives and Records Service—BCARS) and it must be used whenever requesting a copy of that certain picture from the Archives. There are also archive numbers for photos that were obtained from the National Museum.

Photo sources:
1. Mattie Frank Collection
3. Vera Frank
4. Phylis Bowman
11. Adella Pohle
12. Clarence Michiel
13. Len Bruggeman
16. Vina Eby
17. Annie Noonan
18. Katie O'Neill
25. BC Archives and Records Service
26. Murray Hamer
32. R.J. Phillips
33. Hugh McLarty
34. National Museum of Canada
36. Odney (Sandhals) Irvine
41. Elsie M. Whitlow
46. Vancouver Public Library - Mr. D'Altroy
60. Bill Bennett
65. W. McRae

Photo finishing:
A. BC Archives and Records Service
B. Ken's Photo
C. Gifted by donor

Index